Alana Schoen 757-6800

The publishers wish to thank the following artists for contributing to this book:

Jonathan Adams: pp. 33 (bottom), 36 (right), 52 (center right), 101 (top), 108/109, 116 (left), 131 (left), 137 (top right), 139 (bottom left); Owain Bell: p. 34 (right); Dennis Bosdet: pp. 60 (bottom), 61 (bottom left), 115 (top left); Peter Bull: p. 68; Tony Chance (Garden Studios): p. 76; Kuo Kang Chen: pp. 15, 19 (top), 22 (bottom), 23 (bottom), 25 (top left), 26 (right), 27 (top), 30, 34 (bottom), 44 (top), 51 (bottom right), 61 (center left), 62, 63 (bottom), 75, 76 (left), 77 (left), 78 (center left), 84, 87, 89 (left), 103 (center), 104, 105, 118/119, 121, 123 (bottom right), 126 (top right), 130 (top), 134 (right), 135 (top), 137 (bottom), 138, 140 (top left), 150 (center), 153; Peter Dennis (Linden Artists): pp. 7, 26 (center and top), 28 (bottom), 46/47, 66, 80 (bottom left), 105 (bottom), 125, 131 (center), 148/149; Mark Franklin: pp. 29 (top left), 38 (bottom), 59 (right), 98 (top), 99 (left); Jeremy Gower: pp. 6 (left), 12 (top), 17 (right), 24 (left), 25 (bottom), 35 (top right), 49, 57 (top right), 58, 63 (top), 73, 80, 85 (left), 88 (left), 92, 94, 96 (top), 106, 107 (bottom), 110 (center right), 111 (top), 120 (right), 126 (left), 133, 150 (bottom right), 152; Ian Howatson: p. 65 (left), 77 (right), 100 (top), 102 (top), 107 (left), 142 (top); Valerie Sangster (Linden Artists): pp. 60/61, 115 (top left); Mike Saunders: (Kathy Jakeman Illustration) pp. 10/11, 18 (top), 19 (bottom), 56 (bottom); John Scorey: pp. 28, 95, 136, 145

First American edition 1993

 Published in the United States by Random House, Inc., New York. Originally published in Great Britain by Kingfisher Books, a Grisewood & Dempsey company, in 1993.

LIBRARY OF CONGRESS CATALOGING-IN-PUBLICATION DATA
Ford, Brian J.
First encyclopedia of science / Brian J. Ford. — 1st American ed.
p. cm. — (The Random House library of knowledge)
Includes index.
Summary: Over 400 alphabetical entries, with illustrations, maps, and charts, cover such scientific topics as acid rain, computers, numbers, and sound.
1. Science — Encyclopedias, Juvenile. [1. Science — Encyclopedias.] I. Series.
Q121.F67 1993
503 — dc20 92-44792
ISBN 0-679-83698-5 (trade).
ISBN 0-679-93698-X (lib. bdg.)

Manufactured in Italy 10 9 8 7 6 5 4 3 2 1

Abbreviations

Some words are abbreviated, or shortened, in the encyclopedia. The table below explains what the abbreviations stand for.

Measurements and Abbreviations

in	inch
ft	foot
yd	yard
mi	mile
sq mi	square mile
mph	miles per hour
oz	ounce
lb	pound
qt	quart
gal	gallon
°F	degrees Fahrenheit
K	degrees Kelvin
mm	millimeter
cm	centimeter
m	meter
km	kilometer
km/h	km per hour
g	gram
kg	kilogram
°C	degrees Celsius
c. (before a date)	circa (about)
B.C.	before Christ
A.D.	*anno Domini* (refers to any time after the birth of Christ)

The Random House Library of Knowledge

FIRST ENCYCLOPEDIA OF SCIENCE

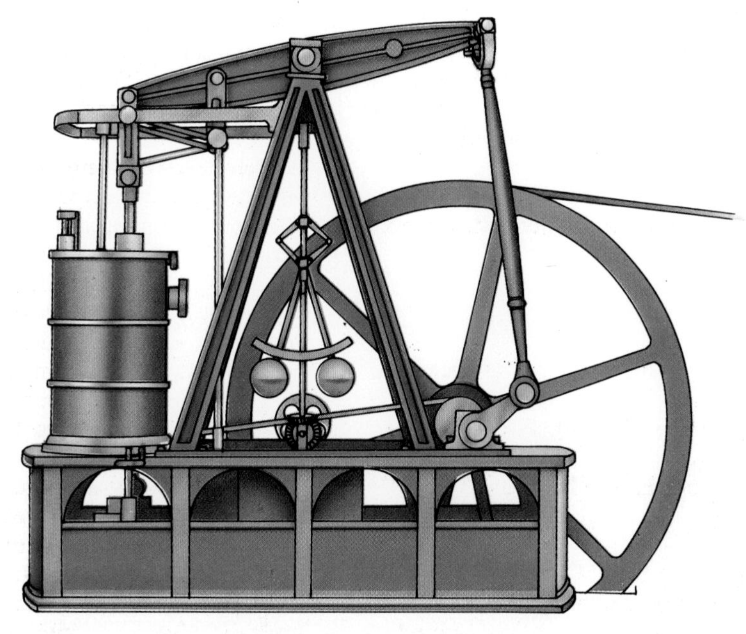

BRIAN J. FORD

Random House New York

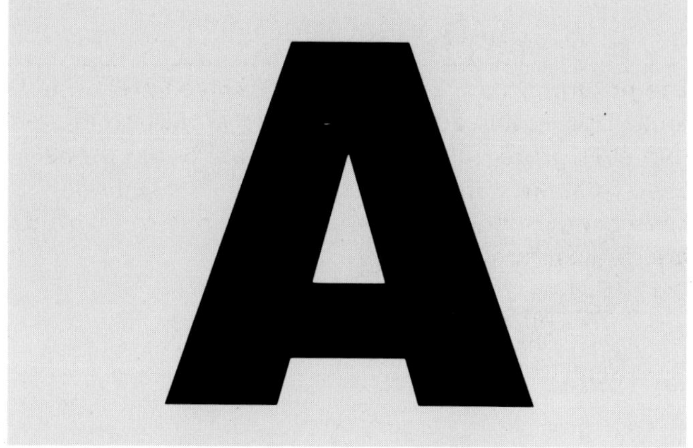

abacus

The abacus is the oldest type of COMPUTER. It is made of beads on wires. The first row of beads stands for ones, the next for tens, next hundreds, and so on. By moving beads to the central bar and adding the beads in each row you can do arithmetic. The first abacus was used in Babylon 5,000 years ago. But Japanese workers still use them in electronics factories. An abacus can sometimes give an answer faster than a CALCULATOR.

▼ Numbers are multiplied or divided by moving beads to the bar. Beads right of the bar stand for five. The totals shown are 136 and 369.

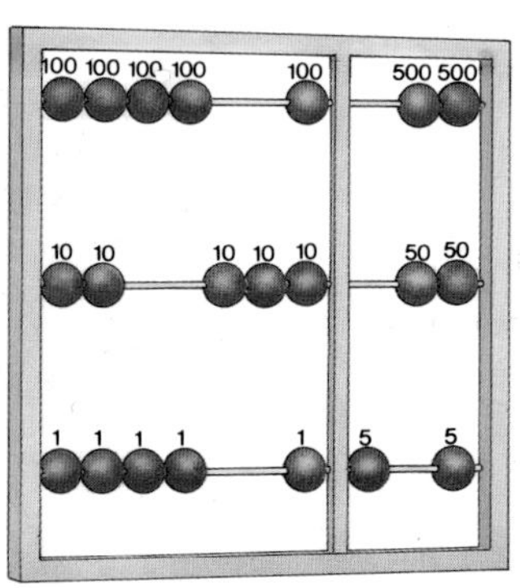

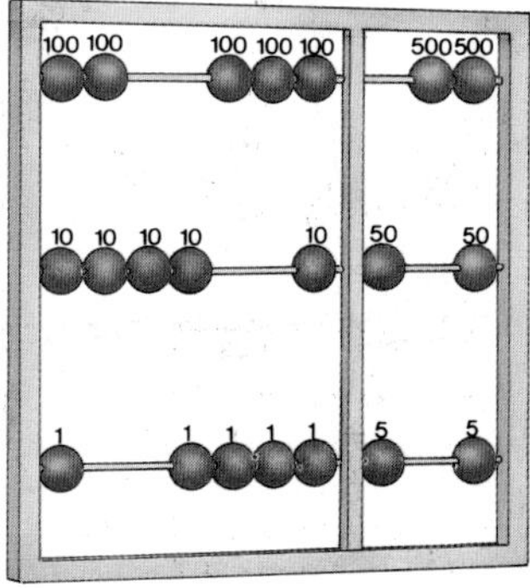

abrasive

Fine, hard substances that wear down solids such as wood or metal are called abrasives. Sandpaper is covered with an abrasive, usually crushed QUARTZ.

absolute zero

Absolute zero is –459°F or –273.16°C. This is the temperature at which there is no HEAT ENERGY present.

absorption

Many substances can soak up a liquid. A towel does this when you dry yourself. This is absorption. HEAT, LIGHT, and SOUND can also be absorbed. Light colors are cooler to wear on a hot day since they absorb less heat than dark colors.

acceleration

Acceleration means "getting faster." If you stop (on your bike, for instance) and then start riding again, you accelerate. When you put on the brakes to slow down the opposite happens — you decelerate.

▼ Boiling a red cabbage in water makes an acid/alkali indicator. Alkalis such as baking powder turn the indicator green. Acids turn it pink.

acids and alkalis

Acids are active chemicals which always contain at least one ATOM of HYDROGEN. But they can pass on this hydrogen very easily. Alkalis are active chemicals which accept hydrogen atoms in exchange for the metal atoms they contain. Acids and alkalis react together to form SALTS and water. Vinegar and lemon juice are weak acids. Baking powder is a weak alkali. Oven cleaners contain very strong alkalis. Strong acids and alkalis burn the skin.

ACID RAIN

RAIN is naturally slightly acidic. It reacts with carbon dioxide in the air and sulfur dioxide released by bacteria to form a weak acid. It measures slightly below 6 on the pH scale, which goes from 0 (acidic) to 14 (alkaline). But acidic fumes from burning COAL and OIL make rain much more acidic. Acid rain measures pH 3 to 5.5 and can damage plant life. Lakes in some countries have lost most of their animal life because of acid rain.

DID YOU KNOW?

The natural acids in rainwater dissolve limestone rock. This is how caves are formed. Pollution makes rain even more acidic so that it attacks the stone used to make buildings. Some famous buildings have been damaged by acid rain. And many statues are now unrecognizable.

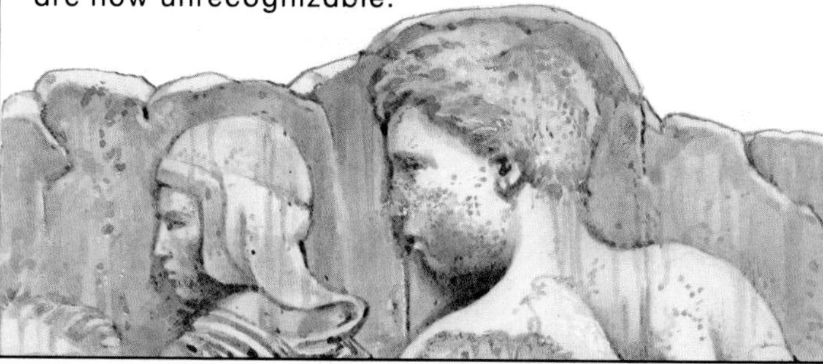

▶ It is our demand for goods and energy that creates acid rain. Power stations, factories, and cars that burn fossil fuels produce huge amounts of acidic gases each day.

The gases from an industrial area can travel thousands of miles before they produce acid rain. Many places suffering from acid rain are far from the countries that cause it.

▶ Acid rain has caused damage in North America, Europe, and Scandinavia.

adhesives

Adhesives make objects stick together. We still do not understand what makes things "sticky." Early glues were made by boiling bones and animal hooves. Some modern glues are made from natural resins; some are man-made.

adsorption

Some substances can adsorb onto a solid. This means that they stick on the outside. If you can smell smoke on your sweater, it is because smoke particles have been adsorbed onto the fibers.

aerosol

An aerosol is a fine mist of particles suspended in a gas. When you sneeze, you make an aerosol of saliva and germs. A scent spray makes an aerosol of perfume. The word aerosol is also used to describe a can filled with a liquid (or powder) product such as paint or deodorant and a pressurized gas called a propellant. When the button is pressed, the pressure inside forces the liquid to spray out in a fine mist. See **chlorofluorocarbons**.

▼ Pressing the button on an aerosol can releases the pressure. The propellant forces the liquid to spray out in a fine mist.

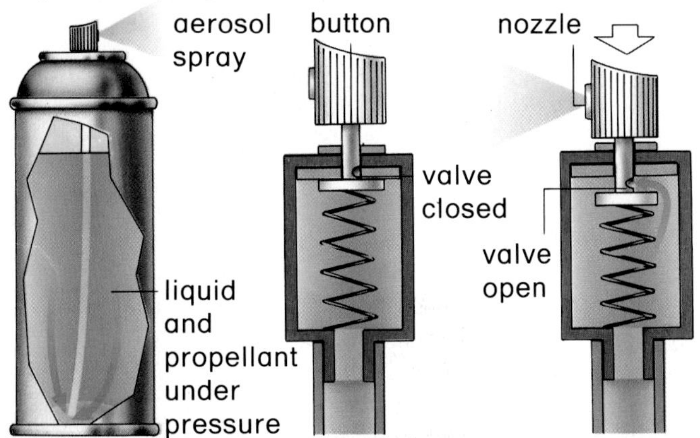

air see **pages 10 and 11**

air conditioning

A REFRIGERATOR system and a HEAT EXCHANGER are used to keep the air in a building at the same TEMPERATURE winter and summer. Air conditioning uses a lot of ENERGY.

aircraft

The first flying machine was designed in the 1400s, but it was not until 1783 that the Montgolfier brothers in France sent up the first manned hot-air BALLOON.

Balloons and airships can fly because they are filled with a gas that is lighter than air. An airplane needs power from its ENGINES and lift from its wings to take off. As the plane speeds along the runway, the AIR rushing over the top of its curved wings is at lower pressure than the air below, and this creates lift.

As the plane flies, hinged flaps on the wings can be lowered to produce extra lift or to slow down the plane when it is about to land. Elevators at the rear of the plane tip the nose up or down, and a rudder on the tail fin is used to turn the plane left or right.

The first airplanes, like the WRIGHT FLYER, had to be very light, as their engines were not very efficient. When better

DID YOU KNOW?

A plane built in 1904 by Horatio Phillips had 20 wings. It looked a bit like a bicycle with a huge venetian blind on top of it. Several years later, Count Caproni built a huge flying houseboat with 18 wings. It was as big as a row of townhouses, but was wrecked when it tried to take off. The first airplane to take off under its own power (carrying a pilot) was the *Eole*, which was flown by Clément Ader in France in 1890.

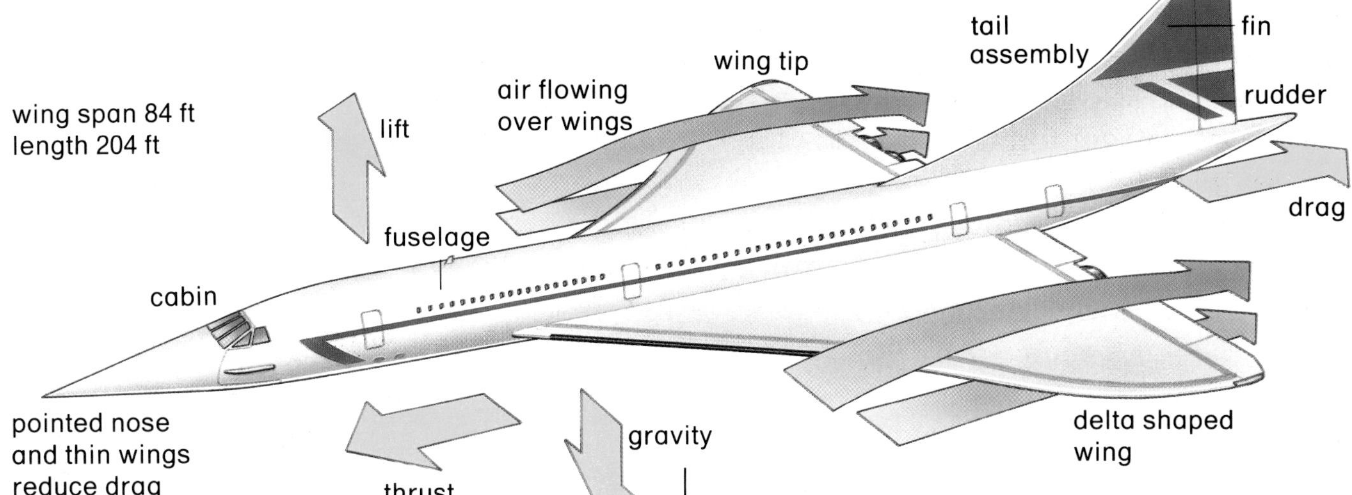

▲ Concorde's engines propel it at more than twice the speed of sound. Its special wings reduce the problems of air resistance.

GASOLINE engines were invented, larger, more powerful aircraft could be built. Today many aircraft are powered by two or more jet engines. There are huge airliners that can carry hundreds of passengers, and fighter planes that travel at three times the speed of sound. Modern aircraft fly in the STRATOSPHERE, where they can avoid clouds and storms.

alcohol

There are many alcohols, from the ethanol in alcoholic drinks to waxy alcohols found in plants. Alcohols are chemicals that contain CARBON, HYDROGEN, and OXYGEN. They are used in many manufacturing processes. Most alcohols are poisonous.

▼ Among the uses of alcohols are the production of plastics, cosmetics, paints, and varnishes.

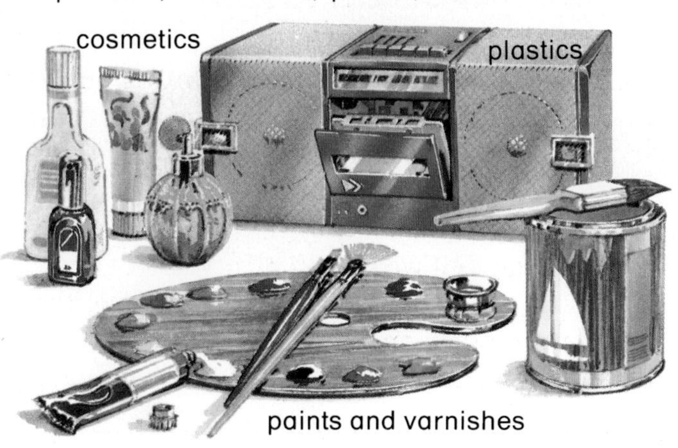

alkali see **acids and alkalis**

alloy

An alloy is a mixture of METALS. Many metals are more useful if they are blended. Brass is an alloy of COPPER and ZINC. Bronze is made out of copper and TIN. ALUMINUM alloys are much stronger than aluminum on its own. NICKEL and copper alloys are used to make coins, because pure copper is too soft and would wear away.

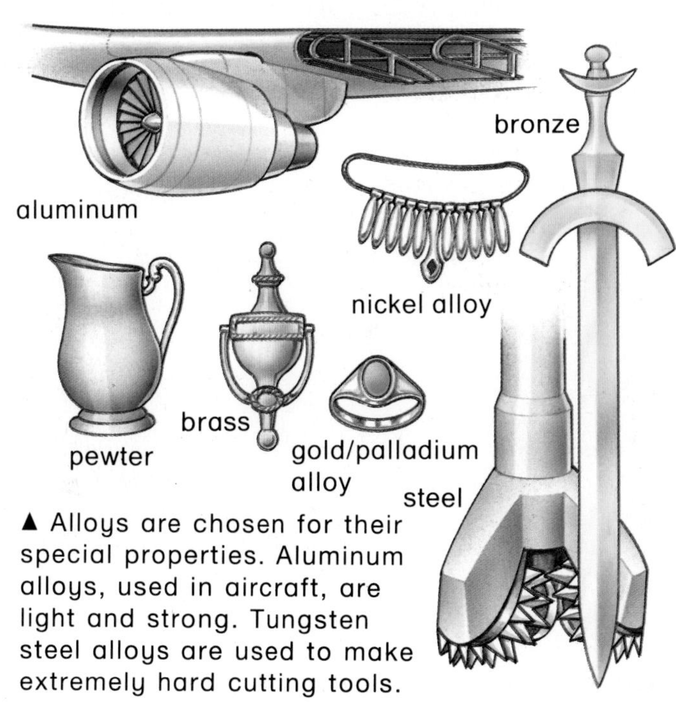

▲ Alloys are chosen for their special properties. Aluminum alloys, used in aircraft, are light and strong. Tungsten steel alloys are used to make extremely hard cutting tools.

A

AIR AND ATMOSPHERE

The Earth is covered by a layer of air. This is the atmosphere. Air is held down by GRAVITY. The atmosphere has several layers. It is thickest at the bottom and gets thinner as you go up. The first layer is about 9 mi (15 km) deep. The top of the thinnest layer reaches about 250 mi (400 km) above the ground.

▶ Imagine the gases in the air all separated out in this balloon. Air is mostly nitrogen, the yellow part. Next is oxygen, colored red. The blue layer is argon. The carbon dioxide is in the bucket hanging over the side.

▶ Satellites orbit 250 mi (400 km) above the Earth. If they were any lower than this, friction with the air would cause them to burn up.

DID YOU KNOW?

Almost four-fifths of the air we breathe is nitrogen. Oxygen, the gas we need to survive, makes up only one-fifth. Argon makes up almost 1 percent. There is only one part of carbon dioxide in 3,500 parts of air — too small to see on this piechart.

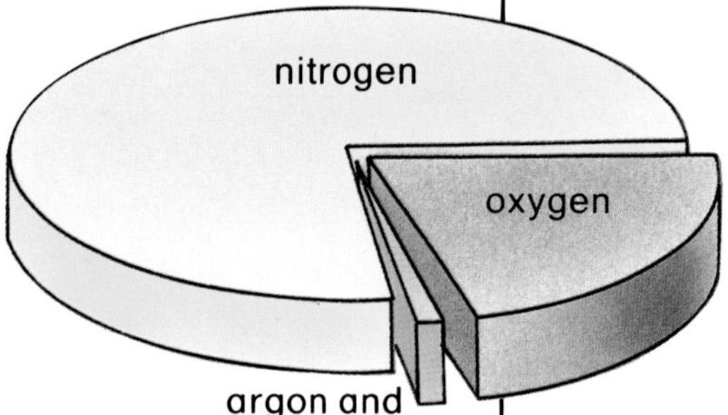

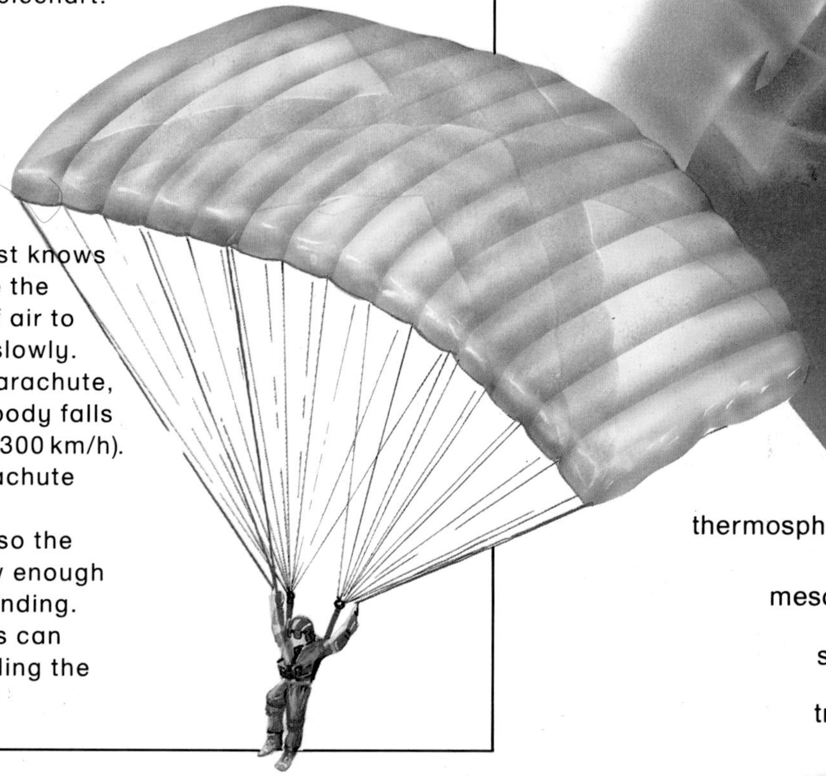

A parachutist knows you can use the thickness of air to float down slowly. Without a parachute, the human body falls at 186 mph (300 km/h). But the parachute provides air resistance, so the speed is low enough for a safe landing. Parachutists can steer by pulling the cords.

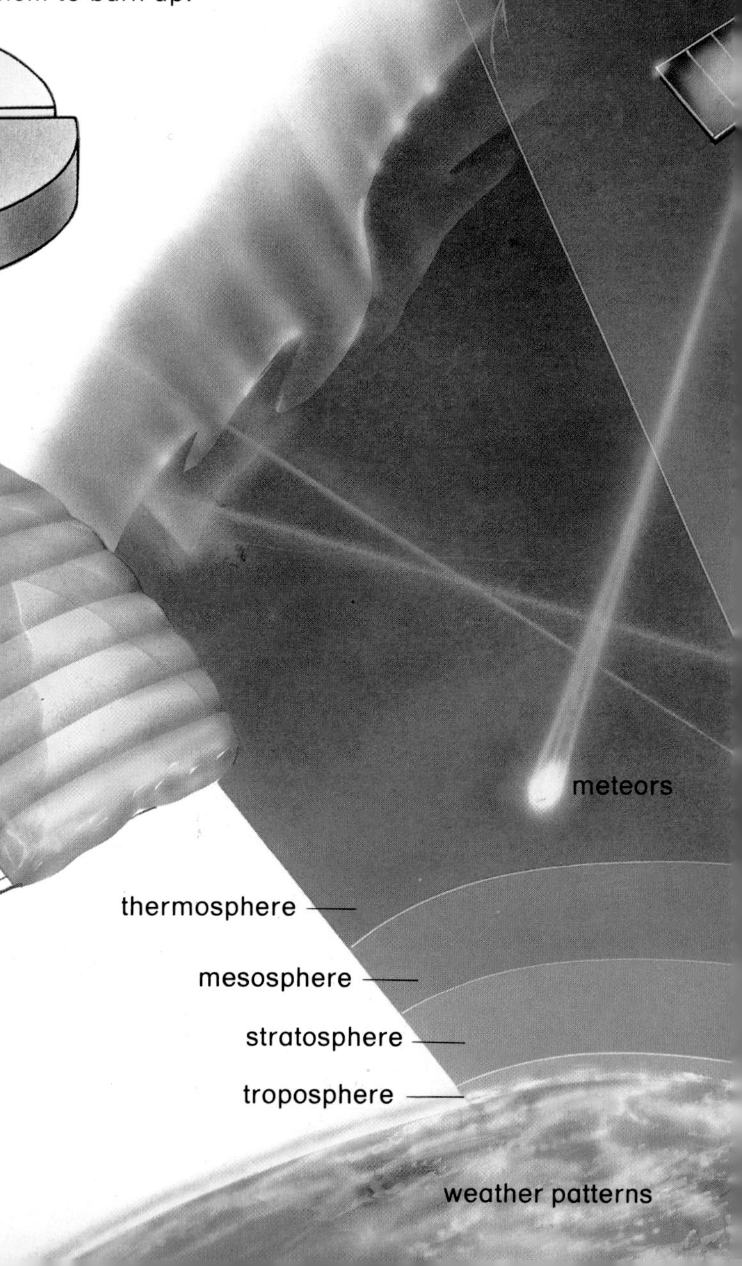

▶ The force of moving air can destroy whole buildings. Tornadoes are violent whirlwinds, with wind speeds of up to 300 mi (500 km) an hour. Winds like this leave a trail of destruction wherever they pass.

◀ The top layer of the atmosphere, 250 mi (400 km) above ground, is the thermosphere. It has just a few molecules of air. This is where the aurora occurs.

◀ At 50 mi (80 km) up, in the mesosphere, the air is thick enough for grains of matter shooting through space to burn up as shooting stars.

◀ Between 11 and 30 miles (17 and 50 km) is the stratosphere, where the Concorde flies. High in the stratosphere is the ozone layer, which protects life on Earth from ultraviolet rays.

◀ The lowest layer is the air with which we are surrounded — the troposphere. It extends from 4 to 11 miles (6 to 17 km) in height.

◀ Compared to the Earth, the atmosphere is not very deep. If the Earth were the size of an apple, the atmosphere would only be as thick as the peel.

A

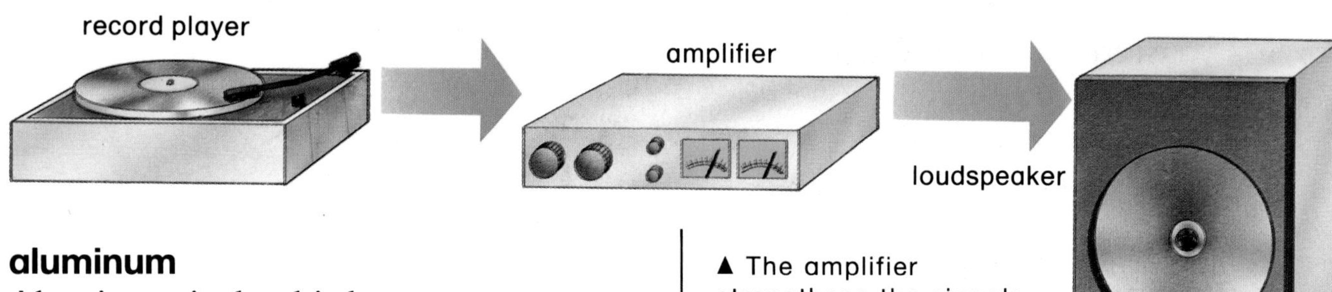

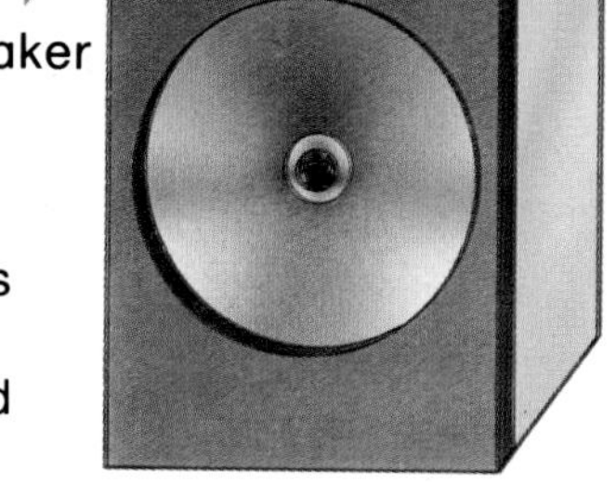

aluminum
Aluminum is the third most common ELEMENT in the EARTH'S crust. It is found as an ORE. It is very light and is used to make AIRCRAFT. When first discovered it was used like a precious METAL, to make jewelry.

▼ Aluminum can be hammered into thin sheets of foil or drawn out into wires to make electrical cables. It is also used to make window frames, soft-drink cans, and firefighters' suits.

ammeter
The flow of a current of ELECTRICITY is measured in amperes (amps), using an ammeter. The symbol for amperes is A.

ammonia
Ammonia is a gas. Each molecule contains one ATOM of NITROGEN and three of HYDROGEN. Its formula is NH_3. It dissolves in water to produce ammonia solution, an ALKALI that gives off choking fumes. Ammonia is used in fertilizers and in coolants for REFRIGERATORS.

▲ The amplifier strengthens the signals produced by a record before they are passed to the speakers.

amplifier
The electrical signals produced by MICROPHONES are weak. To produce sound from a LOUDSPEAKER they must be made stronger, or amplified. Using TRANSISTORS or INTEGRATED CIRCUITS, an amplifier magnifies a weak electrical signal. Musicians who play the electric guitar plug into an "amp" (short for amplifier). Then the small vibrations of the strings can produce a huge sound from the loudspeaker.

analog
An analog is a model. The figures around a watch dial are an analog of the passing of time. The height of the MERCURY in a THERMOMETER is an analog of your temperature. See **digital**.

antifreeze
Some chemicals lower the TEMPERATURE at which water turns to ICE. These chemicals can be used as antifreeze additives. SALT is one example, and in car ENGINES ethylene glycol is used. Ethylene glycol is a very poisonous ALCOHOL.

Aqua-lung
Taking a tank of compressed air under water to supply a diver seems easy. But water PRESSURE increases with depth. If the

air the diver breathes is at a different pressure from the surrounding water, the diver's lungs could easily collapse or burst. The Aqua-lung has a constant-pressure valve that allows the diver to breathe easily at different depths.

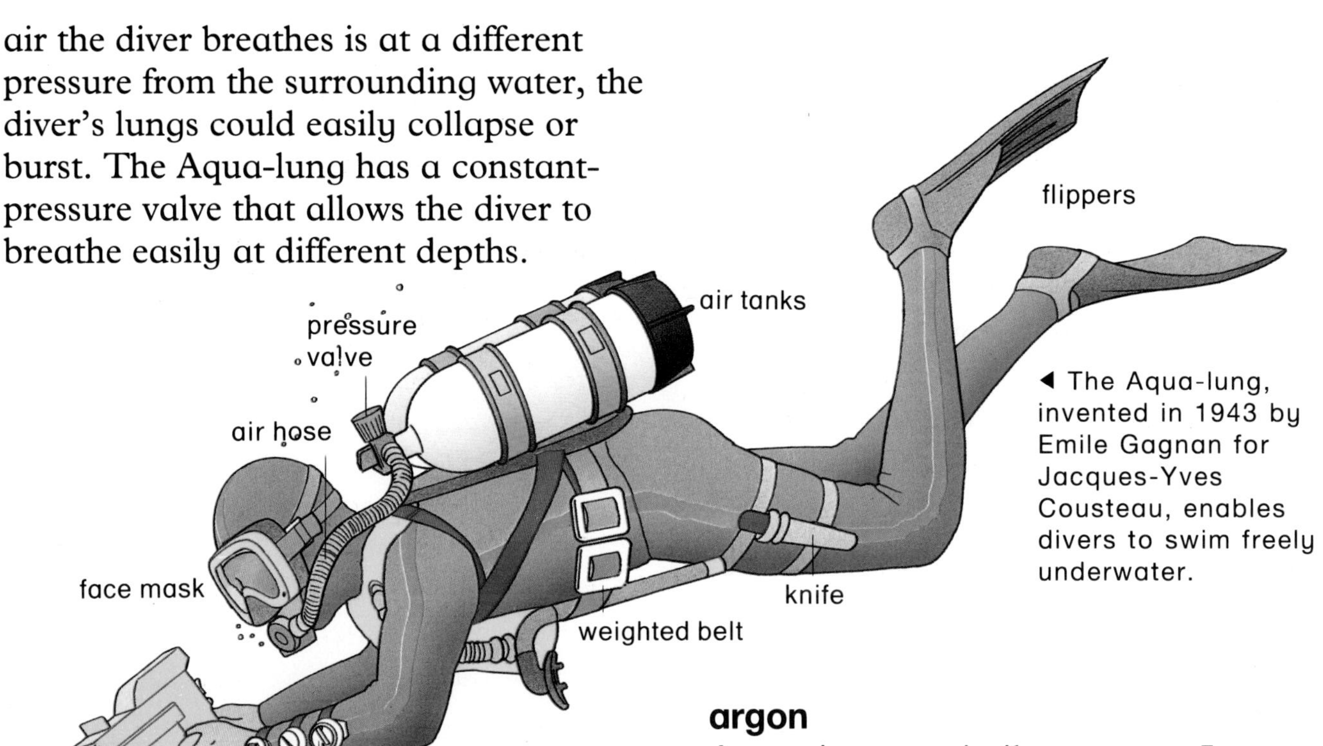

◀ The Aqua-lung, invented in 1943 by Emile Gagnan for Jacques-Yves Cousteau, enables divers to swim freely underwater.

LIFE STORY

Archimedes

Archimedes was a Greek philosopher who lived more than 2,000 years ago. The king had told him to find out whether his new crown had been made with pure GOLD or if some SILVER had been added. Archimedes knew that if the crown contained silver it would be lighter. He thought of comparing the volume of the crown with the volume of a chunk of gold of the same weight. But how could he MEASURE the volume of the crown? The answer came to him one day as he stepped into a full bath and saw the water flow over the edge. He realized that the volume of water the crown would displace would equal the volume of the crown. Archimedes was so excited that he ran home without dressing, shouting "Eureka! Eureka!" (Greek for "I've found it.")

argon

Argon is a gas similar to NEON. It never forms COMPOUNDS and so is called an "inert" or "noble" gas. Argon is the third most common gas in the ATMOSPHERE, making up 1 percent of the air.

arithmetic see **mathematics**

arsenic

Arsenic is an ELEMENT that is a bit like a METAL. It exists in several different forms: metallic arsenic, black or brown arsenic, and yellow arsenic. It is a slow poison and has been used in the past for many famous murders.

artificial intelligence see **computer**

asbestos

There are several types of asbestos. It is a soft fibrous MINERAL that will resist HEAT. One use of asbestos is in brake linings for cars, trains, and planes. It has also been used for heat insulation. But people who breathe in asbestos dust can develop a disease known as asbestosis. We now know that people can even develop cancer many years after breathing the dust. So asbestos is being removed from many buildings. This can leave a lot of dust in the air, so the job must be done carefully.

asteroid see **solar system**

astronaut see **spacecraft**

astronomy

Astronomy is the science of studying space. People long ago used to watch the stars and knew their positions in the night sky. If a new STAR appeared, its position was noted on a star MAP. The first recorded COMET was drawn in this way, over 2,000 years ago. Astronomers use TELESCOPES to study the planets more closely. Today, SPACECRAFT can also land cameras on some of the planets to make close-up studies of their surfaces and ATMOSPHERES.

atmosphere see **pages 10 and 11**

atom see **page 15**

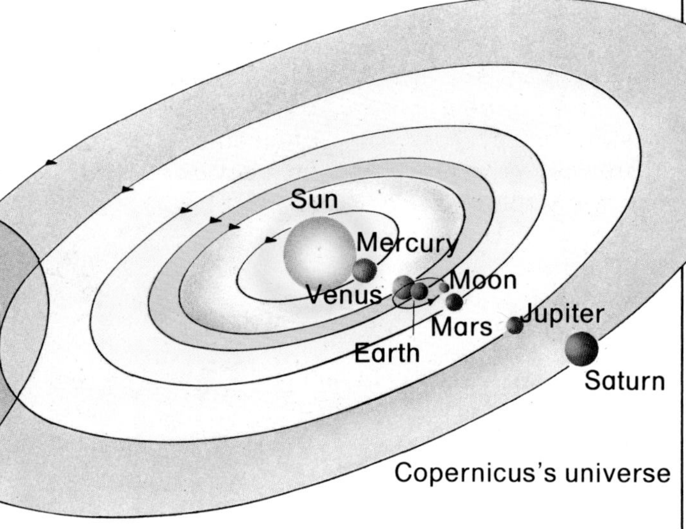

▲ Ancient Greek astronomers believed that the Earth was at the center of the universe. Their ideas survived until the 16th century when a Polish churchman, Nikolai Kopernik (known to us as Copernicus), proved that the Earth and all the other planets revolve around the Sun.

aurora

The Sun sends out waves of ENERGY. This energy is drawn toward the North and South magnetic POLES of the Earth. Sometimes there is enough energy to produce an aurora. This is a flickering curtain of light in the night sky. Auroras are usually seen near the poles, but they can sometimes be seen in countries thousands of miles away.

ATOMS AND MOLECULES

An atom is the smallest piece of an element. A million atoms would measure one millimeter across. The smallest atom is that of HYDROGEN. Among the largest is URANIUM, which is over 200 times heavier than hydrogen. Atoms contain a lot of ENERGY. When they are split, this energy can be released. This principle is used to make nuclear weapons and ELECTRICITY.

▼ The protons have a positive electric charge. The neutrons have no charge at all. Inside each of these particles are three smaller bodies. These are quarks. The forces that stick the quarks together are known as gluons.

▼ The negatively charged electrons orbit at fixed distances from the nucleus. Each layer of electrons makes up an electron shell.

▼ At the center of the atom is the nucleus containing protons and neutrons. Electrons orbit the nucleus. They are much smaller than in this picture. With a nucleus this size, the electrons would be the size of pinheads and would be orbiting over a mile away.

neutron

proton

electron

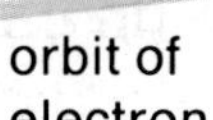

orbit of electron

MOLECULES AND CRYSTALS

Atoms bond together to form molecules. A molecule is the smallest piece of a compound that can exist. The molecule below shows two hydrogen atoms bonded to an atom of oxygen. This forms a molecule of water.

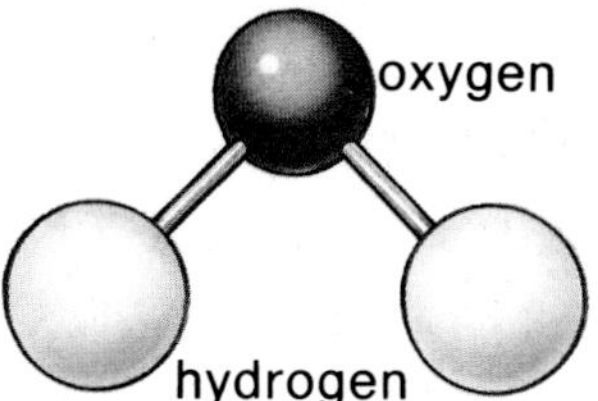

Atoms of sodium and chlorine link to form cubic crystals of salt.

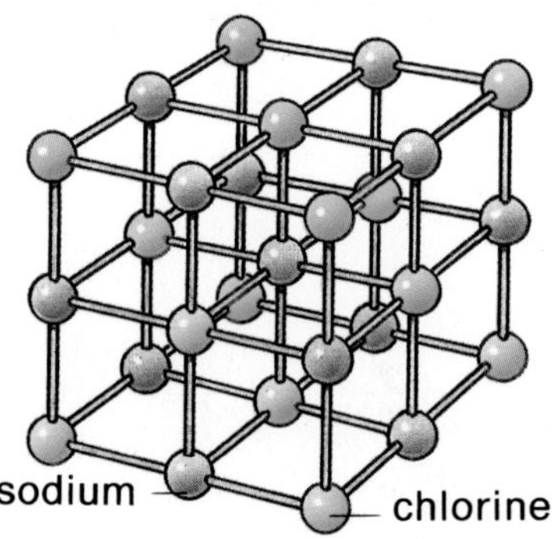

This twisted molecule is the most important for every form of life — DNA.

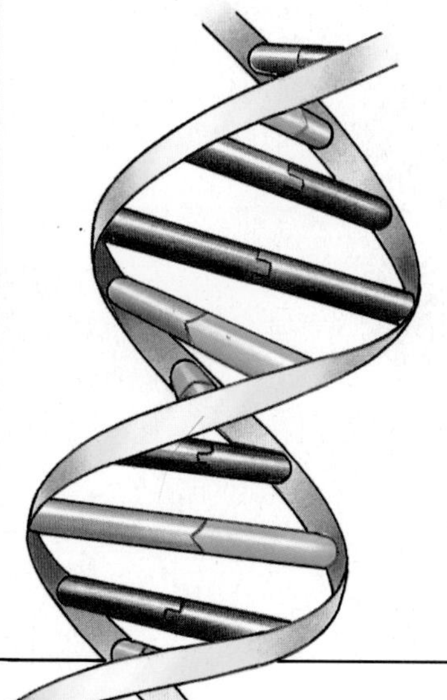

balloon

Two types of balloons can rise in the AIR. One is filled with a gas that is lighter than air, such as HYDROGEN or HELIUM. Hydrogen is lighter than helium, but it catches fire easily. Helium does not burn and is therefore safer to use. The other type is filled with hot air. The balloon rises because hot air is lighter than cold air. A basket underneath the balloon can carry passengers.

bar code see **page 17**

barium

Barium is a metal whose ATOMS block X-RAYS. Doctors give a patient a barium "meal" to swallow when they want to look for any odd shapes in the soft intestines.

barometer

From hour to hour the PRESSURE of the AIR around us changes. If it rises, finer WEATHER is due. If it falls, expect RAIN. A barometer measures air pressure and shows the result on a dial. The first barometers had a column of MERCURY supported by air pressure. The needle of an aneroid barometer moves as flexible chamber walls expand or contract.

battery

A battery contains chemicals that react and produce ELECTRICITY. Dry batteries (used in a flashlight or portable radio) are powered by a chemical paste to produce electricity. They go dead when all the chemicals are used up. Cars have a lead-acid battery, which can be recharged. The first battery was made by Alessandro Volta, an Italian scientist. See **volt**.

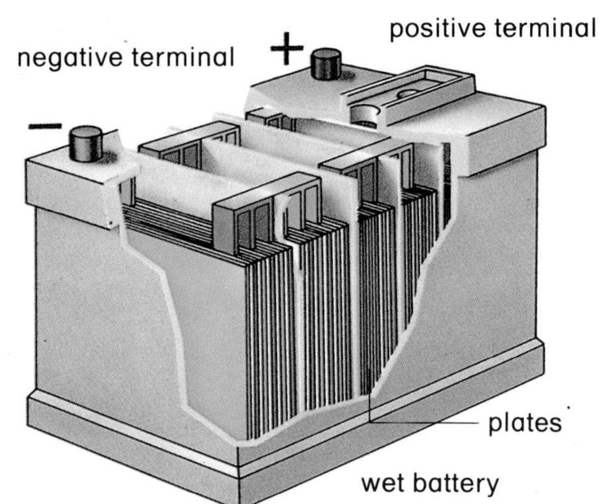

▲ A car battery contains two sets of plates standing in sulfuric acid. One set is made from lead, the other from lead dioxide. Reactions between the acid and the plates produce an electric current.

▼ Flashlights use a type of battery called a dry cell. The acid is in the form of a paste so that it cannot spill out. In one type of dry cell the zinc outer case is one electrode and a carbon rod in the center is the other.

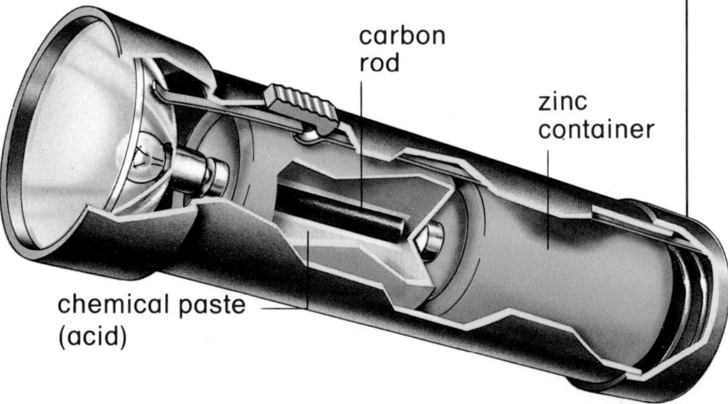

BAR CODES

Bar codes are printed stripes of black and white. They appear on supermarket goods and on books. Bar codes are even used on hospital specimens. They do not hold any mysterious information. They are just a list of code numbers and letters from a catalog. The advantage of using bar codes is that they can be read automatically, by COMPUTER.

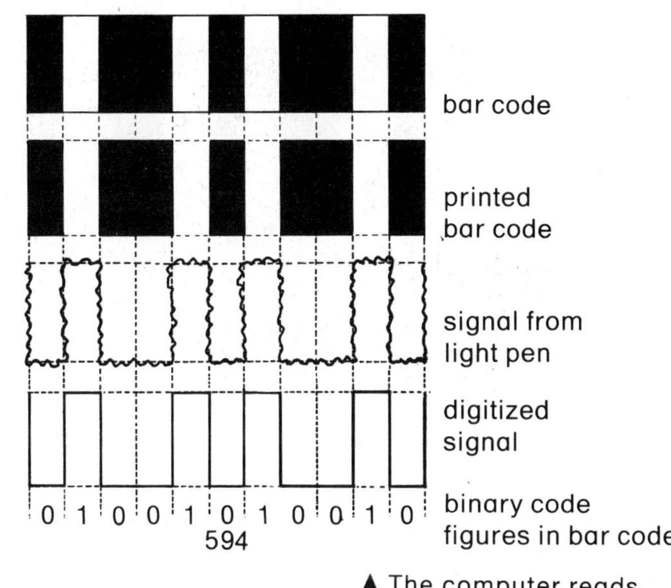

▲ The computer reads the number of bands in a bar code. It measures how wide they are. The computer can then translate the digital signal back into numbers.

▶ Bar codes can be printed upright, or across the item. The upright ones are known as ladder bar codes, because the stripes look like ladder rungs. The horizontal bar codes are called picket fence codes.

picket fence bar code

upright bar code

▲ The check number confirms that the code was read properly.

▲ Here is the catalog number.

◀ This is the number of the company that produced the goods.

◀ The code starts with a digit that indicates the country of origin.

▲ Bar codes can be read with a hand-held wand. A laser beam is shone down the wand. The wand picks up the light reflected from the bars and produces a digital signal which is passed to a computer. The computer can match the information to an entry in the catalog.

reflected light

angled laser beam

▲ The wand must be held at an angle, or the reflection is too bright to be read.

▼ In a supermarket the bar code is read as an item passes over a laser beam. To make sure the code is read properly, the laser beam scans back and forth dozens of times in a fraction of a second. The computer can then check that the readings are correct, and reject any that are incomplete.

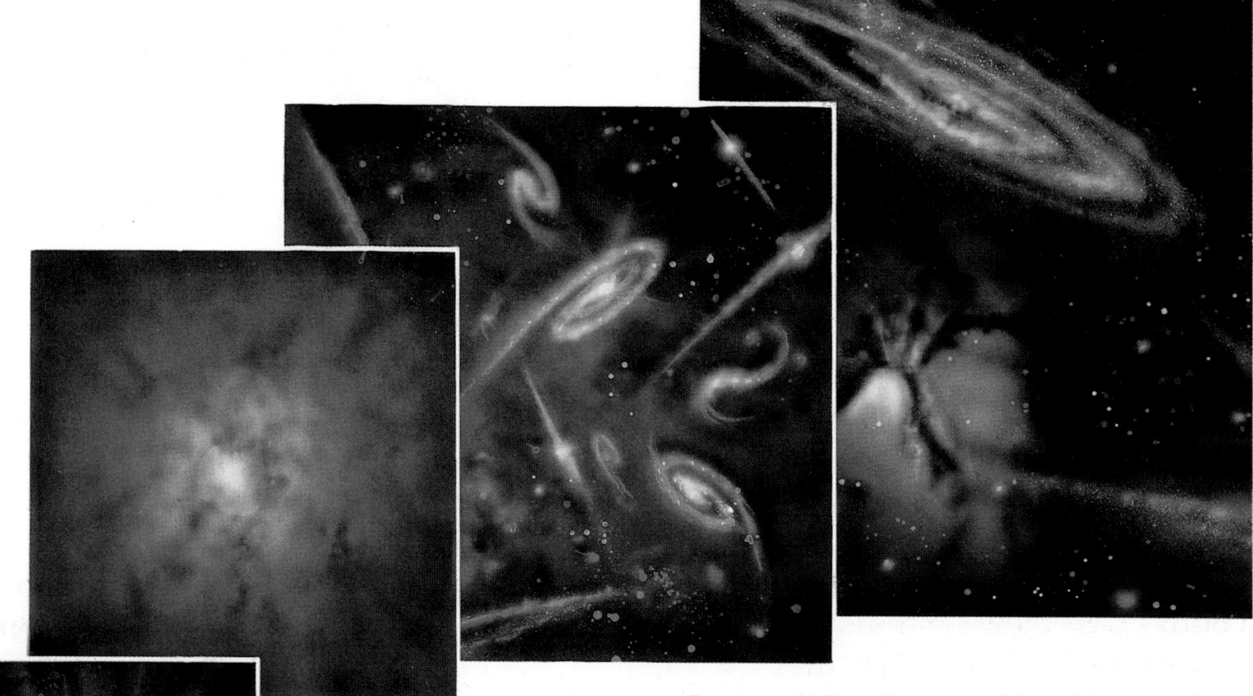

▲ The Big Bang was a vast explosion. Matter and radiation were thrown out in all directions. The universe expanded and cooled, and the galaxies formed.

Big Bang

The Big Bang is the name given to the theory that says the UNIVERSE began with a gigantic explosion 15 billion years ago and that the GALAXIES are still moving apart from the explosion. One piece of evidence for this theory is that distant stars seem to give off red light, which would happen if they are moving away from us. The universe may expand forever, or it might stop and then slowly collapse in on itself.

binary

A binary system has only two positions, "on" (1) and "off" (0). By using combinations of 1 and 0, you can make any figure. "One" would be 001, and "two" 010. "Three" would be one plus two, or 011. This idea lies at the root of the DIGITAL systems used by COMPUTERS and in RECORDINGS.

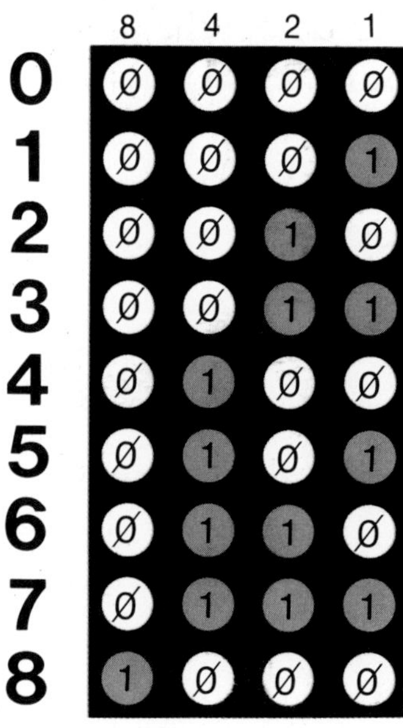

◀ Our counting system is based on the numbers 0 to 9, ten numbers in all. Binary code is a counting system based on the number two. It is better suited to computers because their circuits have two states, off and on. These two states are used to represent the numbers 0 and 1.

binoculars

If you strap two TELESCOPES together you can make a pair of binoculars. Binoculars are easier to use than a telescope because you are using both eyes to look at the same image.

B

biochemistry

Biochemistry is the study of the chemicals connected with life. Living things contain many COMPOUNDS of the ELEMENTS NITROGEN, CARBON, OXYGEN, and HYDROGEN. Biochemists study the structure of these compounds, and what they do. By studying the reactions of these compounds, biochemists have found cures and treatments for many diseases inside the cells of living things.

black hole

When a massive STAR ages it begins to contract. As its MASS shrinks into a smaller VOLUME, its field of GRAVITY gets stronger and stronger. This increased gravitational force makes the star collapse into a smaller and smaller volume. Eventually, the gravity is so strong that even LIGHT cannot escape. Astronomers can only detect the star by its effect on other bodies in space – they cannot see it because no light escapes. This invisible star is a black hole.

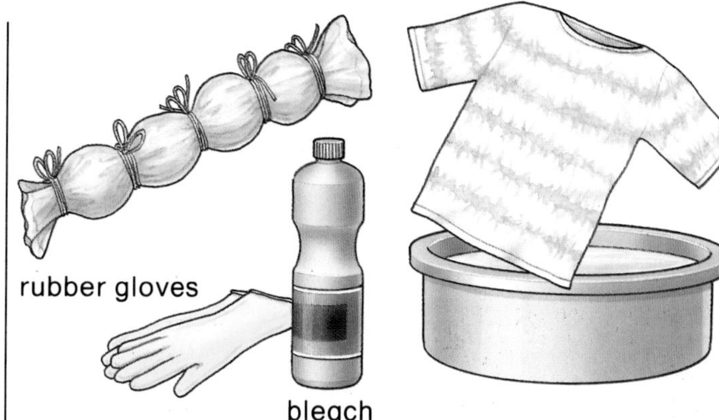

▲ Tie a colored T-shirt with string. Wearing rubber gloves, soak the shirt for 30 minutes in a weak solution of bleach to give a tie-dye effect.

bleach

Many colored chemicals lose their color when they react with OXYGEN. COMPOUNDS that cause this effect are called bleaches. In the home, one common bleach is hydrogen peroxide, used to lighten hair. Another is chlorine bleach, used in the kitchen. Bleach combines with and destroys any biochemical compound. Since germs are made of biochemical MOLECULES, bleach is a valuable aid to killing germs.

▼ The immense strength of gravity in a black hole can distort light from nearby stars.

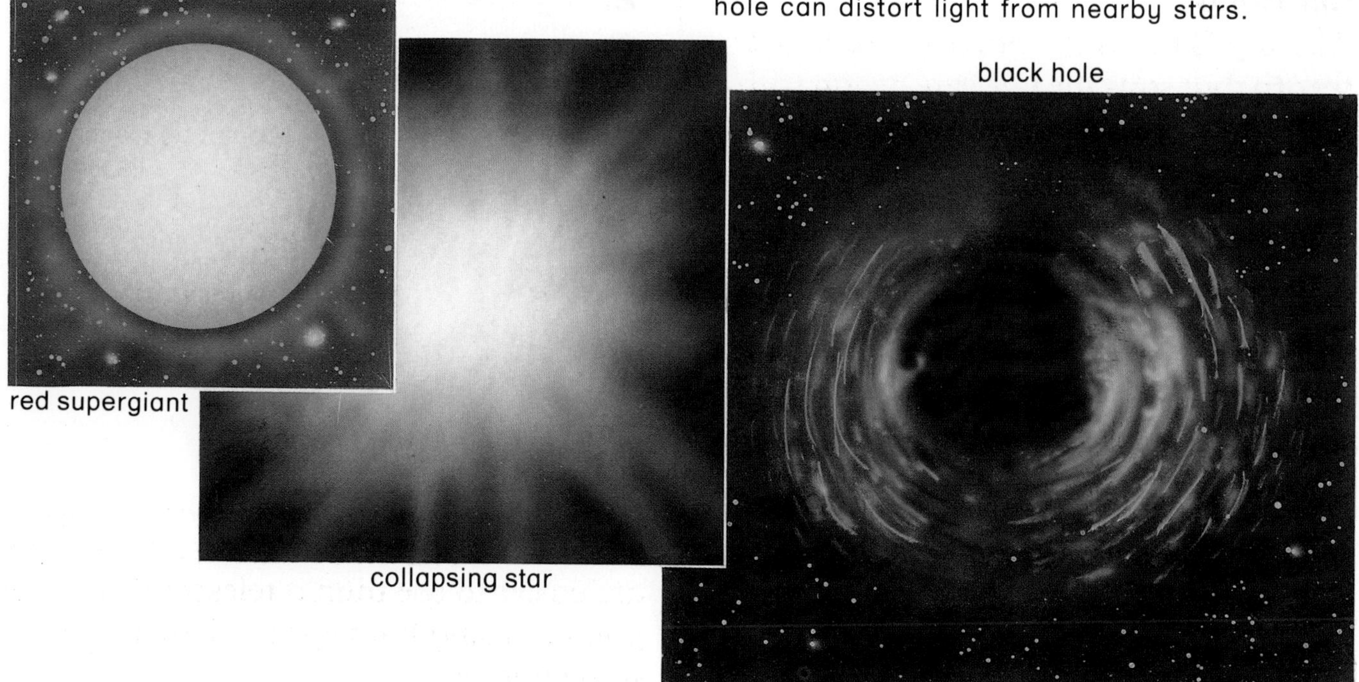

▼ CAT scanners are used to detect problems such as tumors inside a patient's body. X-rays are beamed through a section of the body at different angles. The patient feels nothing. The x-rays are received by detectors and combined by a computer to produce the final image.

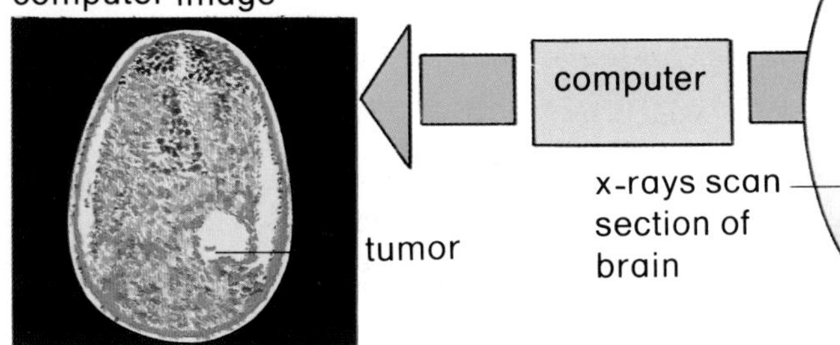

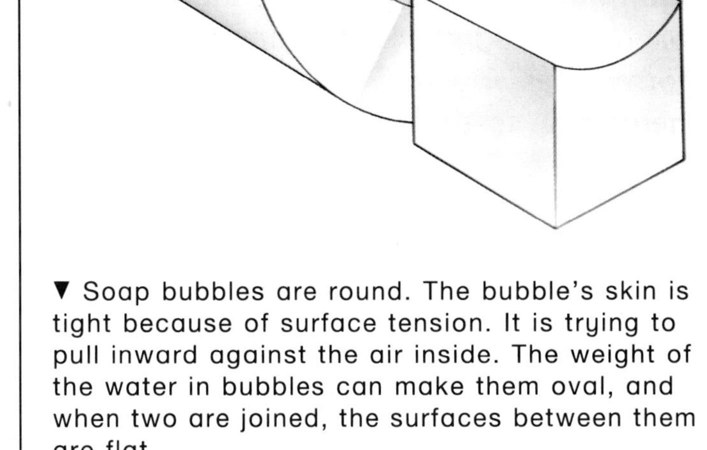

body scanner

A body scanner produces pictures of sections of a living person. The CAT (computer axial tomography) scanner beams X-RAYS through the patient to a detector, which sends the information to a computer that then builds a picture of part of the body. A magnetic resonance scanner uses the PROTON in the HYDROGEN ATOMS of each WATER molecule inside the body. A system of MAGNETS makes the protons RESONATE, and a picture can be made of soft internal organs.

boiling

Boiling happens when a bubbling liquid changes to a gas. The boiling point of WATER is 212°F (100°C).

bubbles

Bubbles are pockets of gas trapped inside a solid or liquid. Some cheeses have bubbles from the microbes that aged them. Bubbles can be made by dipping a wire loop into SOAP solution. If you shape a wire coat hanger, you can make bubbles in unusual shapes — even squares!

burning see **combustion**

▼ Soap bubbles are round. The bubble's skin is tight because of surface tension. It is trying to pull inward against the air inside. The weight of the water in bubbles can make them oval, and when two are joined, the surfaces between them are flat.

liquid detergent

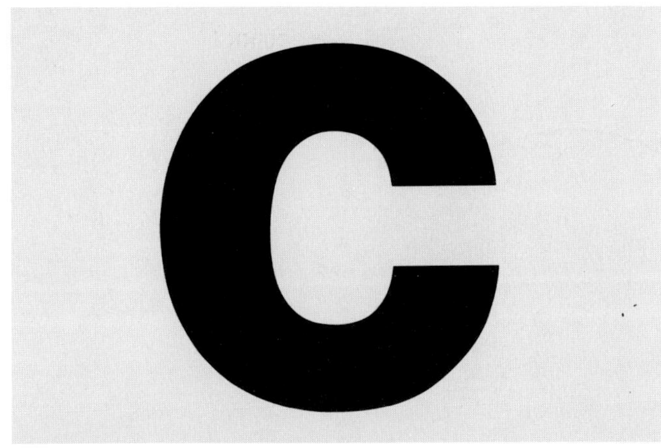

caffeine

Caffea is the Latin name for the coffee plant. Caffeine means "in coffee." It is a DRUG you find in coffee. Pure caffeine forms white crystals. This drug makes the heart beat faster and can also cause headaches. Caffeine keeps people awake. It is found in other drinks too. For instance, a cup of tea and even a glass of cola contain some caffeine!

calcium

Calcium is a very reactive METAL. It is never found on its own in nature. But COMPOUNDS of calcium are very common in rocks, such as limestone and marble. They are also found in dairy foods, like cheese. Calcium is used by the body to make strong bones and teeth, which is why it is important for your health.

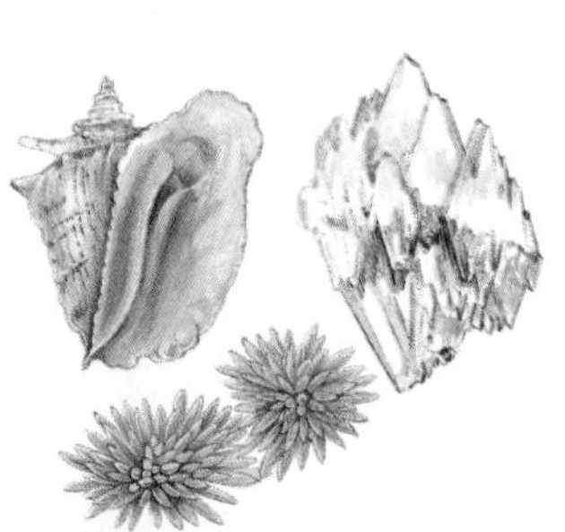

▶ Calcium salts are found in many forms. The white coating that forms in cooking pots is made up of needle-shaped crystals of calcium sulfate. Chalk and seashells contain calcium carbonate.

calculator

Calculators contain a MICROCHIP which can do difficult calculations in an instant. As the chip is very small, a tiny calculator can even be fitted inside a watch. Some calculators are powered by SOLAR ENERGY.

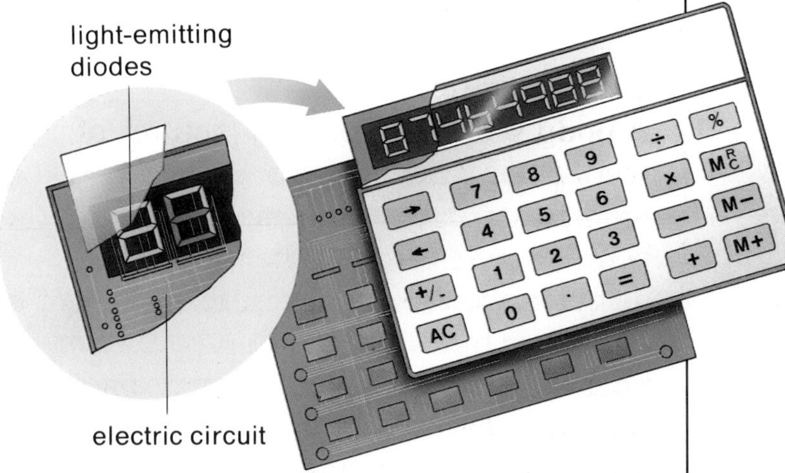

▲ Electronic calculators contain a tiny microchip that can add, subtract, multiply, and divide large numbers in an instant. Scientific calculators can be programmed to do more difficult calculations. Numbers are displayed on light-emitting diodes or a liquid crystal display.

▼ Limestone is a soft rock made from the calcium-rich shells of millions of microscopic sea creatures. Rainwater gradually dissolves the soft rocks, forming channels. In time, these channels join up and form a complicated network of underground tunnels and waterways.

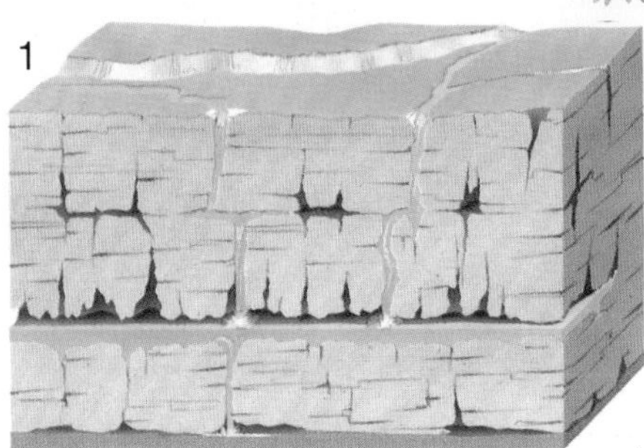

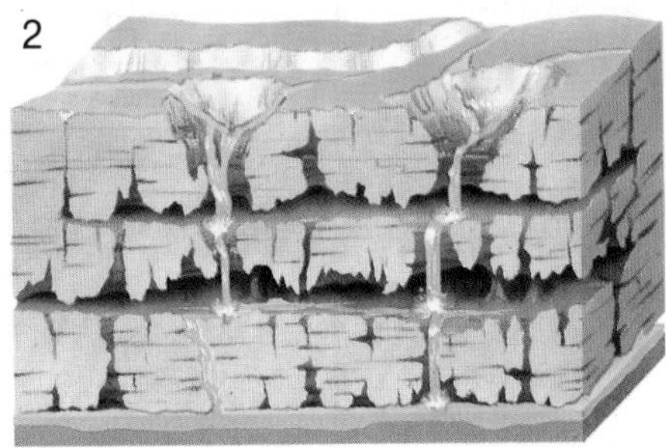

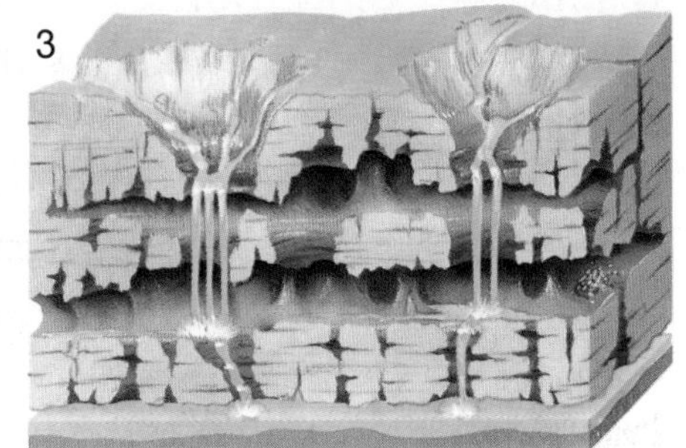

C

calendar

This is how we mark the passing of days: The time it takes the EARTH to go around the Sun is a YEAR, or 365.25 days. The MOON goes around the Earth in 29.53 days. The Earth rotates around its own axis once a DAY. The earliest calendars used the Moon's month to work out the length of a year. But 12 lunar (Moon) months are only 354 days. To make the year add up to 365, most months have 30 or 31 days.

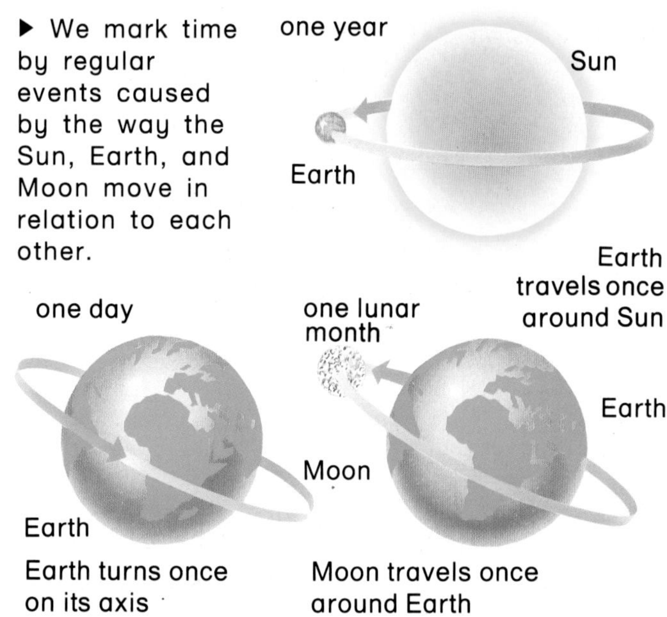

▶ We mark time by regular events caused by the way the Sun, Earth, and Moon move in relation to each other.

camera

Cameras capture an image by focusing LIGHT rays onto a sensitive surface. A VIDEO camera or camcorder records moving pictures by electronics. A camera used for PHOTOGRAPHY takes pictures on film.

carbon

Soot is carbon, and so is coal. Carbon is a nonmetallic ELEMENT. It forms thousands of different COMPOUNDS. Most of the compounds in your body contain carbon.

▶ Graphite, which is the soft "lead" in a pencil, and diamond, one of the hardest substances, are both made of carbon, but with different structures. Graphite is made up of loose sheets of atoms. Diamond is made up of stronger crystals.

carbon dating

Natural carbon contains the ISOTOPE carbon 14, which decays with a HALF-LIFE of 5,760 years. Measuring how much carbon 14 is left determines the age of ancient plant and animal remains.

carbon dioxide

Carbon dioxide is a rare gas in the AIR but a vital one for all life on Earth. There is only one part of carbon dioxide in 3,000 parts of air! Its formula is CO_2 (one carbon atom and two oxygen atoms). See **greenhouse effect**.

cassette see **recording, video**

catalyst

Catalysts are substances that help CHEMICAL reactions to take place or take place faster. The catalyst itself is not changed or used up in the reaction.

▼ A sugar cube makes lemonade fizz violently. It acts like a catalyst, helping bubbles to form.

catalytic converter
Fumes from a car exhaust contain poisonous gases. A catalytic converter in the exhaust helps to turn the poisons into safer gases like water vapor and CARBON DIOXIDE. But although a catalytic converter reduces one sort of pollution, it is no answer to the GREENHOUSE EFFECT.

cathode rays
Cathode rays are beams of ELECTRONS. They can only travel in a vacuum. Cathode rays produce the image in an ELECTRON MICROSCOPE. They also make the picture on a TV screen.

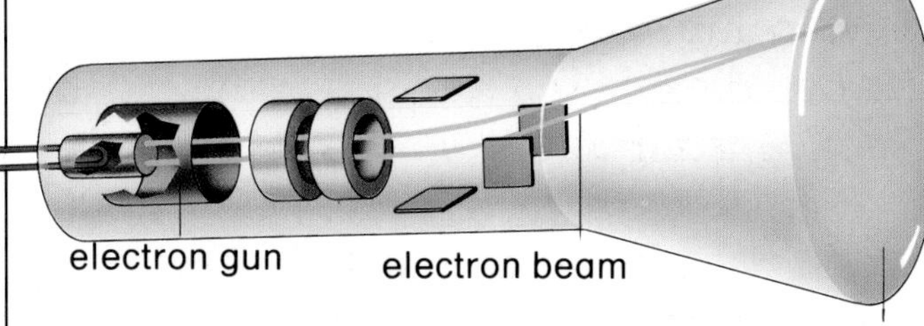

▲ A television picture is formed by cathode rays tracing a series of lines on a screen coated with material that glows when hit by electrons.

cellular phone
Ordinary telephones send messages along wires. But cellular phones use RADIO. They contain a radio transmitter that sends its message to a local relay station. A cellular phone switches automatically to the nearest local station as you travel across the country.

Celsius
Anders Celsius was a Swedish scientist who thought of dividing the TEMPERATURE scale into 100 parts between the boiling and freezing points of water. This led to the scale that most countries use today.

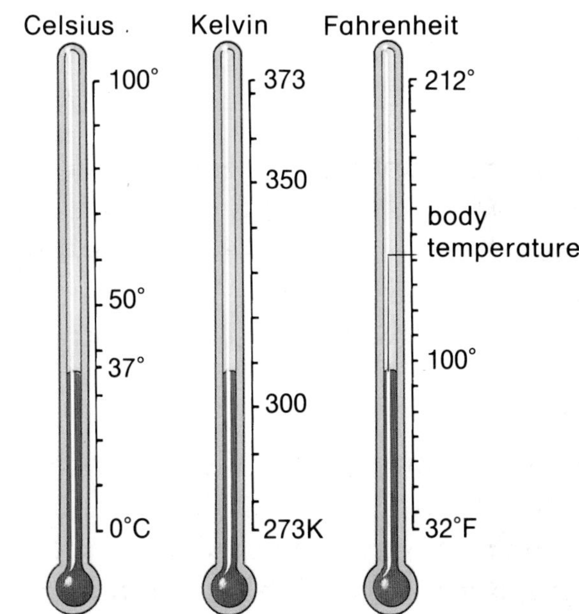

▲ Human body temperature is 37°C on the Celsius scale, 310 K on the Kelvin scale, and 98°F in Fahrenheit.

▼ Each cell has its own relay station which receives calls from a cellular phone.

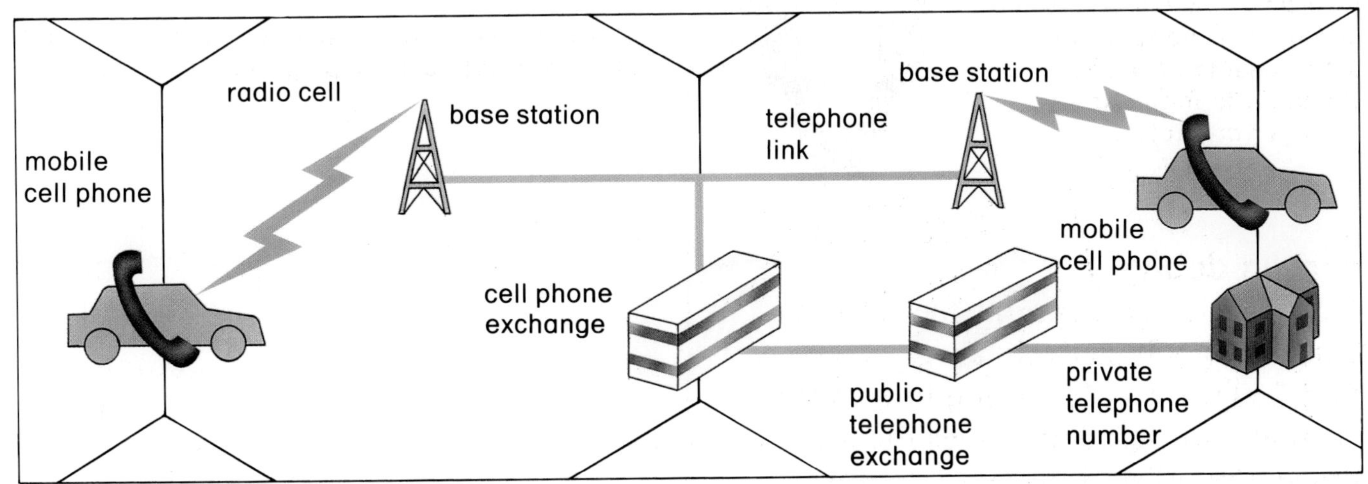

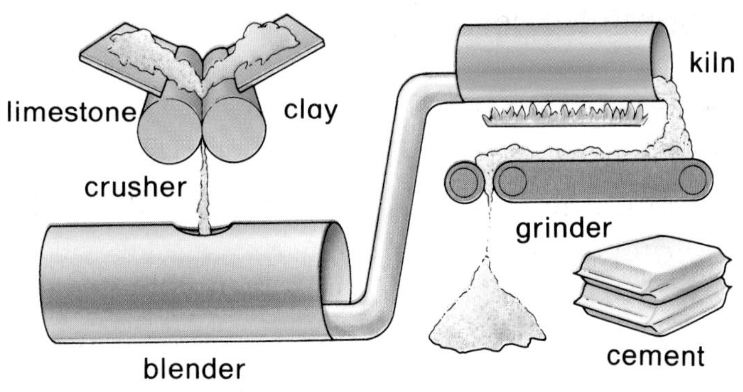

▲ Cement is made by crushing clay and limestone together, heating the mixture, and then grinding it down to make a fine powder.

cement

Cement means "hard glue." Building cement is made by heating limestone and clay. The heat drives off the WATER (H_2O) and CARBON DIOXIDE (CO_2). The cement is ground to a powder, then mixed with water just before use. It changes to its hard, stony form when it dries. As it sets, the HEAT ENERGY originally put in by the cement furnace is given out. This is why setting cement gets warm.

centrifuge

A centrifuge whirls objects around in a circle at a very high speed. It produces centrifugal force, which pushes the objects away from the center as they are spun around. This is what forces water out of wet clothes in a spin drier. Centrifuges can also be used to separate mixtures. If you spin test tubes containing cells, the cells will settle out very quickly. The heavier cells are pushed farther outward and settle at the bottom of the tube. Giant centrifuges are used to train astronauts, as they produce forces similar to those of a ROCKET at blastoff.

◀ Centrifuges are used to separate liquids and particles in a laboratory and to produce the forces that act on pilots and astronauts in flight.

test tube
motor
speed controls
astronaut training in centrifuge

ceramics

Many types of clay are made of tiny grains which melt at high temperatures, just as GLASS does. Ceramic objects are made by firing the molded clays in a kiln, or oven, at high temperatures. Examples include porcelain and china. Some special ceramics are used in electronics.

chalk

Millions of tiny shelled animals made the chalk cliffs you see today. As they died, their minuscule white skeletons or shells built up a thick layer. This hardened to make chalk.

▼ Microscopic shells formed layers at the bottom of the sea and eventually became chalk.

changes of state

Many substances can exist in different forms. The three states are solids, liquids, and gases. If you HEAT a solid it may melt and become a liquid. If you heat a liquid it may boil to become a gas. Each step up

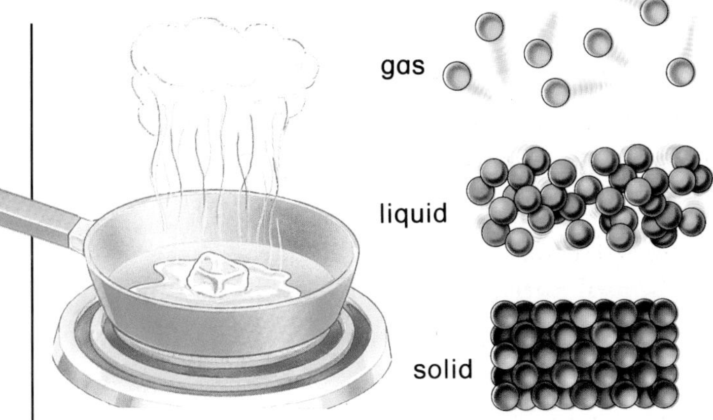

▲ Changes of state are caused by the movement of molecules. When ice is heated the molecules move around and the ice melts to water. On further heating they fly apart, forming a vapor.

uses a lot of HEAT ENERGY. Candle wax can be seen in all three states when it is heated, and so can WATER — as ICE, water, and STEAM. See **combustion.**

charcoal

If you heat wood to a high temperature without letting in OXYGEN, you get charcoal. Charcoal is made of CARBON.

▼ Charcoal is used to purify liquids and gases. As water flows through a filter, impurities are adsorbed on the charcoal, leaving clean water.

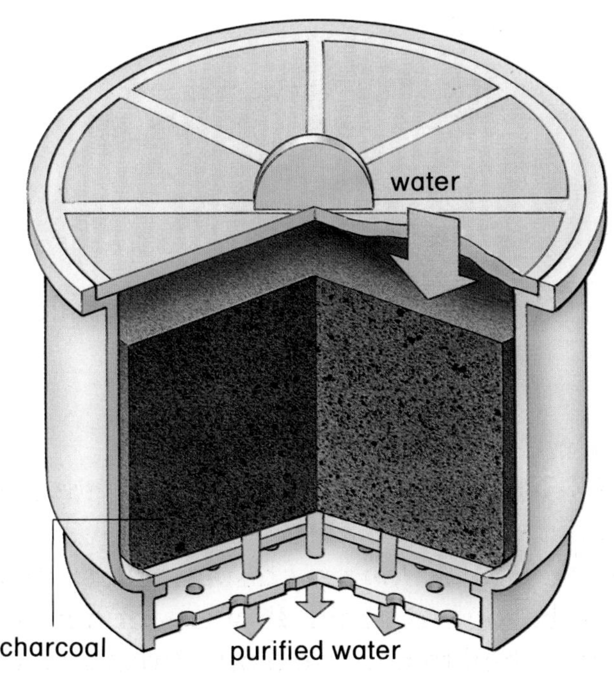

chemistry see **page 26**

chlorine

Chlorine gas is greenish-yellow and is highly poisonous. It has been used to kill soldiers in war. Some kinds of BLEACH give off chlorine, so they can kill the germs in water or around a toilet. Chlorine is also used to kill germs in the water supply. When IONS of chlorine join with SODIUM they form sodium chloride, or common SALT. The sodium and chlorine ions bond together very strongly.

chlorofluorocarbons (CFCs)

Chlorofluorocarbons (CFCs) are gases which contain atoms of CHLORINE, fluorine, and CARBON. If they are put in a can under pressure, they change to liquid form. They were used in REFRIGERATORS and as propellants in AEROSOLS. But many people think CFCs damage the OZONE layer in the Earth's ATMOSPHERE. For this reason, many CFCs are now being banned.

▶ When CFCs float up into the stratosphere, their chlorine atoms react with the ozone molecules.

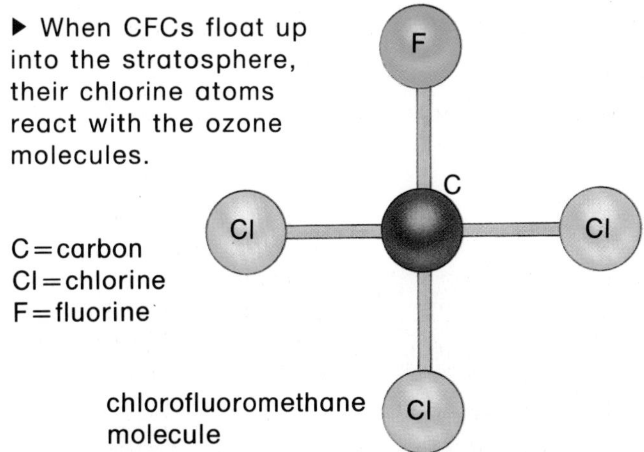

chromium

Chromium is one of the hardest and shiniest metals in the world. It resists corrosion and is used in ELECTROPLATING to coat other metals, and also in ALLOYS.

CHEMISTRY

Chemistry is the study of the ELEMENTS and the COMPOUNDS they form. Chemists study their properties and also how they react with different substances. A substance does not have to be synthetic to be chemical. The food in your kitchen contains chemicals. Medicines are chemicals too, and many of those were developed as extracts from wild plants. One of the most amazing chemical systems we know about is your body.

▼ Products like flour, baking powder, and salt are pure ingredients these days as chemists have developed processes to remove impurities. Ground chalk and even lead oxide used to be found in food.

▼ Baking powder and salt are traditional chemicals in your kitchen. But there are many new products, like margarine and the "creamers" for coffee. Chemical flavorings and preservatives are often added to prepacked foods.

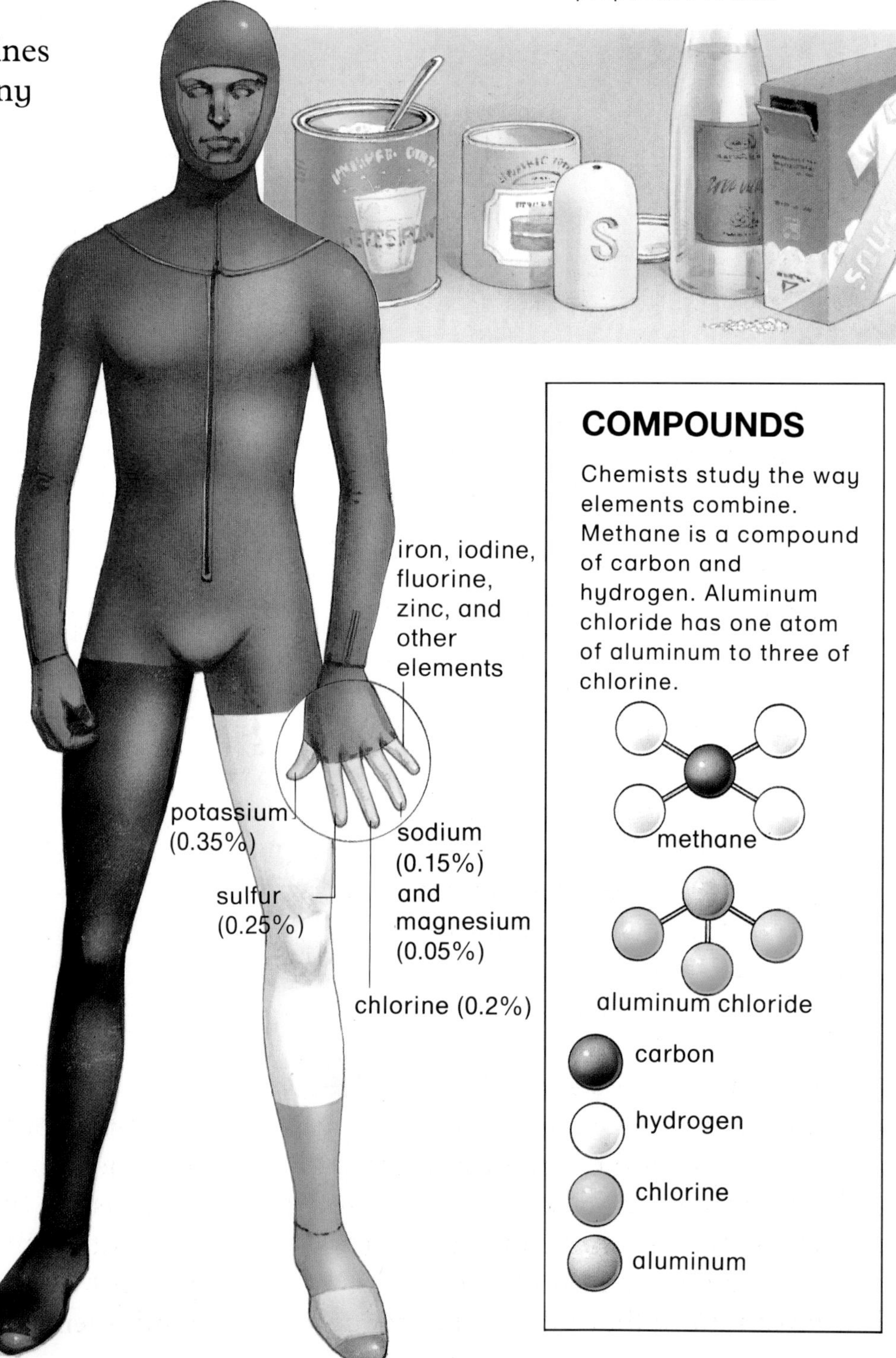

▶ What are the chemical elements in your body? Most of it, 65 percent, is oxygen — shown as the red part in this picture. Carbon, the black part, makes up 18 percent. Next is hydrogen (white) at 9 percent, followed by nitrogen (dark blue), at 3 percent. Two percent of the body is made up of calcium (pale blue) and 1 percent is phosphorus (violet). Two percent is made up of small amounts of other chemicals. Chemical reactions constantly take place inside your body. Food is "burned" with oxygen to give you energy. The vitamins and minerals in your diet are necessary for all the chemical systems to work properly.

COMPOUNDS

Chemists study the way elements combine. Methane is a compound of carbon and hydrogen. Aluminum chloride has one atom of aluminum to three of chlorine.

▲ A movie film is a plastic strip containing many thousands of separate pictures. The wriggling line down one side of the strip is the film's soundtrack.

DID YOU KNOW?

The first movie film ever shown was in 1885, in New York. It was made by Louis le Prince. There is a short film, taken by him in England, which still survives. It shows his father walking in the garden at his house in Leeds. By 1894 the world's first movie house had opened in New York, and in the next year another one opened in Paris. Sound pictures were first demonstrated in London during 1910, and by 1922 public films were being shown in Berlin. Some of the first films were shown in little viewing booths rather than on a big screen. The biggest screen in history was erected for a fair in Paris in 1937. It was 295 feet (90 m) wide and 33 feet (10 m) high. The biggest in use today is in Indonesia. It is 98 feet (30 m) wide and 72 feet (22 m) high.

cinema or motion pictures

Movies work because of a trick. If you see a bright image in your eye, it takes up to a tenth of a second for the image to fade. You can test this by watching a flashlight whirling in a circle at night. Instead of a moving dot, you see a ring of light. This "persistence of vision" explains how movies work. Each picture, or frame, moves the action slightly from the previous one. In motion pictures, films are shown at 24 frames a second, so it seems like one continuous movement. On television, the films are shown at 25 frames a second.

circuit

A circuit is a continuous line — like a racing circuit. A CURRENT of ELECTRICITY can flow around a circuit in a machine. An electrical circuit can be very simple. All you need to make one is a wire connected to the positive end of a BATTERY, a flashlight bulb, and another wire leading back to the negative end of the battery. The current stops if the circuit is broken. COMPUTERS can have thousands of tiny circuits in a single MICROCHIP.

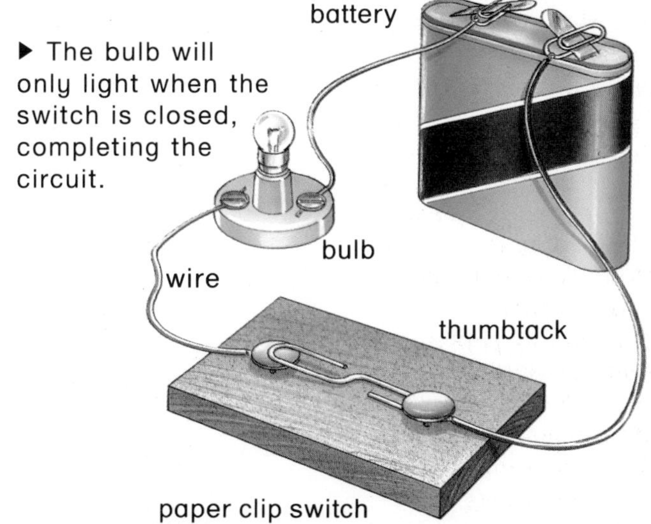

▶ The bulb will only light when the switch is closed, completing the circuit.

circuit breaker

If a CIRCUIT develops a fault that causes an increase in the current, a circuit breaker will cut off the supply of ELECTRICITY to prevent a fire or damage to the equipment. See **fuse**.

CLIMATE

Climate is the long-term behavior of the WEATHER. The bombardment of the ATMOSPHERE by endless heat from the SUN causes the land and sea to heat and cool, and the resulting movement of air and water create the climate. TEMPERATURE and rainfall are the most important factors that determine the climate of a particular area.

WORLD CLIMATES

The world can be divided into climate zones, which depend largely on the distance from the equator. The **polar climates** are the coldest — at the North and South Poles the average temperature never rises above freezing. In high altitudes there are the clear skies and heavy snow typical of **mountain climates**.

The most important climates to humans are the **temperate** and **tropical climate** zones. These areas are where most people live. The temperate climate is typical of areas away from the equator, where the summers are warm and the winters are mild. The tropics are marked by high humidity and high temperatures.

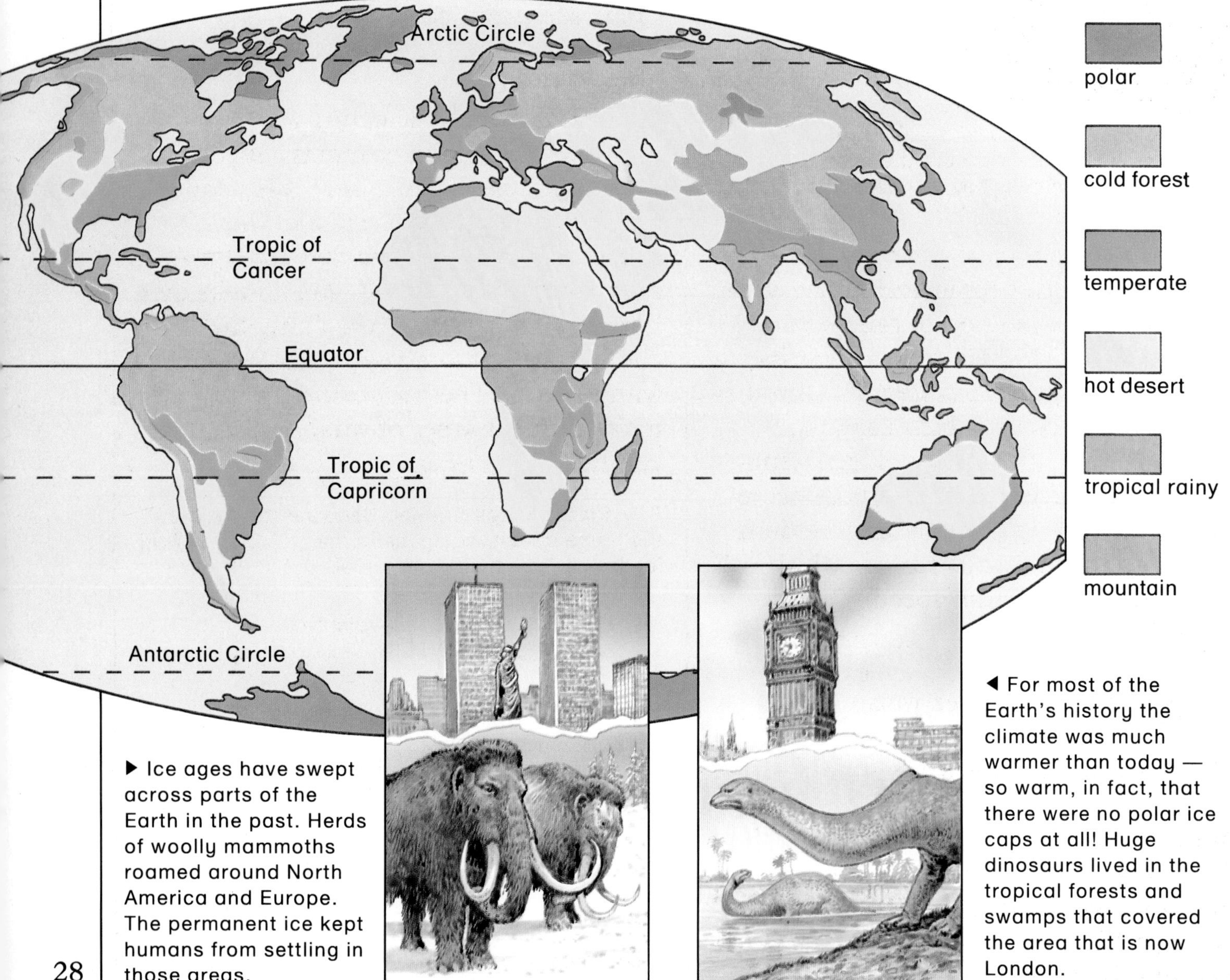

▶ Ice ages have swept across parts of the Earth in the past. Herds of woolly mammoths roamed around North America and Europe. The permanent ice kept humans from settling in those areas.

◀ For most of the Earth's history the climate was much warmer than today — so warm, in fact, that there were no polar ice caps at all! Huge dinosaurs lived in the tropical forests and swamps that covered the area that is now London.

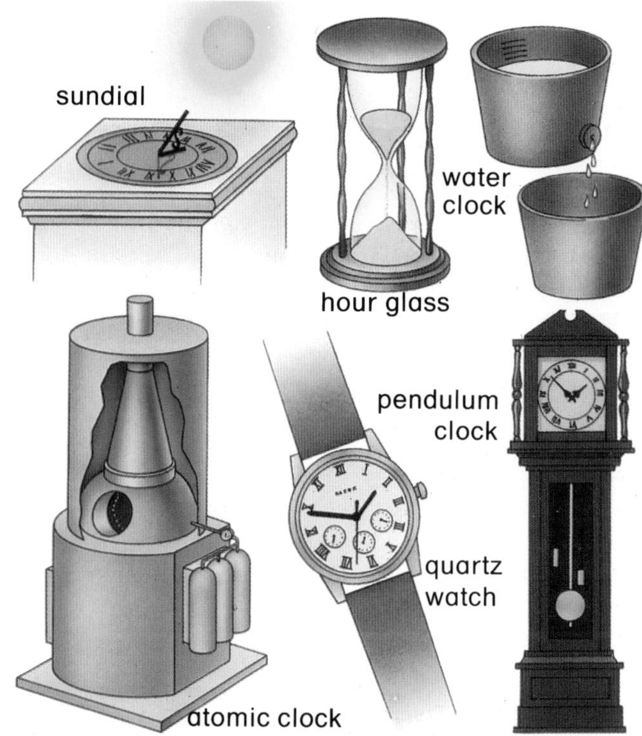

▲ These are just a few of the methods that people have used to measure the passing of time and to divide the day into smaller units of time.

clock

In ancient days, people had many ways of marking the passing of time. One was the water clock, which was a container with water dripping out steadily. Another was a candle clock, which used marks down the side of a candle. When gear-wheels were invented, it was possible to design a wind-up clock. Many modern clocks use a CRYSTAL of QUARTZ, which will RESONATE at a constant speed. Quartz clocks are very precise.

cloth and weaving see **page 30**

cloud see **water, weather**

coal

Three hundred million years ago much of the world was covered with tropical swamps. There was too little OXYGEN in the swamps for the trees to rot away completely when they died, so the CARBON they contained was left behind. This formed coal. Coal is a FOSSIL FUEL.

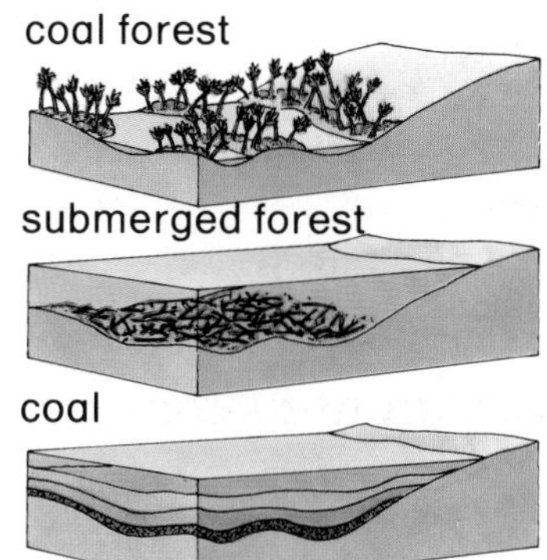

▶ The coal deposits that are mined today were once lush forests. When they died they were buried under mud and then rock. Over millions of years, the rotting plant material changed into coal.

color see **page 32**

combustion

Combustion is the scientific word for burning. If a substance reacts with OXYGEN it may give out HEAT ENERGY. This can be enough to set fire to the rest of the substance. Watch a candle burning. As the FLAME heats the solid wax it melts into liquid oil. The heat of the flame then changes the oil to a vapor, which burns with oxygen. The heat energy given out melts the next layer of wax, and so combustion goes on.

▼ A candle keeps burning because the heat of the flame continuously melts the candle wax and feeds the flame with more fuel.

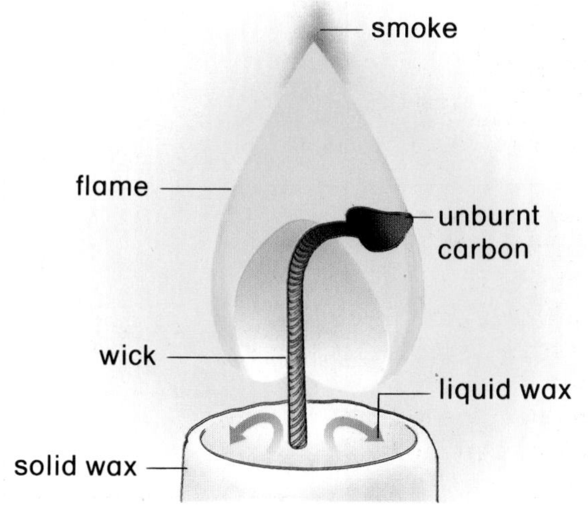

CLOTH AND WEAVING

Cloth is also known as fabric. It is made by weaving, felting, and knitting. Weaving is a process of crossing threads so that they produce a flat, flexible product. Knitting is a way of making cloth with a single string rather than with two sets of threads. Felting involves pressing FIBERS together into a sheet, producing nonwoven fabrics.

▼ You can make a hand loom on a wooden frame, or even with an empty shoebox cut to shape. Wool or acrylic threads are the easiest to use. The threads that run lengthwise are the warp, and the cross threads are the weft. Use a bobbin as the shuttle. A piece of cardboard with alternate slots and holes lifts the warp threads so the shuttle can pass back and forth.

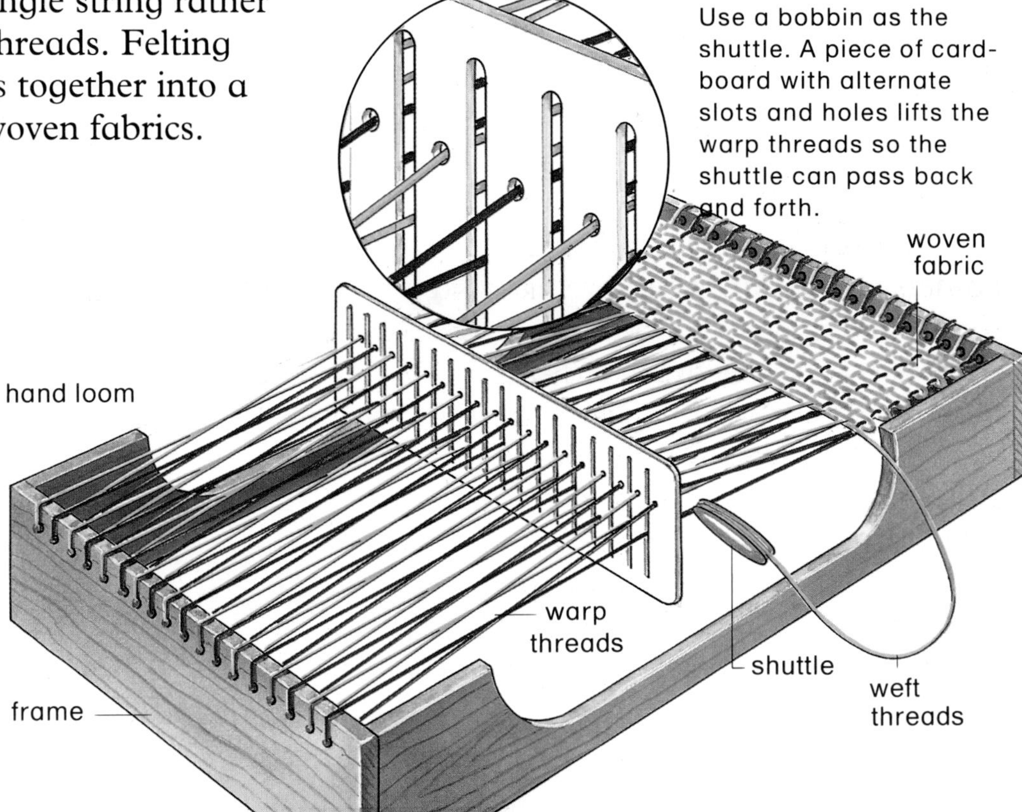

▼ You can see the difference between woven and knitted cloth below. At the top is an example of weaving, with the weft threads crossing over and under the warp. Below is an example of a knitted fabric with linked threads. Fine nylon fibers are knitted together to make tights. Damaged woven cloth tends to form holes. Knitted fabrics run, or ladder, instead.

woven fabric

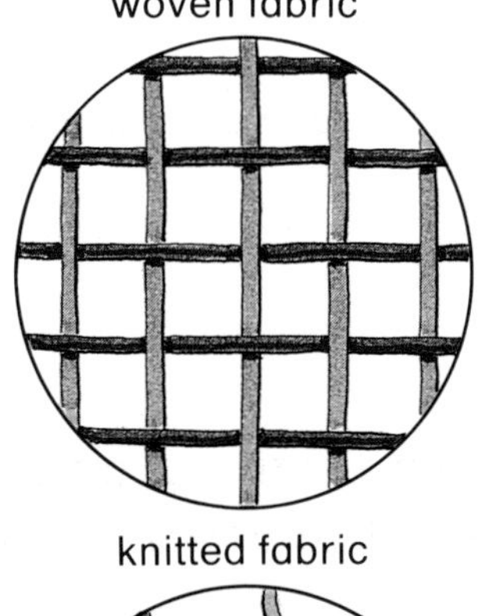

knitted fabric

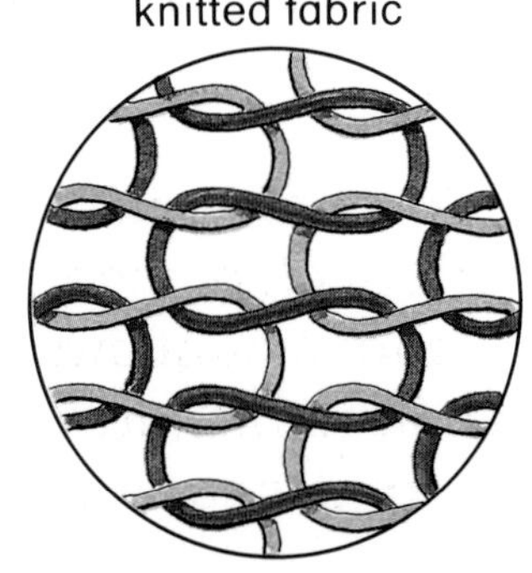

DID YOU KNOW?

Weaving began in Turkey more than 8,000 years ago. There were only slight improvements in weaving looms until Joseph Marie Jacquard invented an automatic loom in 1801. It produced complicated woven patterns that were controlled by a set of punched cards. This gave rise to the data system used on early computers.

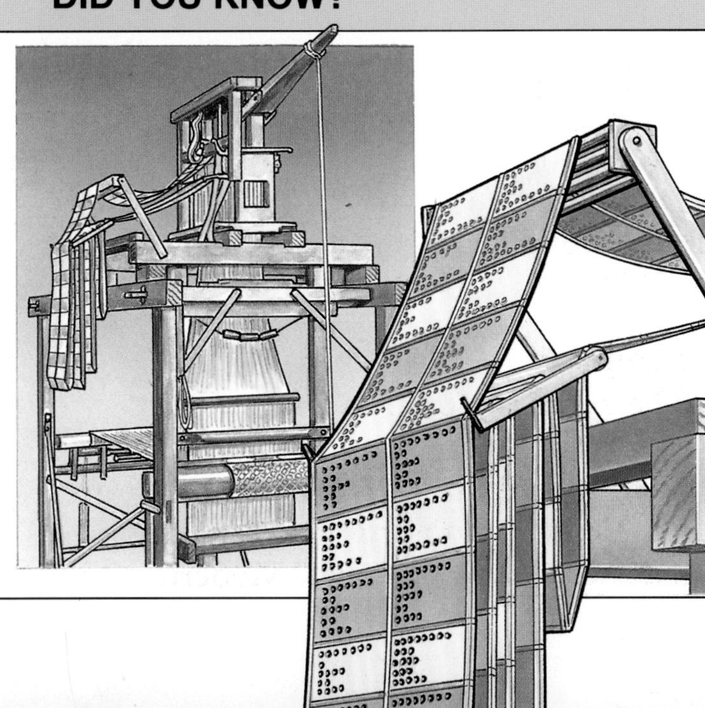

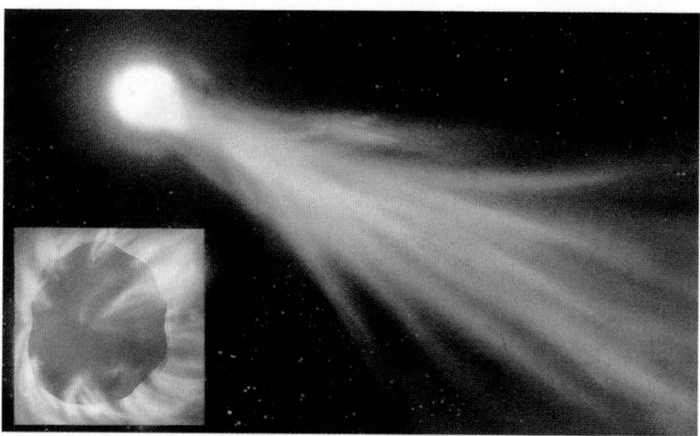

▲ If a comet's orbit brings it close to the Sun, it is heated up, releasing a cloud of dust and gas which then forms the comet's tail.

comet
For thousands of years people have seen comets in the sky. They are ORBITING lumps of rock and ice which travel around the SOLAR SYSTEM. Comets have a tail of gas and dust PARTICLES which may be millions of miles long. In 1682, Sir Edmund Halley saw a comet, and he figured out that it was the same comet seen in 1531 and 1607. Halley said that the comet would come back regularly, and it did. The most recent sighting was in 1986.

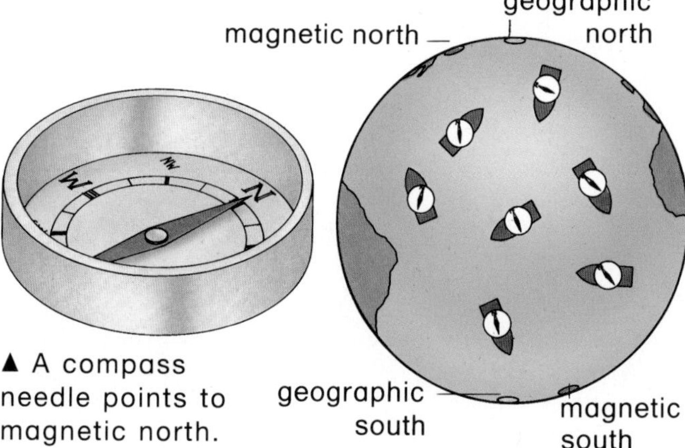

▲ A compass needle points to magnetic north.

compass
The EARTH is a giant MAGNET with a magnetic field. A magnetic needle will point to the Earth's North Pole. Ancient travelers used natural magnets called lodestones as compasses. Modern navigators know that magnetic north is not exactly at the Earth's geographic North Pole and can adjust their course.

compound
A compound is made up of two or more elements. CARBON reacts with OXYGEN to form CARBON DIOXIDE. WATER is a compound of HYDROGEN and oxygen. Oxygen ATOMS form two bonds when they join with other atoms. Carbon forms four, hydrogen only one. That is why there are two oxygen atoms for each carbon atom in carbon dioxide and one oxygen atom with two hydrogen atoms in water.

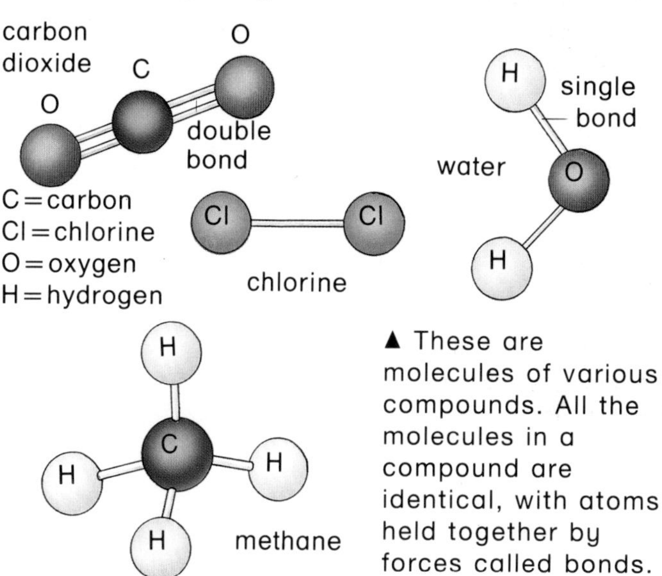

▲ These are molecules of various compounds. All the molecules in a compound are identical, with atoms held together by forces called bonds.

computer see **page 34**

concrete
Concrete is a mix of CEMENT, sand, gravel, and WATER that's harder than cement alone.

conductor
Heat travels from hot places to cooler ones. It moves quickly through a good conductor. An electric conductor allows a CURRENT to pass through it. METALS are good conductors of HEAT and ELECTRICITY.

C

COLOR

The effect of color is caused by LIGHT. Light is made up of different wavelengths. We see each wavelength as a different color. The longer wavelengths are what we call red, the shortest ones are blue and violet. Objects reflect different amounts of each type of light and so they appear to be different colors.

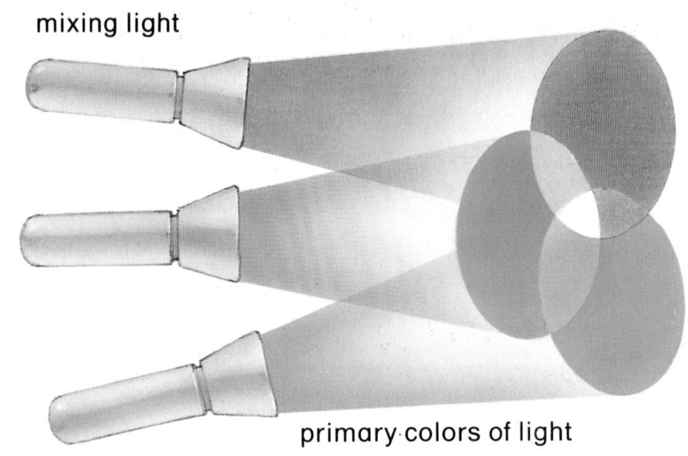

▼ Some people fail to see all colors properly. Their condition is known as colorblindness. A test using tiny colored circles can detect colorblindness.

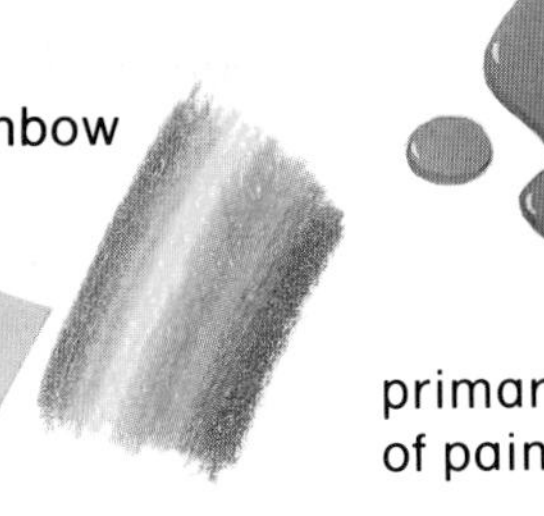

▲ The beveled glass at the edge of a mirror can split light into its separate colors. This rainbow effect is the spectrum. The seven main colors of the spectrum are red, orange, yellow, green, blue, indigo, and violet.

▲ The primary colors of light are red, green, and blue. Together they produce white light. The primary colors of paint or printing ink are red, yellow, and blue. Mixed together in exactly equal amounts they make black.

▲ Brightness affects the way we see colors. If you look at the cross above in bright light, it appears bright red on a dark background. In a dim room at dusk, the cross looks black against the palest blue.

DID YOU KNOW?

People always thought that cats and dogs were colorblind. But recent research shows they can see blue and yellow. Some insects can see colors in the ultraviolet range, which is invisible to us. This picture shows how the same flower appears to a dog, a bee, and a person.

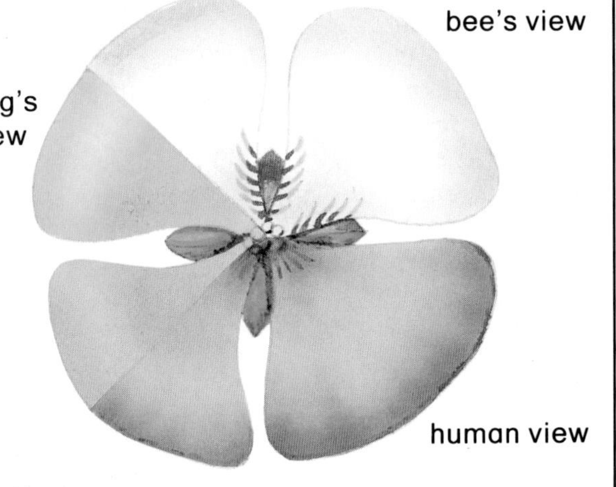

conservation

Conserving means saving. In the past people have captured animals and harvested plants until there were none left. The passenger pigeon was once common in the U.S. A flock seen in 1810 contained more than two billion birds. But by the year 1900, nearly all the pigeons had been killed. The last one died in 1914. If we are more careful we can keep this from happening to other animals.

Today, many species of plants and animals are in danger of becoming extinct. To conserve them, we need to study their life history. For example, the panda is in danger not because people kill it but because the bamboo forests in which it lives and feeds are being destroyed. Otters are now rare in Europe because the rivers are polluted. Many species are endangered because the world's rainforests are being cleared. These forests are so rich in life that scientists have yet to discover many of the species that live in them. These precious habitats need careful management if they and the animals that live in them are to survive.

▶ It is important to conserve plants. Many of them are medically useful. This Madagascar periwinkle, for example, has already given us two drugs used to treat cancer. Scientists hope to find other drugs in plants from the rainforests.

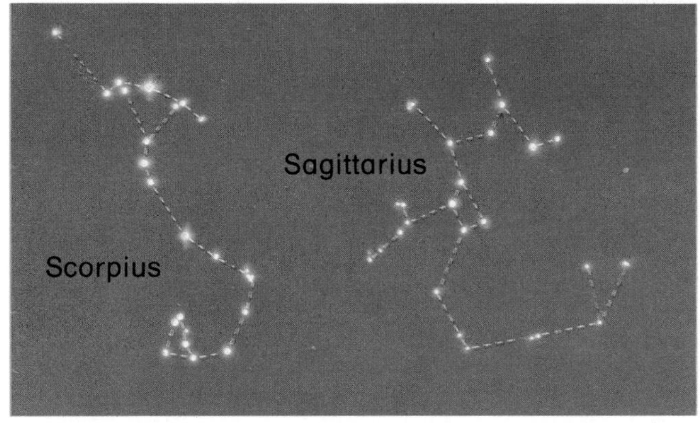

▲ Scorpio and Sagittarius are two of the constellations in the zodiac. The zodiac is an imaginary zone across the sky. The Sun, Moon, and planets appear within this zone and seem to pass through the constellations.

constellation

If you look at the night sky you will see that the STARS make patterns. In ancient times people thought these patterns, or constellations, were the marks of gods watching over them, so they gave the star patterns names. In northern skies there is a group of clustered stars called the Seven Sisters, or Pleiades. Another group looks like a saucepan with a bent handle — this is the Big Dipper, or Great Bear. Three stars in a row are Orion's Belt. The Southern Cross is a constellation in the skies of the Southern Hemisphere.

continent

The huge masses of land on the Earth's surface are the continents. At the South Pole is the continent of Antarctica. Russia and China cover most of Asia, and America is split into two halves, North and South. India, in the south of Asia, is so large that it is called a subcontinent. About 300 million years ago, the continents were in one big mass. This mass slowly broke up and drifted apart to form the separate continents we know today. See **plate tectonics**.

COMPUTERS

The first small electronic computers were built in Berlin around 1940. A larger machine, called Colossus, was secretly working in wartime Great Britain in 1943. It had 1,500 ELECTRON tubes to make calculations. TRANSISTORS replaced tubes in the 1950s. Since the development of the MICROCHIP in the 1970s, small home computers have become available. The computer at school or in your home has more computing power than all the early models put together.

DID YOU KNOW?

Charles Babbage, a British scientist, was a pioneer of computers. He built a "difference engine" in 1822 to do long calculations, and then went on to design an "analytical engine" to work out mathematical problems. Sadly, Babbage could not raise enough money for his project and it was never finished.

▼ Business computers used to hold data on large spools of tape. All computers have a central processing unit (CPU) to handle data and a memory to store the information. The data is stored on chips.

▼ A desk-top computer is a vast improvement on the computers of the 1960s. If cars had developed as fast, they could carry hundreds of people at the speed of the Concorde using only a spoonful of fuel!

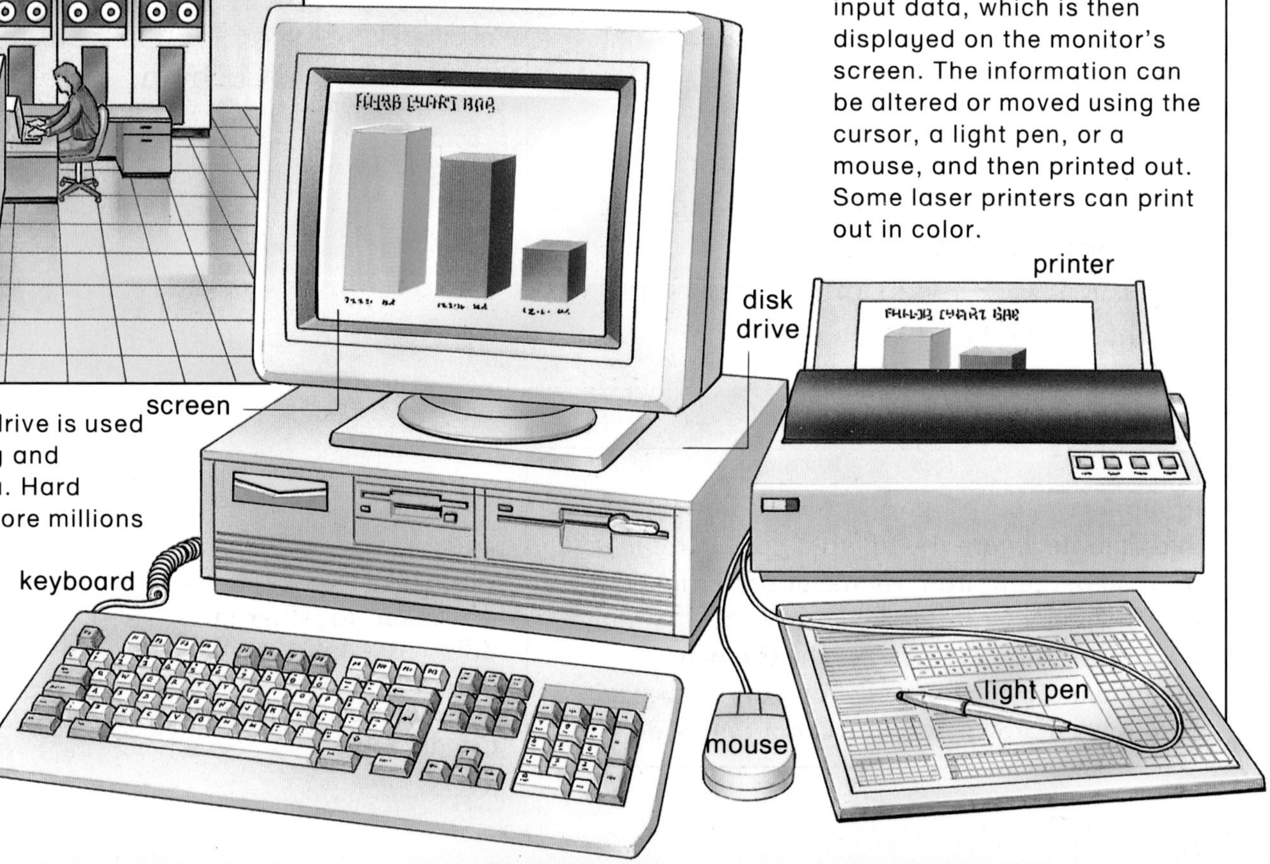

▼ The keyboard is used to input data, which is then displayed on the monitor's screen. The information can be altered or moved using the cursor, a light pen, or a mouse, and then printed out. Some laser printers can print out in color.

▶ The disk drive is used for inputting and storing data. Hard disks can store millions of words.

monitor
printer
disk drive
screen
keyboard
floppy disks
light pen
mouse

convection

HEAT can spread through a room by convection. Newly warmed air expands, and so it weighs less than cold air. As a result, it rises. Cooler air then moves in below, and is also warmed.

◀ The electrical element inside a kettle heats the water around it. The water expands as it warms. It becomes less dense than the water above it and floats up through the cooler water. The cool water sinks to the bottom, where it is heated, and so convection currents are formed.

copper

Copper is a reddish, rather soft METAL, and a good CONDUCTOR of heat and electricity. It can be drawn out into fine wires. Copper has long been used to make water pipes. Copper ALLOYS are used to make coins.

corrosion

METALS do not always stay bright. They may be damaged by the AIR or by RAIN. IRON forms RUST if it is exposed to water and air; this is corrosion. CHROMIUM metal rarely corrodes.

DID YOU KNOW?

Iron only rusts if air and water are both present. In a climate where the humidity of the air is less than 40 percent, iron will never rust! Aluminum forms a thin layer of oxide as soon as it comes in contact with air. This is the reason why aluminum always looks slightly dull — but with this built-in protection it will not corrode.

cosmic rays

We are surrounded by RADIATION all our lives. Some comes from space, and this radiation is called "cosmic rays." The atmosphere protects us from most of the cosmic rays.

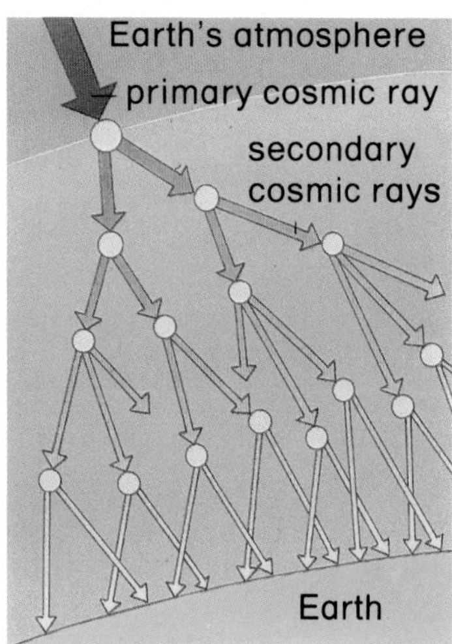

◀ When cosmic rays enter the Earth's atmosphere they collide with atmospheric particles and secondary cosmic rays are created. An "avalanche" may continue until the rays reach the ground.

crystals

If MOLECULES or ATOMS stack up in a neat pattern, a crystal may form. You can see ancient crystals of minerals in rocks. At the seashore you may find a dried-up rock pool of seawater in which SALT crystals are left behind.

▲ Crystals exist in different forms because their atoms or molecules are linked together in different ways. Calcite, pyrite, and sulfur show three forms. Snowflakes are also crystals.

C

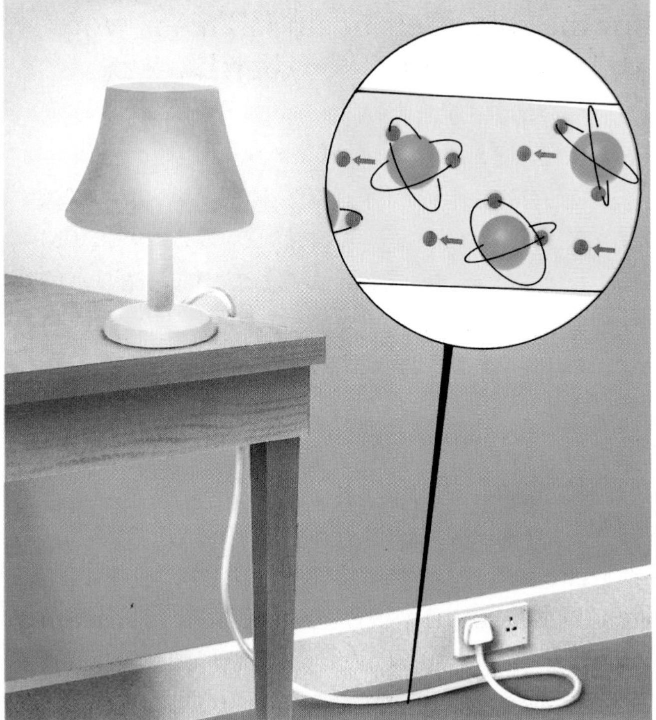

▲ When an electric light is switched on, electrons which normally orbit atoms in the wire are forced to jump from atom to atom. This forms an electric current.

current

An electric current is a flow of electric charge. It is driven by a POWER source such as a BATTERY. The power source causes ELECTRONS to jump from one ATOM in the wire to the next. The electrons carry an electric charge, and a current flows along the wire. See **electricity, volt**.

cyclone

A cyclone is a HURRICANE storm with strong WINDS and heavy RAIN. In METEOROLOGY, an anticyclone is an area of high air PRESSURE with winds moving in a circle. An area of low pressure, a cyclone, has winds moving in the other direction. It is also known as a "depression." Cyclonic winds blow counterclockwise in the Northern Hemisphere but clockwise in the Southern Hemisphere. See **isobar, weather**.

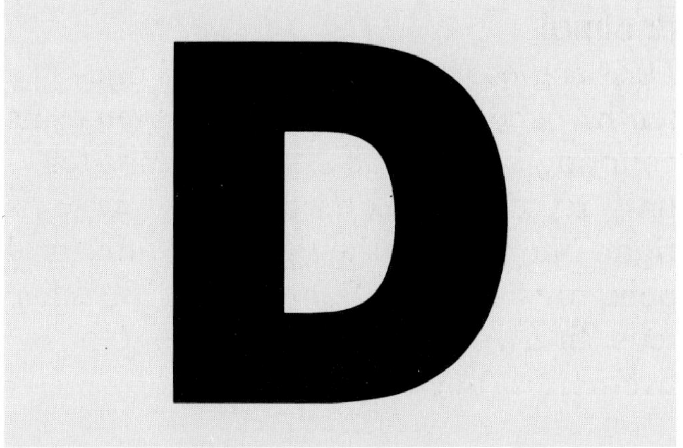

day and night

The planet EARTH turns on its axis as it ORBITS the SUN. The Sun constantly shines LIGHT at the Earth. The half of the planet that is facing the Sun has day. And the half facing away from the Sun has night.

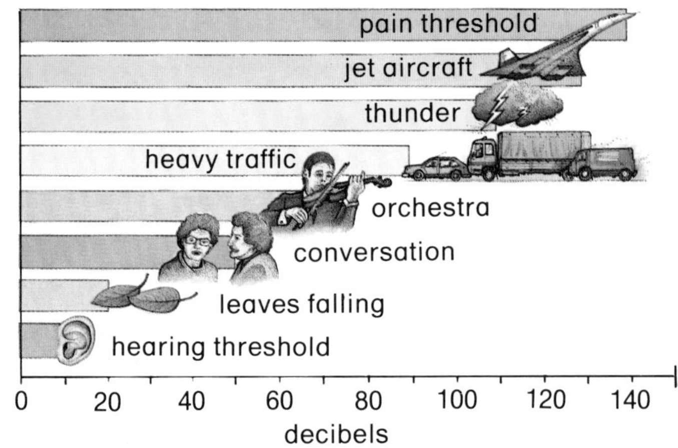

▲ The decibel scale measures sound. Sounds above 140 decibels are dangerous.

decibel

A decibel is one-tenth of a bel. It is a measure of SOUND PRESSURE. The higher the pressure, the louder the sound. If a sound reading goes up by ten decibels it means the sound is ten times louder. The bel was named after Alexander Graham Bell. He invented the TELEPHONE and an early phonograph.

D

decimal

Deci- comes from the Latin for "one-tenth." The decimal system uses ten as its counting base. Each NUMBER stands for units ten times greater than the one to its right. Numbers to the right of the decimal point are fractions. For example, 50 is five tens (fifty), 5.0 is five ones (five), 0.5 is five-tenths (one half).

density

Density is the MASS of a certain volume of a substance. Which do you think weighs more, a pound of feathers or a pound of lead? Both weigh the same. But the lead has the greater density.

▼ A submarine dives by flooding its "ballast" tanks to make it denser than the surrounding water. It surfaces by forcing the water out.

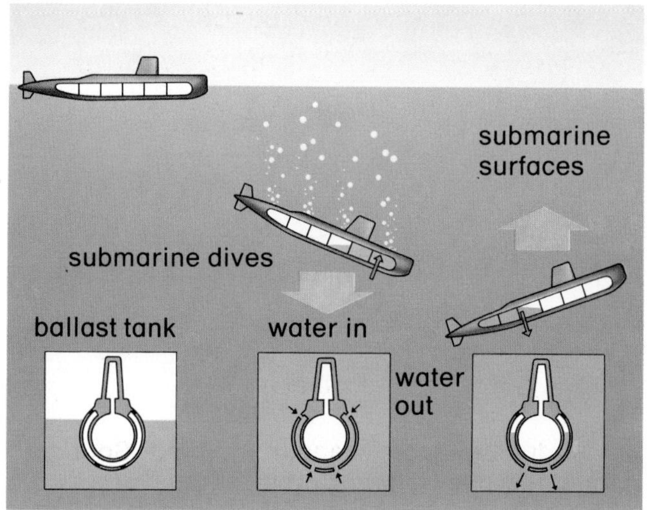

desalination

Desalination is the process of removing SALT from sea water. To purify sea water it can be BOILED to produce water vapor. When the vapor cools it condenses to form pure water. Another method of desalination uses thin membranes to hold back the salt from the water. Desalination happens all the time in nature. SOLAR ENERGY evaporates water from the seas, but the salt is left behind. This is why rainwater is fresh. See **distillation**.

desert

Some parts of the EARTH have very little RAIN. Nothing much grows there. These are the desert areas. Sometimes when it does rain, masses of beautiful flowers open for just long enough to make seeds.

desertification

Soil contains vegetable and animal matter and lots of microscopic life. In a desert this living part of the soil is missing. Intensive farming can damage soils and cause desertification. A warmer, drier CLIMATE also helps deserts to spread.

detergent

Dirt clings to clothing, and water is usually not enough to remove it. This is because dirt and water often do not mix. Detergents have long MOLECULES. One end of the molecule will stick to grease and dirt, and the other end holds onto the WATER. The molecules of detergent surround the dirt and draw it away. A range of detergents are used. Some are made for washing clothes, others for dishes.

1

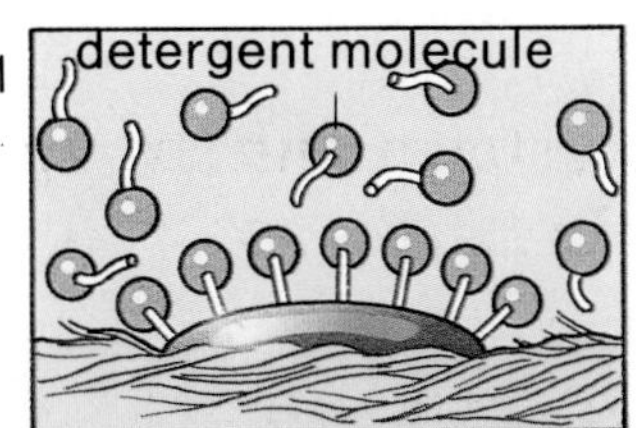

◀ Detergent molecules clean clothes by surrounding particles of grease and dirt. They lift the dirt off so it can be rinsed away.

2

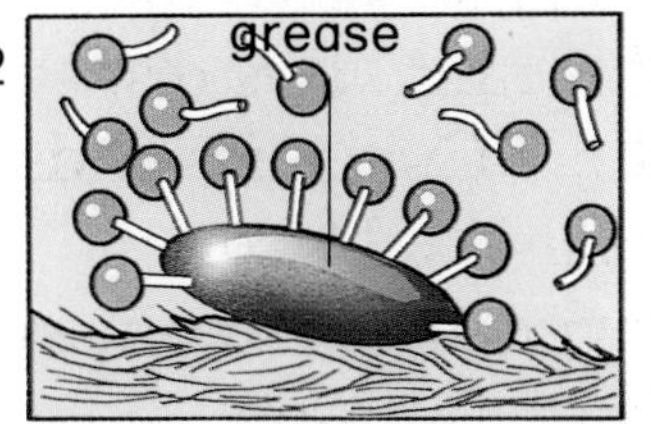

3

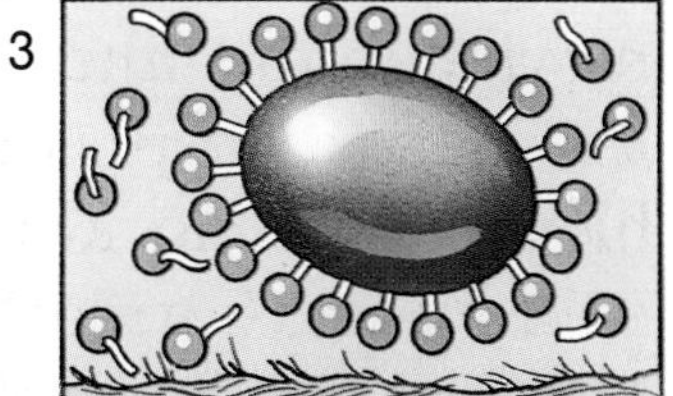

D

diamond

ATOMS of CARBON joined in a three-dimensional pattern form CRYSTALS of diamond. Diamond is the hardest substance in the world. The only thing that can cut it is another diamond.

diesel

In 1892 Rudolf Diesel, a German engineer, designed an INTERNAL-COMBUSTION ENGINE that could run on COAL dust (CARBON). Later, the design was changed so that the engine could run on heavy OIL instead. There is no spark plug in a diesel engine. Instead, the fuel heats up as it is compressed and explodes by itself, driving the pistons up and down.

▼ In a diesel engine, the up-down motion of the pistons is changed into the rotating motion of the crankshaft which drives the wheels.

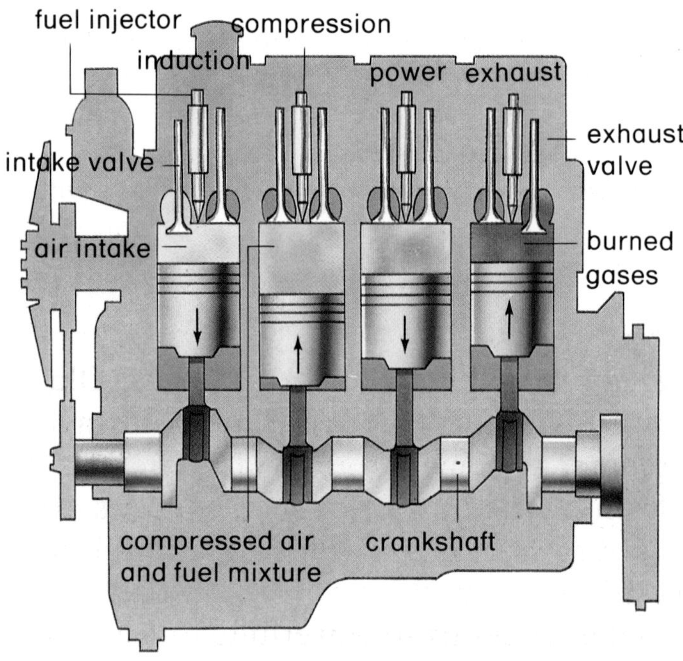

digital

Digital systems turn information into BINARY code. A sound RECORDING may store digitized information. Each digital value says how loud or how high a note might

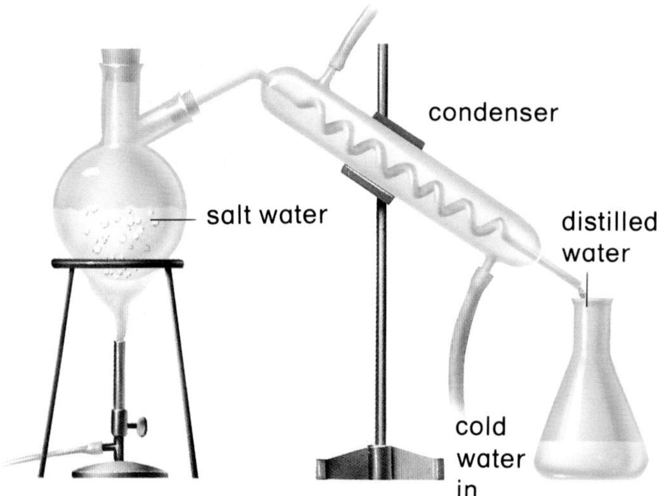

▲ Fresh water can be distilled from boiling salt water. The salt is left behind as the water evaporates. The water vapor is cooled in a condenser, and pure water drips into a flask.

be. From this a whole orchestral concert can be played back. The quality of digital recordings is very high. The pattern of dots you can see in a newspaper photograph shows a digitized image.

distillation

Distillation is used to separate a liquid from another substance. DESALINATION uses distillation. The process is also used to separate ALCOHOL from WATER. Ethanol boils at a lower temperature than water. So, when the mixture is heated, the alcohol EVAPORATES first and can be cooled and collected.

Doppler effect

Sound WAVES travel outward from their source. If the source is moving toward you, the SOUND waves are pushed together and the frequency of the pitch goes up. When the source is moving away from you, the sound waves are farther apart. You can hear this when an ambulance goes past with its siren on. The pitch gets higher as it approaches and lower as the

D

◀ Sound waves are squashed up in front of an ambulance, so the siren sounds higher as it travels toward you.

ambulance speeds away. This is called the Doppler effect, after the Austrian scientist Johann Christian Doppler, who first explained it in 1842.

drug

Drugs are CHEMICALS that alter the body. Some, such as aspirin, are used to control pain. Antibiotics help to fight infections. Some drugs are used to alter people's moods. CAFFEINE, NICOTINE, and ALCOHOL are all drugs. Many drugs have dangerous side-effects, and some are very addictive.

▶ Plants are the source of many modern medicines. The drugs digitalis and digoxin can be obtained from the dried leaves of the foxglove plant. These drugs are used to treat heart failure. The foxglove is called *Digitalis*, because its flowers fit on your fingers, or digits.

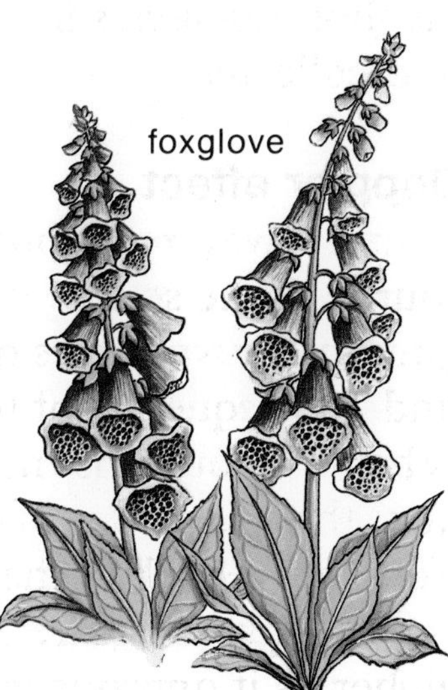

DID YOU KNOW?

Many important drugs were found in plants. Many of them have been used for hundreds of years by ancient tribes. The Madagascar periwinkle provides two drugs that are used to treat cancer. Curare, used to relax patients during major surgery, was used on poison darts by Amazon hunters. And the licorice plant has given us a drug for the treatment of stomach ulcers! Aspirin was found in willow trees. The bark was used for centuries to treat people with fever. We use aspirin for the same purpose today.

dye

A dye alters the COLOR of an object. Old-fashioned dyes often come from strange places. Cochineal (red food color) comes from crushed insects. Chemical dyes are used to color CLOTH. Older dyes used to wash out from the cloth, but many modern dyes fix so powerfully to the FIBERS that they never fade.

dynamo

A dynamo is a device that turns mechanical motion into ELECTRICITY. See **generator**.

Earth see **Solar System**

earthquake

When rock masses slip against each other they vibrate. These vibrations can spread over vast distances. This is an earthquake. Earthquakes usually occur in places where the moving plates on the Earth's crust rub together. About 10,000 earthquakes are felt each year. The most famous earthquake zone is in California, along the San Andreas fault. Most are small, but there is a large tremor somewhere every week. See **plate tectonics**, **Richter scale**.

▼ Many modern buildings, especially in areas where earthquakes can be expected, are built to withstand the shock of an earthquake, but older buildings sometimes collapse.

echo

SOUND waves can bounce back from a solid surface. You hear the sound a second time a little later and more faintly. This is an echo. See **sonar**.

eclipse

The SUN is much larger than the MOON. But because the Moon is nearer to Earth, both seem about the same size in the sky. Sometimes the Moon passes between us and the Sun. When this happens, the Moon blocks the Sun out. This is a solar eclipse. Some nights the Moon passes

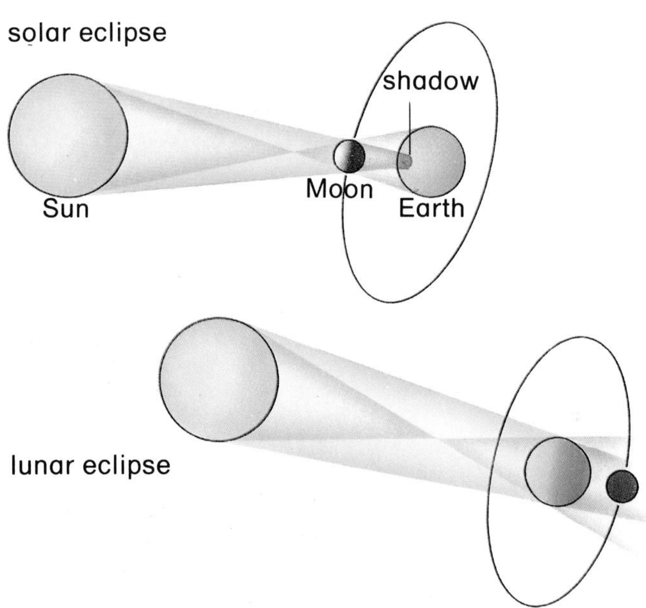

▲ The Moon disappears in the Earth's shadow during a lunar eclipse. The solar eclipse occurs when the Moon passes between the Earth and Sun and blots out the Sun for several minutes.

through the Earth's own shadow. When this happens the Sun can no longer shine on the Moon. The result is an eclipse of the Moon.

LIFE STORY

Edison

Thomas Alva Edison was born in 1847 in a small town in Ohio. He became one of the greatest scientific inventors. Communications fascinated him, and he set up a telegraph business, wiring messages across America. He worked on electric lights, the typewriter, methods of duplicating documents, and many other ideas. Edison did not always invent things. Often he took an invention and improved it. One of these was the TELEPHONE. This led him to invent the phonograph, which could record the human voice for the first time.

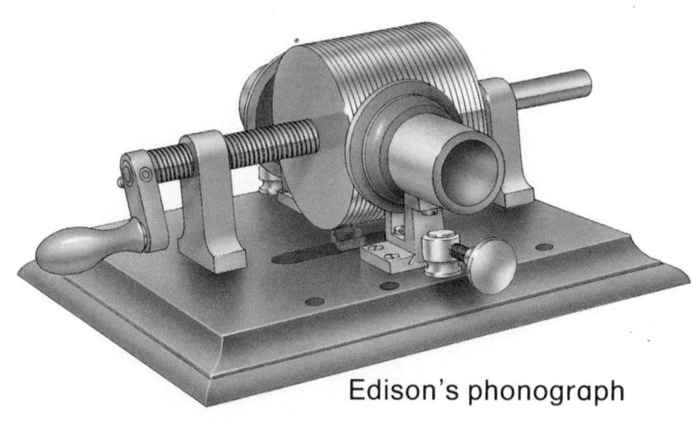

Edison's phonograph

electricity see **pages 42 and 43**

electromagnetism

Electromagnetism is the study of MAGNETS and electric CURRENTS. An electromagnet is made with a core of iron and a wire coil wrapped around it. When an electric current flows in the coil, the iron becomes a magnet. Beams of electrons in the CATHODE RAY tube of a TV set can be focused onto the screen with magnetic fields, using an electromagnetic lens. Geologists even use electromagnets to find metal ORES under the ground. This is called electromagnetic prospecting.

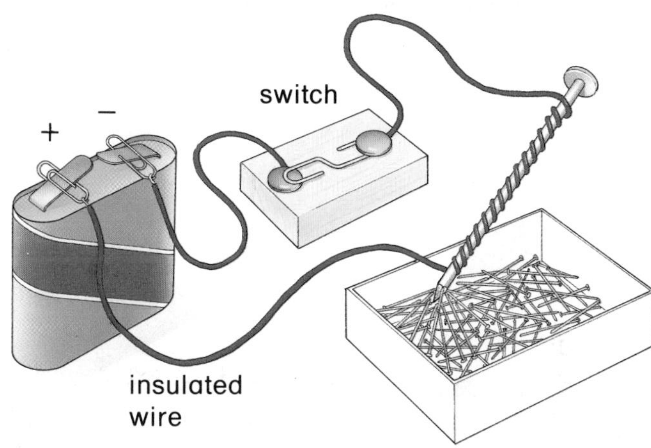

▲ You can make an electromagnet by wrapping a wire around an iron nail and connecting it to a battery. Try using it to pick up small nails.

electron

An electron is a tiny particle in an ATOM. Each electron has a single negative ELECTRIC charge. Beams of electrons are also called CATHODE RAYS.

electron microscope

An ELECTRON microscope uses beams of electrons to produce a magnified view of a specimen. It produces a far more detailed image than a light MICROSCOPE, but it cannot be used to study living things as a light microsope can. The electron beams are focused with ELECTROMAGNETIC lenses. In a scanning electron microscope we look at the electrons reflected from a solid specimen. This gives a detailed view of the surface with highlights and shadows, so CRYSTALS, insects, and other solid specimens look three-dimensional.

ELECTRICITY

Electricity results from the build-up or movement of ELECTRONS. If they collect in one place, static electricity builds up. But if they move along, an electric CURRENT is produced. People sometimes mistakenly speak of electricity as a "fuel." OIL, GASOLINE, and COAL are fuels, but electricity is a form of ENERGY. It can be produced by a GENERATOR using any kind of fuel. The electrons are moved about by some outside form of energy.

▼ A magnetic field is created between the poles of a magnet. If the field is cut by a moving wire coil, then electrons will move along the wire. If the wire is part of a circuit, an electric current will flow. This is a simple electric generator. The same effect works in the opposite direction. If you pass a current of electricity through a wire coil in a magnetic field, then the wire will move. An electric motor uses this effect to turn electrical energy into mechanical energy.

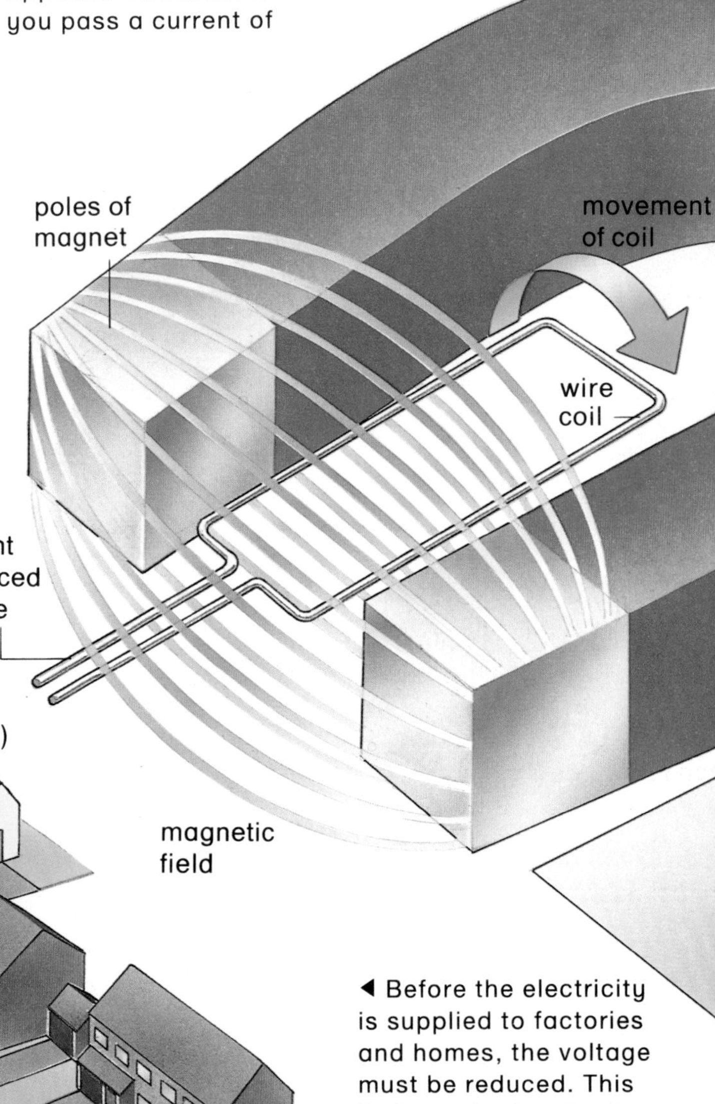

▼ Power stations burn fuel to make steam. The steam turns blades in the generator and produces electricity. In order to deliver as much power as possible the electricity is sent out at an extremely high voltage.

▼ Electricity is sent along power cables supported by pylons. The high voltage is very dangerous. But it allows the cables to carry large amounts of electricity without overheating.

power station

industry (10–30kV)

transformer

pylon

substation

domestic supply (100 or 240V)

◀ Before the electricity is supplied to factories and homes, the voltage must be reduced. This is done at a local substation in residential areas and industrial centers. Household voltage is a thousand times lower than that of cross-country cables — but it can still kill.

DID YOU KNOW?

Household electricity is used to power many objects: the microwave oven, power drill, toaster, and iron are examples. Flashlights and portable cassette players can run on batteries.

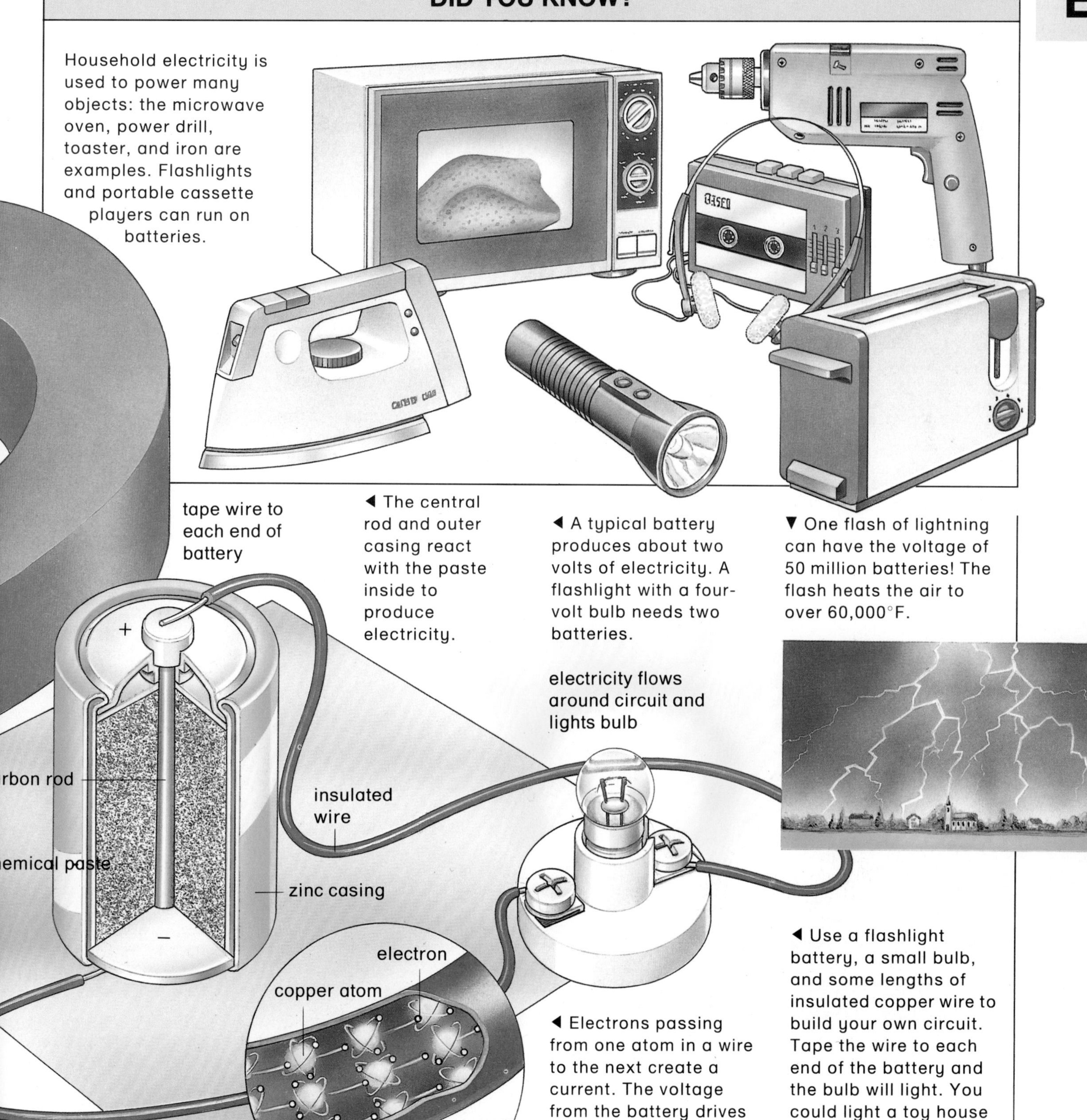

◀ The central rod and outer casing react with the paste inside to produce electricity.

◀ A typical battery produces about two volts of electricity. A flashlight with a four-volt bulb needs two batteries.

▼ One flash of lightning can have the voltage of 50 million batteries! The flash heats the air to over 60,000°F.

◀ Electrons passing from one atom in a wire to the next create a current. The voltage from the battery drives them around the circuit.

◀ Use a flashlight battery, a small bulb, and some lengths of insulated copper wire to build your own circuit. Tape the wire to each end of the battery and the bulb will light. You could light a toy house like this.

E

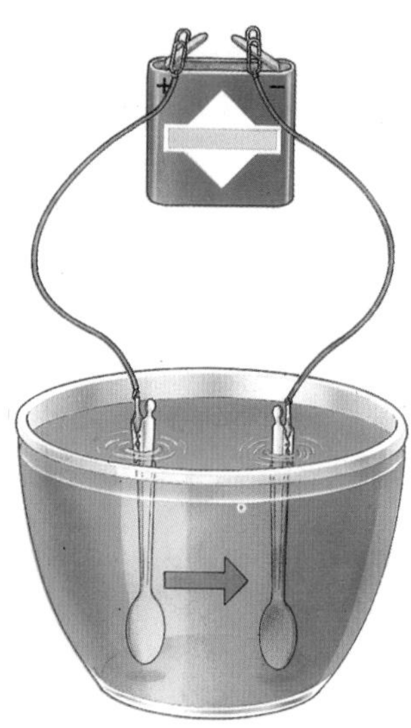

▶ You can make your own electroplating bath by dipping two old spoons in a copper sulfate solution and connecting them to a battery. The electric current flows through the solution, carrying particles of copper onto the spoon connected to the battery's negative terminal. This spoon turns reddish as it is plated with copper.

electroplating

Some metals, such as CHROMIUM and SILVER, are very useful for coating others. Electroplating uses an electric CURRENT to carry IONS of the METAL onto the object to be coated. Metal objects are often electroplated to protect them from CORROSION.

element

There are 109 known elements. These elements are the basic ATOMS from which COMPOUNDS are made. All the atoms in an element are exactly the same. Each element has a chemical symbol. OXYGEN is O, NITROGEN is N, and HYDROGEN is H. Au is the symbol for gold, from the Latin word *aurum*. The elements are listed in the periodic table according to the number of protons their atoms contain. Hydrogen, number one, has one PROTON in its nucleus; HELIUM has two. The elements in each column, or group, have much in common. Lithium, SODIUM, and POTASSIUM in the first group are all soft, reactive metals.

▶ The periodic table groups the elements. The atomic number (above each symbol) is the number of protons each atom contains.

energy see **pages 46 and 47**

engine

Engines burn fuel to release ENERGY. The energy is then used to do work, like turning wheels or driving a propeller. Early engines were powered by wind (windmills) or water (waterwheels). Later, fuels such as COAL were burned to heat water and produce STEAM to drive powerful steam engines. Engineers then realized that it was even better to burn the fuel inside the engine as the energy could be produced immediately. This is how an INTERNAL-COMBUSTION ENGINE works.

alkali metals — inner transition metals — transition metals — nonmetals

1	2							
1 Hydrogen H								
3 Lithium Li	4 Beryllium Be							
11 Sodium Na	12 Magnesium Mg							
19 Potassium K	20 Calcium Ca	21 Scandium Sc	22 Titanium Ti	23 Vanadium V	24 Chromium Cr	25 Manganese Mn	26 Iron Fe	27 Cobalt Co
37 Rubidium Rb	38 Strontium Sr	39 Yttrium Y	40 Zirconium Zr	41 Niobium Nb	42 Molybdenum Mo	43 Technetium Tc	44 Ruthenium Ru	45 Rhodiur Rh
55 Cesium Cs	56 Barium Ba	57–71 Lanthanide series	72 Hafnium Hf	73 Tantalum Ta	74 Tungsten W	75 Rhenium Re	76 Osmium Os	77 Iridiur Ir
87 Francium Fr	88 Radium Ra	89–103 Actinide series	104 Element 104	105 Element 105	106 Element 106	107 Element 107	108 Element 108	109 Elemer 109

57 Lanthanum La	58 Cerium Ce	59 Praseodym-ium Pr	60 Neodymium Nd	61 Prometheum Pm	62 Samarium Sm	63 Europium Eu	64 Gadolinium Gd	65 Terbiur Tb
89 Actinium Ac	90 Thorium Th	91 Protactinium Pa	92 Uranium U	93 Neptunium Np	94 Plutonium Pu	95 Americium Am	96 Curium Cm	97 Berkeli Bk

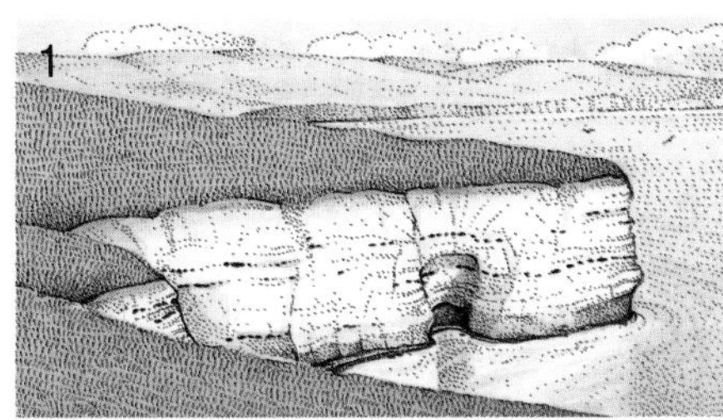

▲ The battering of waves can wear a hole into a cliff (1) or even all the way through (2). If the roof falls in, a rock tower is left standing alone (3).

erosion

Erosion means "a wearing away." Wind, WATER, and ICE can erode solid rock, cutting deep river valleys and shaping the coastline. Wind and RAIN can cause soil erosion on cultivated land. The topsoil is blown or washed away, leaving bare land where no crops can grow.

groups of elements

			3	4	5	6	7	8
								2 Helium He
			5 Boron B	6 Carbon C	7 Nitrogen N	8 Oxygen O	9 Fluorine F	10 Neon Ne
			13 Aluminum Al	14 Silicon Si	15 Phosphorus P	16 Sulfur S	17 Chlorine Cl	18 Argon Ar
28 Nickel Ni	29 Copper Cu	30 Zinc Zn	31 Gallium Ga	32 Germanium Ge	33 Arsenic As	34 Selenium Se	35 Bromine Br	36 Krypton Kr
46 alladium Pd	47 Silver Ag	48 Cadmium Cd	49 Indium In	50 Tin Sn	51 Antimony Sb	52 Tellurium Te	53 Iodine I	54 Xenon Xe
78 latinum Pt	79 Gold Au	80 Mercury Hg	81 Thallium Tl	82 Lead Pb	83 Bismuth Bi	84 Polonium Po	85 Astatine At	86 Radon Rn

66 sprosium Dy	67 Holmium Ho	68 Erbium Er	69 Thulium Tm	70 Ytterbium Yb	71 Lutetium Lu
98 ifornium Cf	99 Einsteinium Es	100 Fermium Fm	101 Mendelev-ium Md	102 Nobelium No	103 Lawrencium Lr

escape velocity

A spacecraft has to reach a certain speed to escape the pull of the Earth's GRAVITY. The exact speed is the escape VELOCITY, which is 6.96 mi (11.2 km) per second.

evaporation

Evaporation is the CHANGE OF STATE from liquid to gas. Evaporation uses up HEAT ENERGY, which is why sweat evaporating from your skin cools you down.

expansion

Most substances get larger when they are heated. This increase in volume or length is known as expansion. Water is unusual because it expands as it freezes, which is why ice can burst pipes.

explosives

Chemical explosives are high in ENERGY and need HEAT or a physical shock to set them off. Once the reaction starts, the heat produced sets off the whole explosion. A vast amount of heat and gas are released with great force. NITROGLYCERINE is a common explosive used to make dynamite. Ammonium nitrate is used in mines. Gunpowder is an explosive used to make FIREWORKS. The biggest man-made explosions have been made by nuclear weapons.

ENERGY

Energy is everywhere, and it is constantly changing from one form to another. The energy from fuels is used in a power plant to turn water into STEAM to turn turbines and make electrical energy. You use the energy in your food to move around and keep warm. The SUN is beaming energy at us too. Energy allows work to be done. The energy of a moving object is called *kinetic energy*. A brick on top of a wall has *potential energy*. This energy was stored in the brick when it was put there in the first place and is released when you push it off the wall. The chemicals in fireworks react together to release the energy that shoots them into the air.

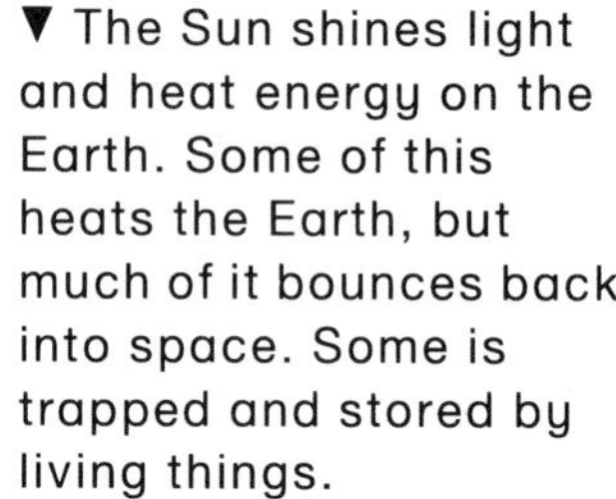

▼ The Sun shines light and heat energy on the Earth. Some of this heats the Earth, but much of it bounces back into space. Some is trapped and stored by living things.

▼ The only living things that can trap solar energy as they grow are green plants. Plants use the sunlight to make food out of water and carbon dioxide in their leaves.

▼ Earthworms are an energy-rich food. We do not appreciate them, but chickens and ducks like to eat worms whenever they can.

▼ A chicken sandwich gives you energy to grow on. The energy came from the chicken's diet of grain and, of course, those earthworms.

▼ When we burn coal or oil we use stored energy from the sunlight that shone millions of years ago. When the trees in the ancient forests died, they formed such huge piles that there was not enough oxygen for them to rot away. They turned into coal.

▼ The ancient forest plants stood a hundred feet tall. In the swamps where they grew, the layer of dead plants grew steadily thicker. The solar energy which gave them life was trapped in the huge tree trunks when they died.

▼ In time, the pressure of new layers of plants and rock turned the plant remains into coal. Huge seams of coal have been found, some deep underground.

▼ Coal is mined from the underground seams. It is full of energy and burns easily. The heat can be used to produce steam at a power plant.

▼ Some crops produce a pound of new growth per square foot in a season. Plants are used as an energy source by grazing animals such as rabbits, sheep, and cows.

▼ Unluckily for rabbits, foxes like to use small animals as their own energy source. The energy that is stored in the rabbit's body then becomes food for the fox.

▼A dead fox is an ideal food for a scavenger, such as a crow. The rest of the fox's body provides energy for tiny creatures in the soil. The solar energy has now been used four times!

▼ As well as feeding teeming masses of microscopic organisms, decaying animals and plants make the soil a rich source of food for the earthworms. They too become food in time.

▼ The energy from this chain of events is what you use to live, to move, even to throw stones at cans on the top of a wall. It all came from the Sun.

▼ The stone missed! The energy used to throw the stone is transferred to a window, which breaks. The energy chain ends in trouble.

▼ After its long journey, through five kinds of animals (from rabbits to people) the solar energy ends up as the energy which breaks a window and makes the sound of a loud crash!

▼ The steam is used to drive giant turbines. In this way a coal-fired power plant turns the solar energy first trapped by the coal forests, into electricity.

▼ Microphones, motors, and even some cars can be powered by electricity. So can burglar alarms. An alarm has been set off by the broken window.

▶ The energy used to throw the stone and break the window set off the alarm. The alarm itself is powered by electricity made from the solar energy stored underground in coal for millions of years.

F

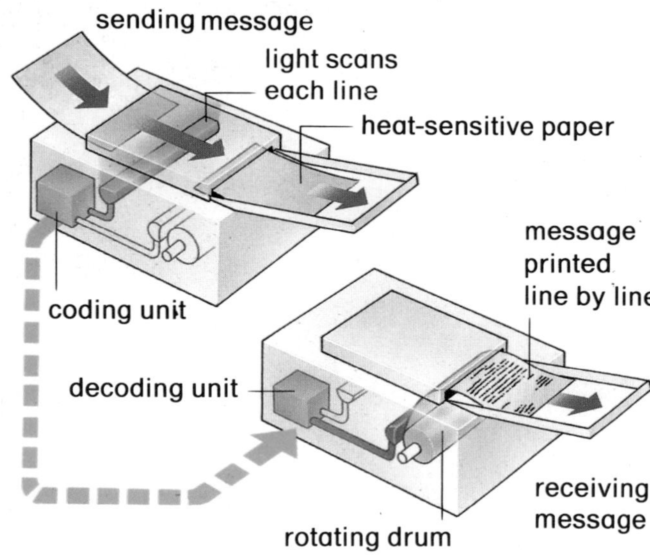

▲ A fax machine changes a page of information into a sound code. Another fax machine uses the code to create a copy. The fax sends pictures and text down a telephone line.

fax

"Fax" is short for facsimile. It is a way of sending images on paper by TELEPHONE. A beam of light scans across the images or message on a sheet of paper. The reflected beam is converted into DIGITAL signals. These are sent down the wire like a normal telephone transmission. At the other end, the signals are fed to a line of tiny metal probes. These get hot where the signal indicates "black" and cold when the signal means "white." A roll of heat-sensitive paper passes across the line of probes. Where it is heated it turns black. Otherwise it stays white. In this way the whole image is built up, line by line.

feedback

Feedback is the way that an action can be controlled by the result it causes. For example, a machine that goes too fast can automatically cut off its own electricity supply, preventing it from going any faster. An early feedback device was the GOVERNOR of a STEAM engine. If the ENGINE went too fast, spinning metal spheres would swing out and cut off the steam supply so that the engine would slow.

fibers

Fibers are fine threads. Natural fibers come from animals and plants. Synthetic fibers, such as NYLON, are made from by-products of the PLASTICS industry. Clothes made from synthetics dry more quickly than natural fibers.

▶ Cloth may be made from animal or plant fibers. Wool and cotton are the most widely used. Silk comes from the silk moth and linen is made from the flax plant.

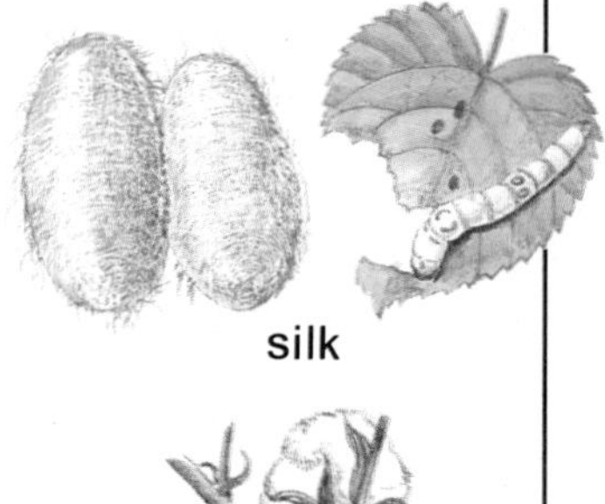

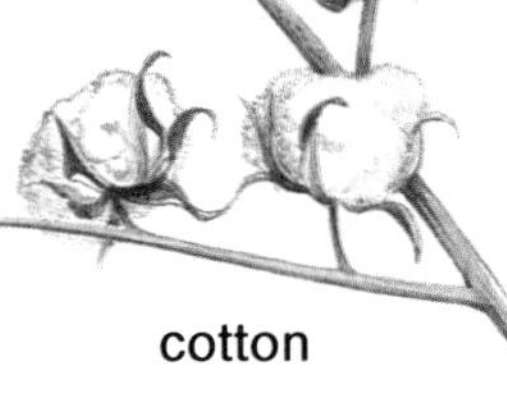

film see **photography**

fire see **combustion**

FIREWORKS

Fireworks are cardboard tubes filled with gunpowder. A chemical inside gives out OXYGEN when it is heated. This lets the charge burn, even though it is shut away inside a tube out of contact with the air. Different chemicals are used for different effects and colors. They might create flower shapes that burst in the air, or flashes of brilliant light. The technical term for the study of fireworks is pyrotechnics. Fireworks can be dangerous and must be handled with care.

Gunpowder fuels the rocket. The chemicals produce different colors. Strontium produces bright red; sodium, yellow; and barium, green.

F

▲ Nuclear fission can be controlled to generate electricity. In a nuclear bomb the chain reaction accelerates uncontrollably due to the amount of uranium present, causing a violent explosion.

fission

Some heavy ATOMS are unstable. They can be broken in two. When this happens NEUTRONS are shot out as the NUCLEUS splits open, releasing a large amount of NUCLEAR ENERGY. Each of these neutrons will in turn split any atom it hits. This gives out still more neutrons, and they split many more atoms. Once this happens, all the atoms start to undergo fission. This is a chain reaction. As the atomic nuclei break up, a large amount of ENERGY is released. This can be used to cause an explosion or, if controlled, to generate NUCLEAR POWER.

flame

A flame is the hot glowing gas formed during COMBUSTION.

flight

Like birds, AIRCRAFT have curved wings. This enables them to produce enough lift for flight. Air rushing over the curved top of the wings has to flow faster than the air below as it has farther to travel. The air pressure below the wing is greater than that above, and this produces lift. Lift must be greater than the force of GRAVITY acting on the plane's weight. Forward thrust is provided by the ENGINES.

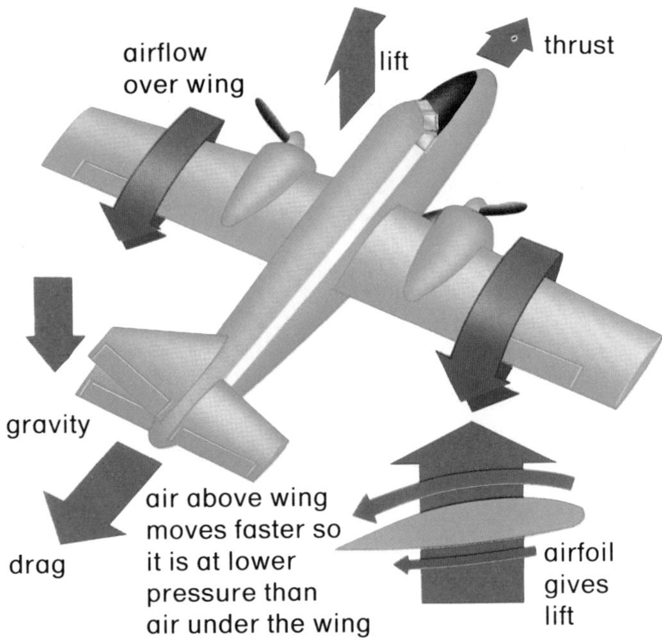

▲▼ Four forces act on a bird or an aircraft in flight. The wings create lift, while the body weight pulls downward. Engines (or bird wings) create thrust, while air resistance causes drag.

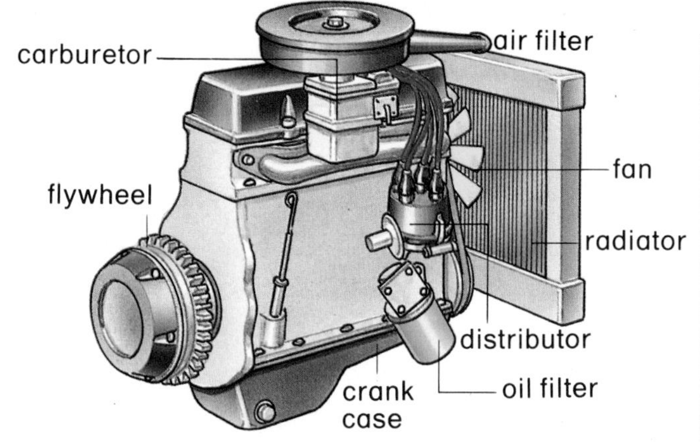

▲ The flywheel is so heavy it spins at a steady speed. This keeps the engine running smoothly.

flywheel

A flywheel is a heavy wheel. Once it is spinning around, it will keep spinning until something stops it. This is because it has INERTIA. Without a flywheel a car engine would run roughly, because INTERNAL-COMBUSTION ENGINES have a series of EXPLOSIONS going on inside. But the heavy flywheel in the engine absorbs the irregularities and keeps the engine turning smoothly. See **gyroscope**.

fog

Fog is a grayish cloud which stops you from seeing very far. It is an AEROSOL of tiny droplets of water in the AIR close to the ground. If you can see through it easily, it is a mist. When a fog is combined with smoke particles it may be called smog. Photochemical smog forms when sunlight acts on traffic and factory fumes in cities. See **pollution**.

▼ A warm wind blowing over cold water collects vapor from the water. When the moist wind meets the land, it cools and the vapor it carries changes back into water droplets. This is fog.

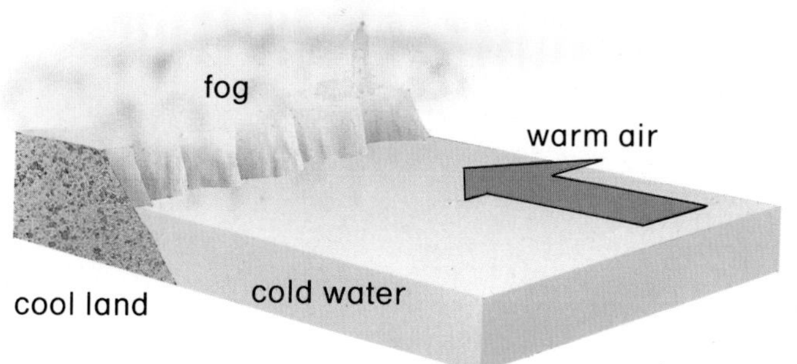

force

Any kind of action that makes an object start moving, or changes the way it moves, is a force. Your hand pushing and the wind blowing are both forces.

forensics

Science can be used to solve crime. Evidence is gathered from the scene of the crime and is analyzed by forensic scientists. They can look at fingerprints under a MICROSCOPE and identify a suspect because everyone's fingerprints are unique. Grains of pollen on clothing may prove what the wearer was doing. Chemical tests can identify explosives. The smallest piece of matter might offer a clue. Using DNA fingerprinting, genes from human cells can be compared to those of a suspect.

▼ A criminal may be identified by matching a fingerprint found at the scene of a crime.

F

formula

Formulas show the make-up of a chemical COMPOUND. The symbols for the ELEMENTS are used with numbers to show how they combine. CARBON DIOXIDE's formula is CO_2. This means it has one atom of CARBON and two of OXYGEN. Formulas in equations show how chemical reactions work. When a fuel releases carbon it combines with two ATOMS of oxygen to form carbon dioxide, but when the oxygen supply is low it bonds with one atom and forms harmful carbon monoxide:

$C + O_2 \rightarrow CO_2$ carbon dioxide
$C + O \rightarrow CO$ carbon monoxide

fossil

Fossil remains of plants and animals may be millions of years old. Some were buried in mud or silt after they died. In time, their hard parts, such as bones or the veins of leaves, turned to stone. The soft parts rotted and the impressions they left behind in rocks became trace fossils.

▼ Millions of years ago the remains of plants and dead animals were covered with mud and turned into stone. The fossils are revealed when the rocks above them erode.

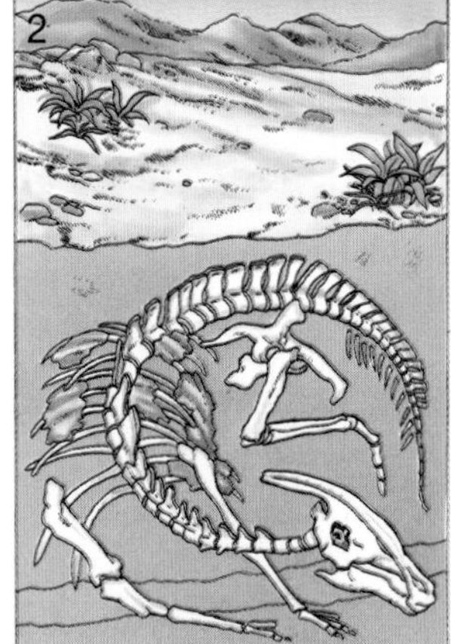

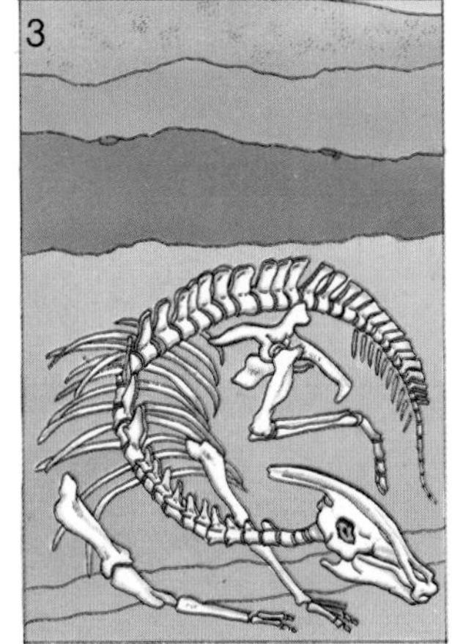

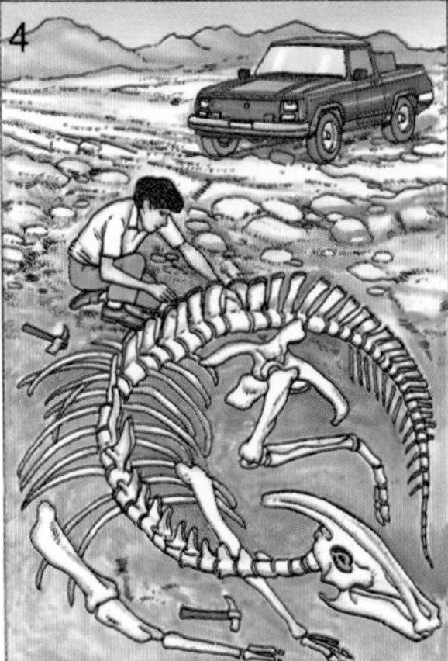

fossil fuels

Some fossilized plant remains can burn. Examples are COAL and OIL. Coal is fossilized trees, and oil is formed from tiny plants and animals that lived in the sea millions of years ago. Because these are the remains of early forms of life, we call them fossil fuels. See **fossil**.

LIFE STORY

Foucault

Jean Bernard Léon Foucault was a French scientist who invented the GYROSCOPE. In 1851 he set up an experiment to show that the Earth rotates. He hung up a long PENDULUM in Paris and set it swinging. He marked the position on the ground when it started to swing. As hours went by, the pendulum moved from the mark. In fact, it was still swinging in the same direction — it was the Earth that had turned.

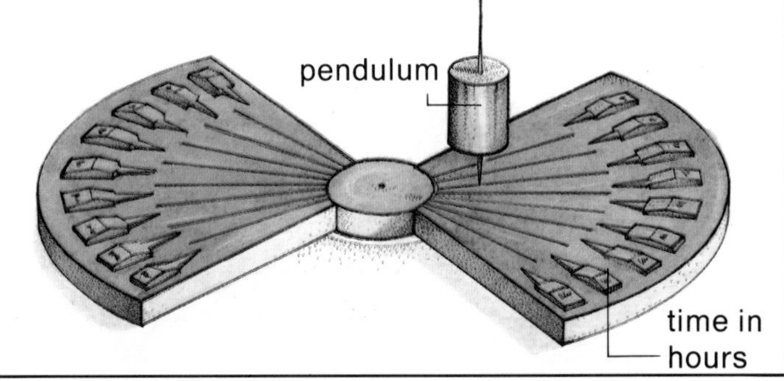

freeze-drying

Freeze-drying is a way of preserving food. If frozen food is placed in a vacuum, the ICE will then sublime away — it will evaporate without melting. The food is left in its original state but bone dry and permanently preserved.

freezing

Freezing happens when a liquid becomes solid as it cools. WATER freezes to ICE at a temperature of 32°F (0°C).

friction

Friction is the FORCE that stops surfaces from sliding easily against each other. If you slide your hand across a brick wall, there is high friction. But wet soap in the shower slips around with low friction. A LUBRICANT, like OIL, can help to reduce friction in machinery. But the soles of your shoes are designed to have high friction. You need friction to walk safely. If you have ever walked on smooth ICE (which has very low friction) you'll know how important friction can be.

▼ Bicycle brakes work by friction. When the rider squeezes the brake lever, a pair of brake blocks are pressed against the wheel. The grip steals energy from the wheel and slows it down.

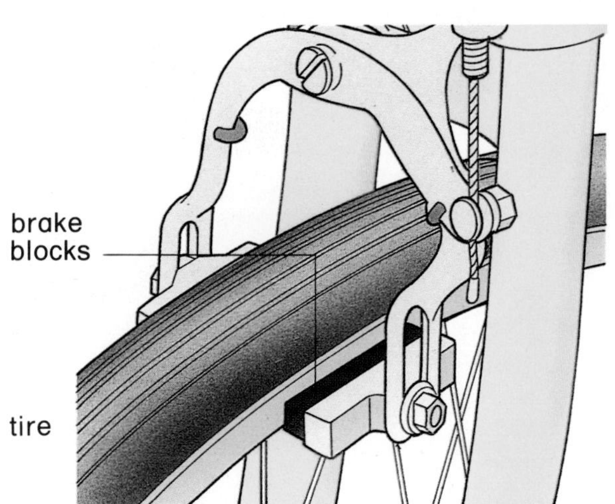

fuel

Fuels are substances that burn to give out HEAT ENERGY. COAL, wood, and ALCOHOL can be used as fuels. Energy can also be obtained without actual burning taking place. In a fuel cell, HYDROGEN and OXYGEN will react without ever producing a FLAME. The ATOMS join to form MOLECULES of WATER, and ELECTRICITY is produced. Fuel injection is a system that squirts fuel into an ENGINE to produce extra POWER.

fuse

Fusing means melting. A fuse is a piece of wire in a CIRCUIT that melts if the CURRENT is too strong. See **circuit breaker**.

▶ Electric current flows through a fuse wire unless the current is greater than a certain value. If the current is larger than this value, the fuse wire heats up and melts, or "blows," and the circuit is broken.

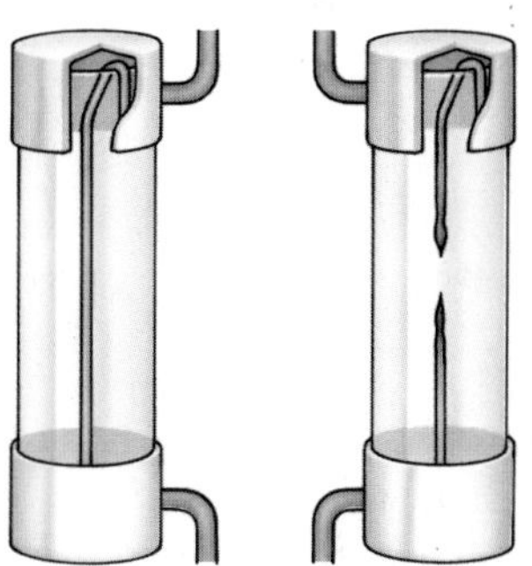

fusion

Nuclear FISSION releases ENERGY when heavy atomic nuclei split. But energy is also released when light nuclei join to form bigger ones. This is fusion power. When ATOMS of heavy ISOTOPES of HYDROGEN react together they join to form HELIUM, and energy is released. This is the reaction that takes place in the SUN. It has been used to make the HYDROGEN BOMB.

Fusion power requires temperatures too high for most reactors, but in 1991, the Joint European Torus (JET) produced the first harnessed fusion energy. One day we may be able to use this idea to make ELECTRICITY. See **nuclear power**.

galaxy
A galaxy is a collection of STARS. There are about a hundred million galaxies in the visible universe. If you look at the night sky, many of the "stars" you see are actually galaxies. And each galaxy contains millions of stars.

galvanizing
Galvanizing is the process of coating steel with ZINC. This delays CORROSION.

gasoline
Gasoline is a fuel that is distilled from crude OIL. See **petrochemicals**.

gas turbine
Normal TURBINES spin around when they are driven. A gas turbine spins by using energy that it releases inside itself. The best example of a gas turbine is a jet ENGINE. Gas turbines are used in planes and power stations and have been used in experimental cars.

Geiger counter
The most common apparatus for measuring nuclear RADIATION is a Geiger counter. It converts radiation into pulses of electricity which can be heard as clicks when amplified.

▲ Viewed edge-on, a spiral galaxy is a flat disk of stars with a bulge at its middle. From above (right), its spiral arms snake out into space.

gem
Gems are MINERALS that look beautiful. The most valuable is DIAMOND, the hardest mineral in the world. Other gems include sapphire, ruby, opal, and emerald. Some have practical uses. For example, ruby is used to make LASERS.

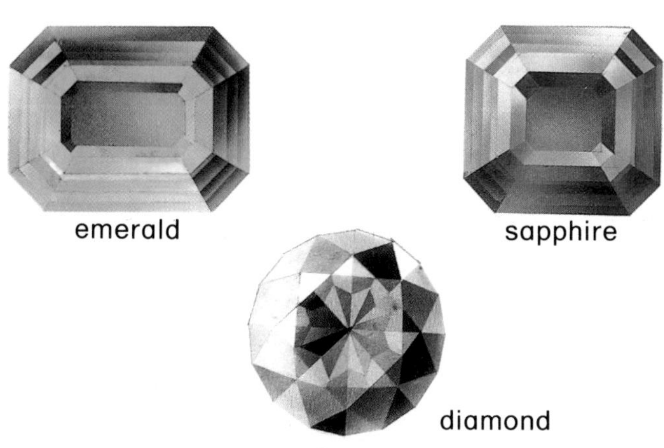

▲ When gems are mined, they are usually irregular lumps of dull crystal. Hard gems are transformed into sparkling precious stones by cutting and polishing.

generator

If you turn a wire coil in a MAGNETIC field, then you generate ELECTRICITY. Simple generators are used to power bicycle lights. In this kind of generator, known as a DYNAMO, the magnet spins and the coil stays still.

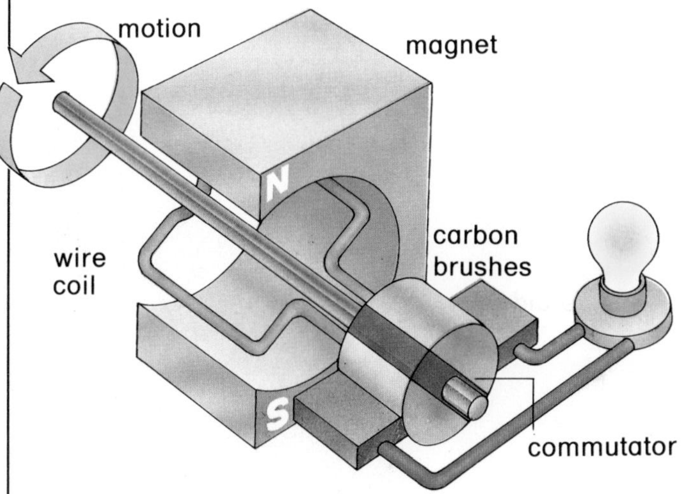

▲ An electricity generator works by spinning a coil of wire in a magnetic field. As the wire cuts through the magnetic field, an electric current flows through the coil and, here, lights a bulb.

geography

Geo- is Greek for the Earth, and *graphikos* means drawing. So geography is the recording of the Earth's surface.

geology

Geology is the study of the ROCKS and MINERALS in the Earth's crust and of the processes that form and shape the planet.

▼ Geologists study the Earth's rocks. Rocks are formed when lava hardens, or when layers of rocks or sediments are heated or compressed.

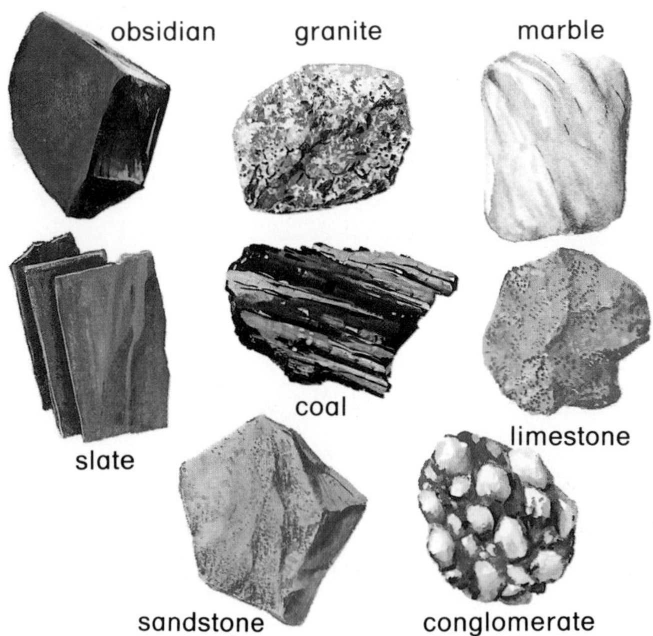

geometry

Metrès is Greek for "measurer." *Geo-* means Earth. So geometry started out as the MEASURING of the EARTH. It has moved on to be the measurement of shapes in general. Circles, squares, and triangles have been studied for thousands of years, and they are the basis of the part of MATHEMATICS called geometry.

geothermal

Thermal means "heat." Geothermal describes the heat ENERGY inside the EARTH. It can be used as a source of POWER.

▸ If underground water meets hot rocks and boils suddenly, the result is a geyser — a jet of steam and water gushing out of the ground. Geysers are often found where there are or were volcanoes. They are common in New Zealand, Iceland, and parts of the United States.

geyser

WATER deep inside layers of ROCK below ground is sometimes heated by VOLCANIC activity. Then the water boils and shoots out of cracks, forming a geyser.

glacier

Glaciers form when huge masses of ICE build up in mountain valleys. The PRESSURE of the glacier melts the ice underneath, so the whole mass moves downhill at up to 65 ft (20 m) a day.

▼ As a glacier moves downhill it drags rocks and mud, building up ridges called moraines. Lakes are formed in hollows in the valley.

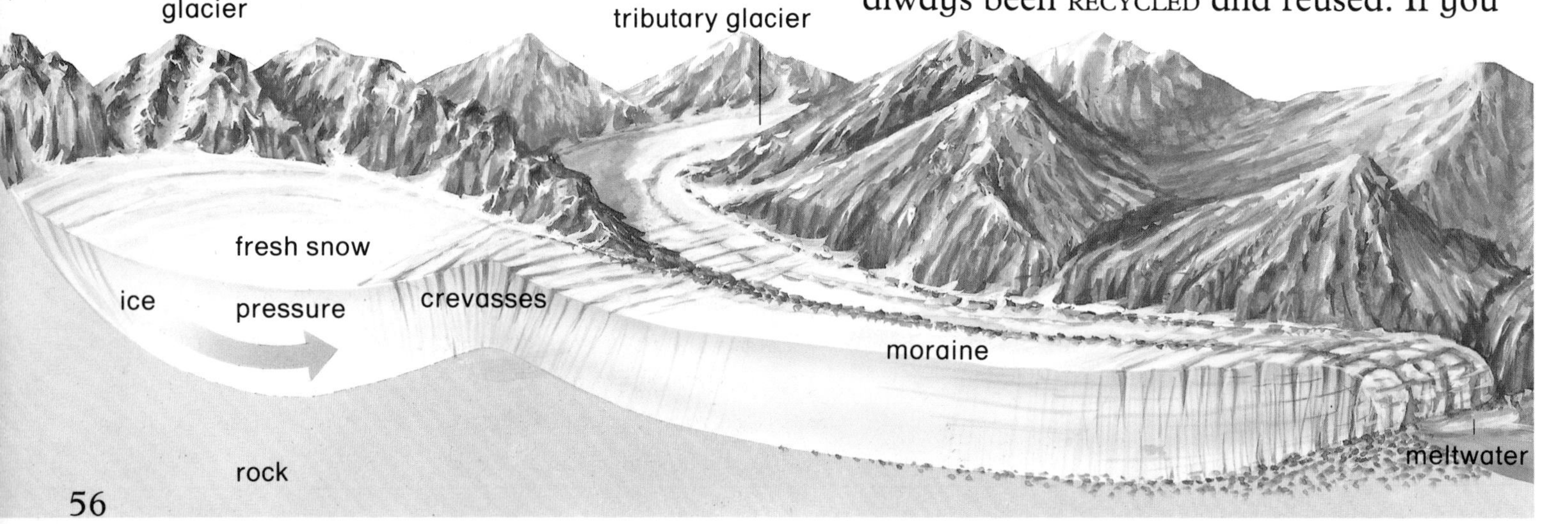

glass

Glass is a blend of silica (silicon dioxide), the mineral in sand. Commercial glass is made by melting a mixture of sand and sodium carbonate with a little limestone to help it melt. Glass has no fixed melting point. It simply gets softer as it heats up. While it is hot it can be molded or blown into shape before it is allowed to cool and set hard.

▶ Gold is an inert metal and will not react with most substances. Gold reflects heat. A thin wrapping of gold protected the Lunar Module from getting too hot.

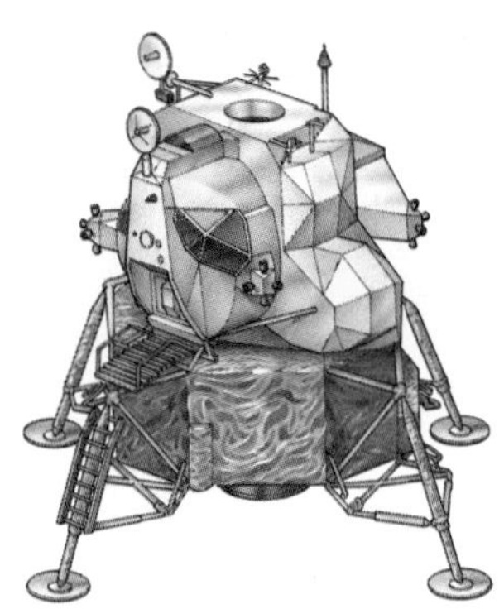

gold

Gold is a precious yellow METAL that has been known for thousands of years. It is not affected by most of the ACIDS and gases that attack other metals. Gold can be hammered so thin that light shines through it. In this form, gold leaf, it is used to cover objects with a thin layer of the metal. Because gold is so valuable it has always been RECYCLED and reused. If you have some gold at home it may include gold from the Spanish conquest of Mexico, in the 16th century.

governor

A governor is a device for controlling speed. The first governors were on STEAM engines. They kept the ENGINE from going too fast. See **feedback**.

graph

Often the clearest way to see information in MATHEMATICS is to draw it out on squared paper, or on a COMPUTER. Values are plotted as points on the graph, then joined up to make a curve. A graph shows how one value changes with time or compares to another value.

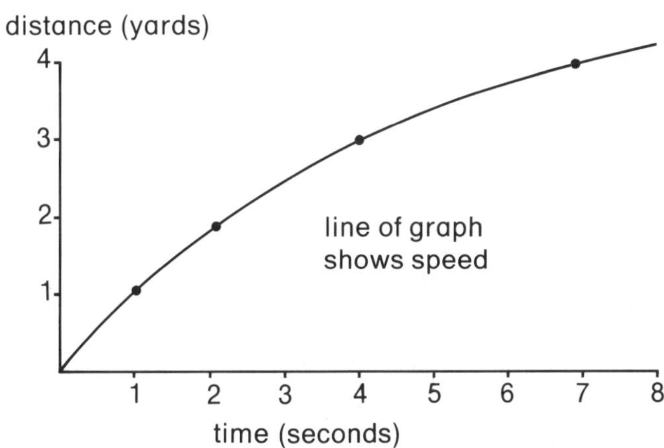

▲ A graph showing the speed of a moving object is drawn by plotting the distance traveled against time. The shape of the curve shows how the speed changes.

gravity

Gravity is the force that pulls objects toward the ground. Large amounts of MASS pull other masses toward them. The Earth's gravity keeps you from floating up toward the ceiling. The laws of gravity were said to have been worked out by Isaac Newton, after an apple fell from a tree. He realized that the MOON didn't fall, although it was very heavy. This gave him the idea of gravity pulling downward, matched by the VELOCITY of the Moon keeping it in ORBIT.

▶ Gravity pulls the Earth and Moon toward each other. The Earth is much larger than the Moon, and its gravitational force is six times as strong.

greenhouse effect see **page 58**

gunpowder

Gunpowder is a mixture of sulfur, CHARCOAL, and saltpeter (potassium nitrate). This EXPLOSIVE was known to the ancient Chinese, who used it to make FIREWORKS.

gyroscope

Everyone is fascinated by gyroscopes. A gyroscope is a spinning metal FLYWHEEL. It will resist any FORCE that tries to tilt it, and the wheel axle will always point in the same direction as when it started to spin. Gyroscopes are used for navigating on planes and ships. The wheel is spun with the axle pointing north. Whatever the direction of the ship, the gyroscope will always show north.

▶ A spinning gyroscope can be balanced on the tip of a pencil as long as its flywheel is spinning. The gyroscope falls over when the flywheel slows down.

GREENHOUSE EFFECT

ENERGY shines onto the Earth from the SUN. It is reflected back again as HEAT, but much of it is trapped by gases in the ATMOSPHERE and cannot escape. This greenhouse effect keeps our climate balanced. Not all the gases in the air trap the heat equally. CARBON DIOXIDE traps a large amount of heat. The burning of FOSSIL FUELS, in cars and power stations, adds to the carbon dioxide in the atmosphere. As a result, more heat is trapped, and the world may be getting warmer.

▼ The extra heat trapped by the greenhouse gases may be heating the atmosphere by 2°F every thirty years. This small change in temperature could have dramatic effects on the climate. If the ice and snow melted, the sea could rise and flood a lot of land. The only answer is to cut back on the release of greenhouse gases.

▶ Half of the global warming is caused by carbon dioxide, 15 percent is caused by methane, 25 percent by CFCs, and the rest by nitrogen oxides.

◀ We call this the greenhouse effect because gases such as carbon dioxide and methane act like the glass in a greenhouse. The layer of glass prevents the Sun's heat from escaping, so the greenhouse stays warm.

half-life
The ATOMS of unstable ISOTOPES break down into simpler atoms as time goes by. At first they break down frequently, but as there are fewer atoms left they break down more rarely. The half-life is the time it takes for half of the atoms to break down. For some materials, like plutonium, the half-life is millions of years. But for an isotope of lithium the half-life is less than a billionth of a billionth of a second.

hardness
The hardness of water depends on the amount of lime dissolved in it. The hardness of solids is measured on the Mohs scale. The softest mineral is talc, numbered one on the scale. Talc is so soft it can be scratched with a fingernail. The hardest mineral is DIAMOND, which is number ten on the scale. Each mineral can scratch the next one down the list, and so on down the scale.

hardware see **computers, software**

heat see **pages 60 and 61**

heat exchanger
A heat exchanger is a device for moving HEAT from one place to another. The "radiator" of a car cools the engine by exchanging its heat with the cold air blowing over it from the outside.

▼ A car radiator is a heat exchanger. Water absorbs heat from the engine. Cold air is drawn through the radiator to cool the water again.

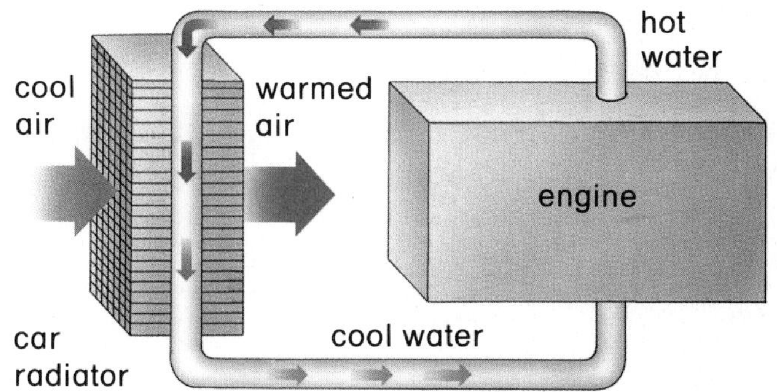

heat pump
A heat pump is like a REFRIGERATOR running in reverse. A heat pump collects the low level of HEAT in a river or in the soil and takes it through a series of pipes. The fluid in the pipes is compressed to release the heat. In this way a nearby river can be used to heat a house.

▼ The Mohs scale is used to measure hardness. Materials are compared to ten minerals. A material that scratches apatite but is scratched by orthoclase has a hardness rating of 5.5.

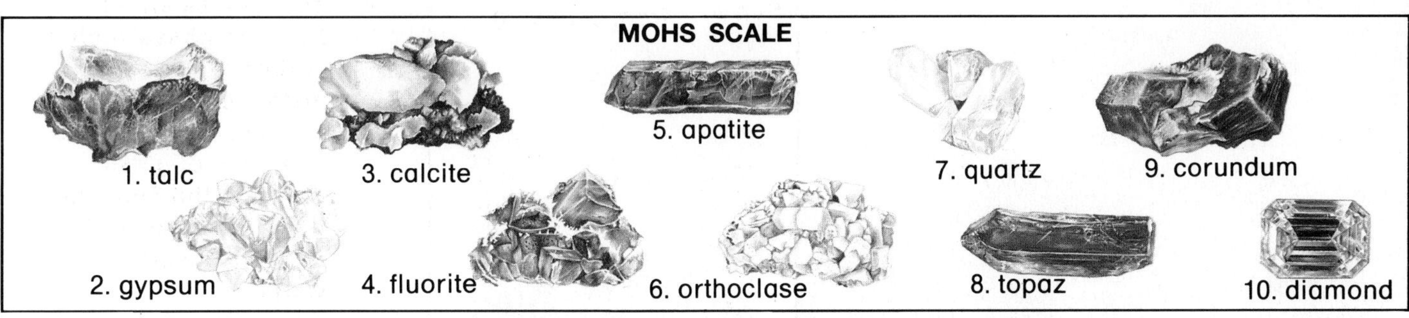

HEAT

Heat is a form of ENERGY. It spreads in three ways. One is by slowly spreading through a substance, like warmth along a metal spoon. This is conduction. A second is CONVECTION, which occurs when a hot liquid or gas expands and rises. Colder liquid or gas takes its place, and (after being heated) rises in its turn, forming a convection current. The third way, radiation, is in the form of INFRARED rays shining across a space. It is how the energy from the SUN reaches Earth across the empty space that lies between.

▼ When you heat a saucepan of water, the metal pan is heated by conduction. Then the water inside is heated by convection currents.

TEMPERATURE

Temperature tells you how hot something is, but not how much heat it contains. Two objects could be the same temperature but the one that stays hot longer has more heat energy. The lowest temperature possible is absolute zero (−459.69°F and −273.16°C). Even outer space is warmer than this. The nearest anyone has come to absolute zero is two trillionths of a degree above it.

▶ Here, one person is feeling heat radiated from the Sun. The other feels it radiated from the heater. Their backs heat up, too. Heat radiating between the two of them causes "local heating."

DID YOU KNOW?

As a substance is heated, the atoms or molecules of which it is made become more agitated. They jiggle about more as the temperature goes higher. The top picture of the three shows them totally still. This would be absolute zero. The middle picture shows them as they might be when at room temperature. And the lowest picture shows them jiggling furiously, when very hot.

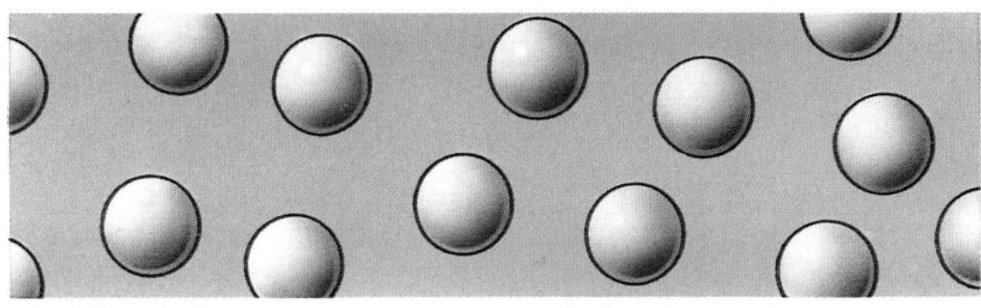

absolute zero

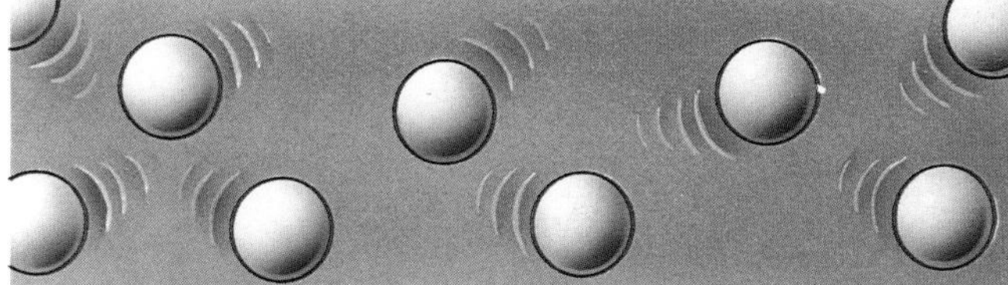

room temperature

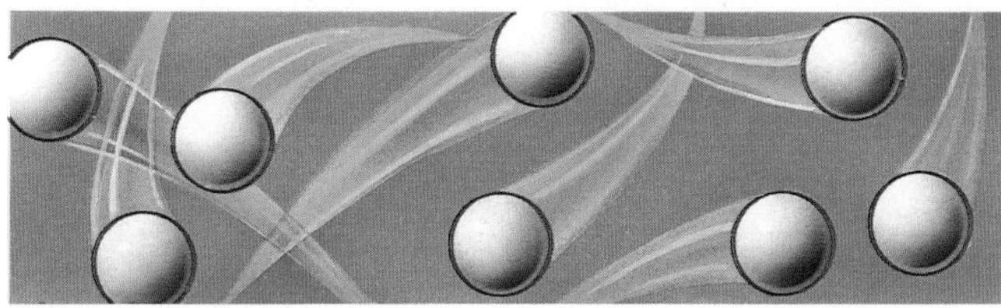

hot

▼ Local heating takes place where two radiating bodies face each other closely. On an electric heater the hottest loops in the coil are those closest together. You may notice that the hottest places in a coal or wood fire are in between the lumps of fuel. This is because the pieces of fuel reflect heat to each other, and the temperature builds up in between. An example of local heating is in a barbecue fire. The hot spots are between the coals. Move the coals apart and the fire dies.

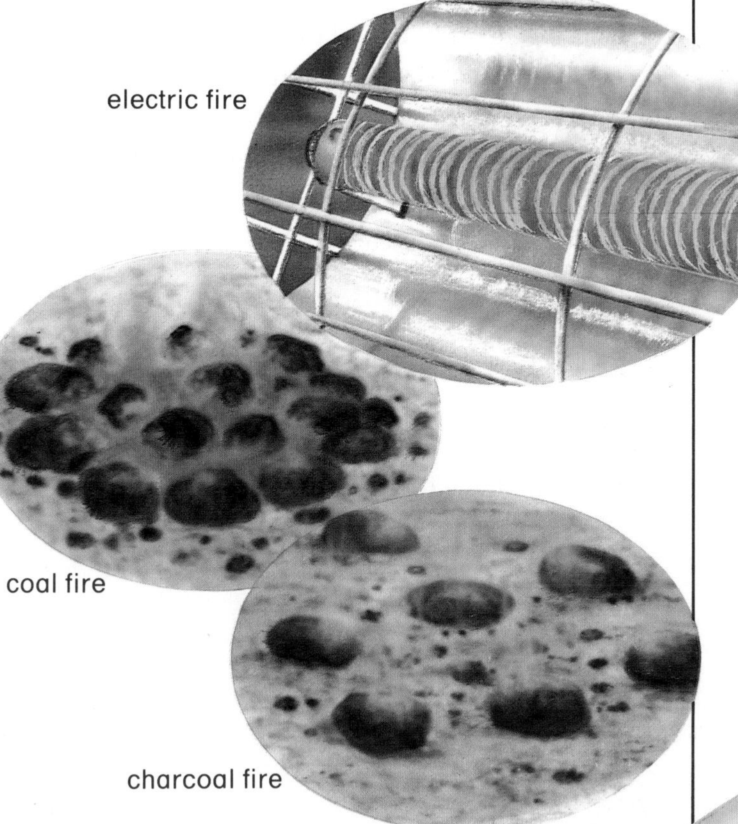

electric fire

coal fire

charcoal fire

The temperature that something reaches depends on how much infrared energy it absorbs. Infrared is reflected from a white surface, and absorbed by a dark one. Try this experiment one sunny day. Stand with one bare foot on a white tile and the other on one that is black. The white tile will feel much cooler.

▼ Chemical reactions take place more rapidly in hot water than in cold. Dissolve two fizzy tablets, one in hot water and one in cold, and you can see which one reacts quickest.

cold water

hot water

heavy water

A MOLECULE of normal WATER is made of two ATOMS of HYDROGEN and one of OXYGEN to make the COMPOUND H_2O. Heavy water has an unusual hydrogen atom with a NEUTRON in the nucleus. It is also known as deuterium oxide, abbreviated D_2O. Heavy water is used in some NUCLEAR reactors.

helicopter

A helicopter is an AIRCRAFT in which lift is produced by a large propeller on the top. This propeller is known as the rotor, and it takes the place of wings. It allows the helicopter to take off vertically and hover in the air, as lift can be produced without the helicopter traveling forward.

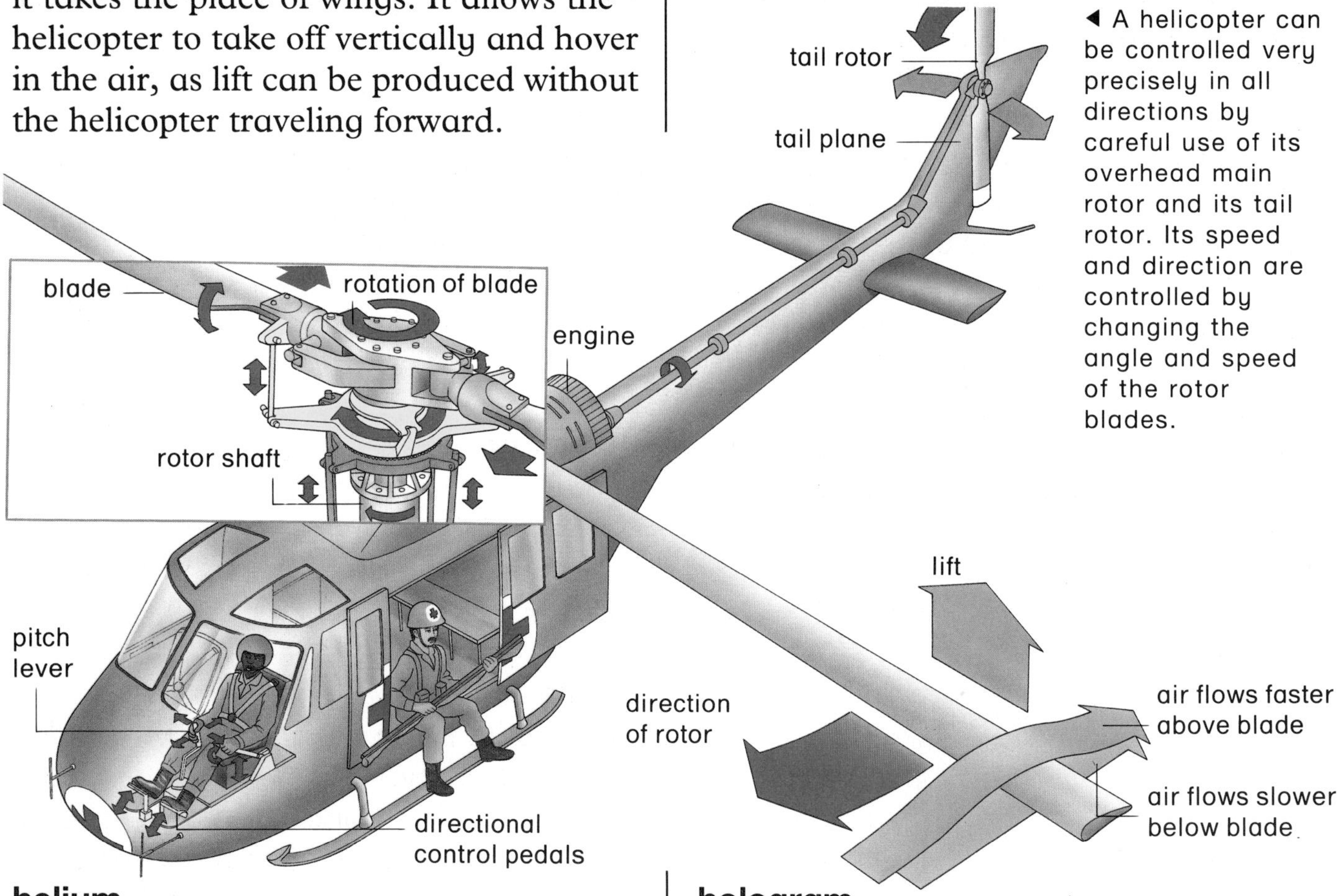

◄ A helicopter can be controlled very precisely in all directions by careful use of its overhead main rotor and its tail rotor. Its speed and direction are controlled by changing the angle and speed of the rotor blades.

helium

HYDROGEN is the simplest ATOM, with a single PROTON in the nucleus. Helium is next, with two protons and two NEUTRONS. Its symbol is He. Helium is the second lightest gas after hydrogen. It was first detected by analyzing the LIGHT of the SUN, and later discovered on Earth. Unlike hydrogen, helium does not catch fire, so it is used as the lighter-than-air gas in BALLOONS and airships.

hertz

Electromagnetic WAVES (such as RADIO waves) were first produced by the German physicist Heinrich Hertz in the 1880's. The SI UNIT that measures the frequency of waves is named hertz (Hz) after him. One vibration, or cycle per second, equals 1 Hz.

hologram

A hologram is a recording of the pattern formed when laser light is reflected from an object and "interferes" with the original laser beam. The result is a three-dimensional image.

▶ One horse can work at a rate of one horsepower. When engines replaced horses, engine power was still measured in horsepower. It was calculated from the size and number of cylinders in the engine. Engine power is now measured more accurately in brake horsepower (bhp) — the power needed to brake the engine. It is measured by a device called a dynamometer.

type of vehicle	hp	type of vehicle	hp
	1		300–500 bhp
	4		4,500 bhp
	75–85 bhp		
	80–105 bhp		280,000 bhp

horsepower

Horsepower was the power of a single horse. But (since there are strong and weak horses) it is now set at 745.7 WATTS.

hovercraft (air-cushion vehicle)

A hovercraft is a vehicle that is held above the surface by a cushion of air. Hovercraft can glide straight from land to sea. The air cushion reduces FRICTION between the hovercraft and the sea, so it glides quickly along with very little effort. The first successful hovercraft was designed in England by a boat builder named Christopher Cockerell in 1955. His first experiments were done with a coffee can and a hair drier.

▼ A hovercraft rides on top of a cushion of air blown out beneath the craft by a large fan.

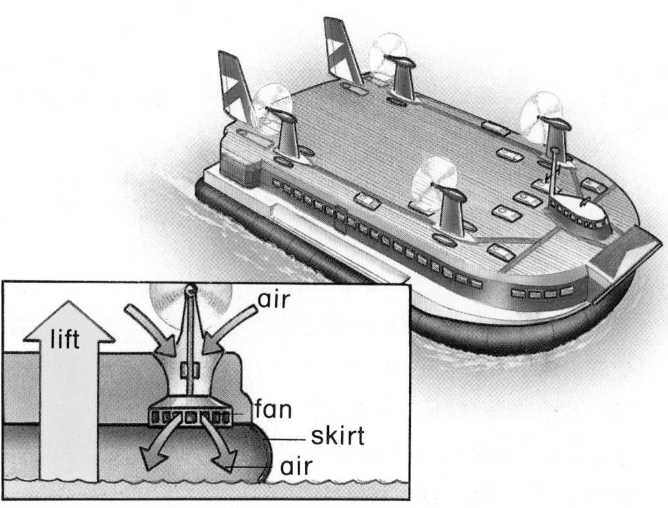

humidity

Humidity is a measure of the moisture in the air. When the air cannot hold any more moisture, the humidity is 100 percent. Hot air can hold more water than cold air. When warm, damp air cools, the water condenses to form FOG.

hurricane

A hurricane is a tropical storm with strong WINDS spinning round a center of low PRESSURE at 74 mph (125 km) or faster. See **air and atmosphere**.

hydraulics

Hydraulics is the science of how liquids flow. You cannot compress liquids. If you force liquid down one end of a pipe then the same amount of liquid must come out of the other end. You can use this idea to make a foot pedal operate a brake some distance away. A large movement of a small piston can make a large piston move a little way. This is how a hydraulic jack lifts a car.

▲ This is a surface-piercing hydrofoil; the underwater wings are not completely submerged.

hydrofoil

A hydrofoil is a kind of wing that works under water. The word is also used to describe a ship with strong "wings" underneath. When going fast, they make the ship rise out of the water. This cuts down FRICTION and allows the hydrofoil to travel easily across the water.

hydrogen

Hydrogen has the simplest ATOM possible. A hydrogen atom has a single PROTON in the NUCLEUS and a single ELECTRON in ORBIT around it. It is the lightest ELEMENT in the universe and also the most plentiful. See **heavy water, helium**.

hydrogen bomb

At very high levels of energy, hydrogen ISOTOPES can join together to form HELIUM. This reaction gives out large amounts of ENERGY. It is the source of energy inside the SUN. Powerful hydrogen bombs which use this reaction to produce a huge explosion have been tested but they were never used in warfare. See **fusion**.

hydrometer

A hydrometer is a device for measuring the DENSITY of a liquid compared to water, which has a density of one.

hydroponics

Hydroponics is a way of growing plants without soil. Instead of rooting plants in soil, hydroponic farmers grow them in water containing all the chemicals that they need. Many commercial crops, such as tomatoes, are grown in this way.

▼ Growing mustard and watercress seeds on wet kitchen paper is one form of hydroponics, a method for growing plants without using soil.

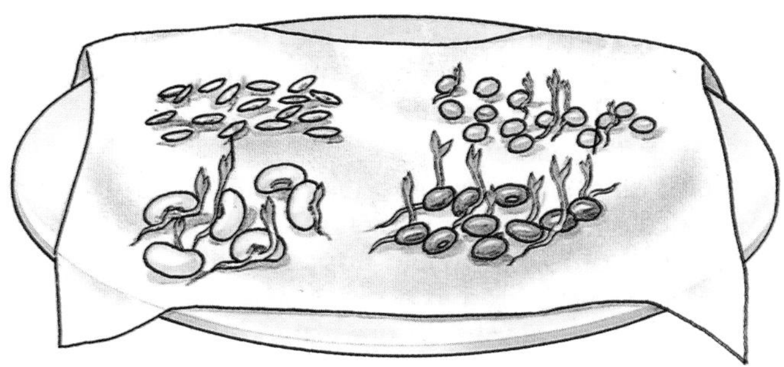

hygrometer

A hygrometer is a device for measuring the HUMIDITY of the air. Have you noticed how your hair changes depending on whether the air is wet or dry? Scientists noticed this too — which is why there is usually a hair inside a hygrometer.

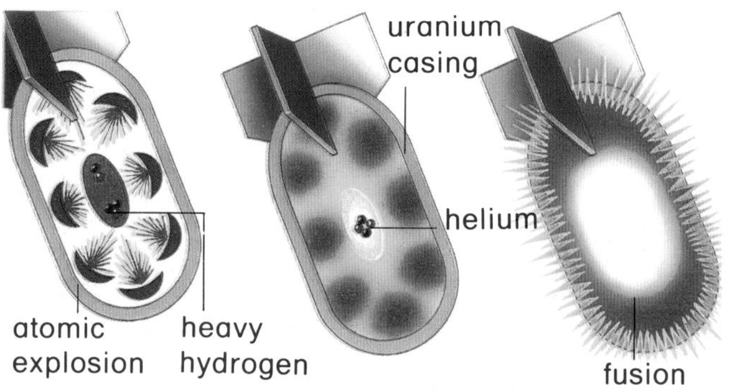

▲ A hydrogen bomb is triggered by an atomic explosion. Heavy hydrogen atoms are forced together, forming helium and releasing energy.

ice and snow see **page 66**

implosion

An implosion is the opposite of an EXPLOSION. An implosion occurs when something collapses inward.

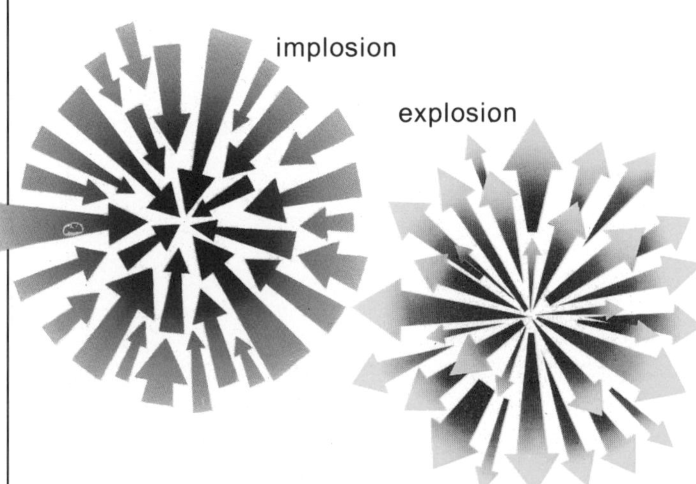

▲ The force of an implosion is directed in toward a central point. Compare this with an explosion, in which the energy bursts outward.

indicator

In chemistry, an indicator is a substance whose color is changed by ACIDS AND ALKALIS. LITMUS is the best known indicator. In an alkali it is blue and in an acid it turns red. In pure water, which is neutral, it is purple. Universal indicator is a mixture of different indicators which tells you exactly how acid (or alkaline) something is by the color it turns the solution. This is measured on the pH scale. A pH of 0 is very acidic, pH 7 is neutral, and pH 14 is very strongly alkaline.

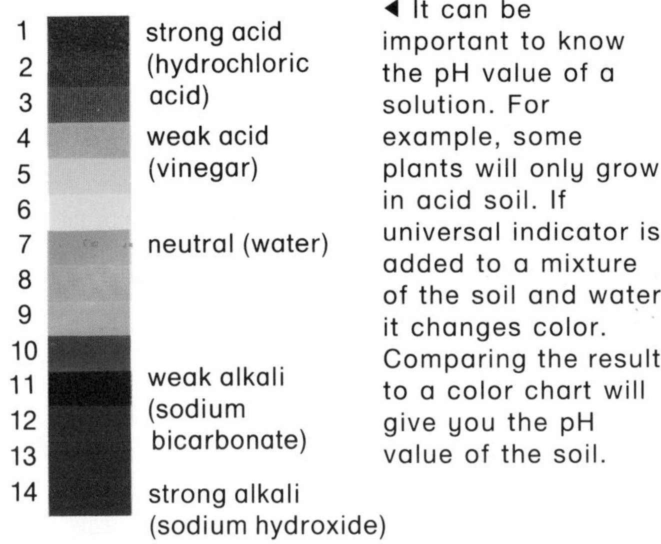

◀ It can be important to know the pH value of a solution. For example, some plants will only grow in acid soil. If universal indicator is added to a mixture of the soil and water it changes color. Comparing the result to a color chart will give you the pH value of the soil.

inertia

An object that is at rest likes to stay that way. It takes ENERGY to make it move. Once moving, it takes energy to make it stop. This tendency to keep doing the same thing is called inertia.

infinity

Infinity goes on for ever. The number of stars in the universe is limited. So is the number of sand grains in the world. But infinity never ends. You cannot imagine it, because everything you experience ends somewhere, even the universe.

information technology

Information technology is the study of methods of handling data. See **computers, fax, telephone**.

infrared

Infrared waves are the electromagnetic wavelengths that lie beyond the red end of the visible spectrum. HEAT rays are infrared. See **light, radiation**.

ICE AND SNOW

Ice is an amazing substance. If you freeze a normal liquid, the solid form always sinks. But when WATER freezes the ice floats. This is because water expands as it freezes, so the ice is lighter than water. Pure water freezes at 32°F (0°C), but adding an impurity such as SALT lowers the freezing point. That is why salt is put on roads in winter to melt the ice.

DID YOU KNOW?

Cold air cannot hold as much water vapor as warm air. As air rises, the vapor may condense to form clouds and rain. But on a cold day snow crystals will form.

When damp air condenses at ground level it forms hoarfrost. You can study the lacy patterns of hoarfrost on a frozen window, or, using a lens, frozen dew on a spider's web.

▶ If the air is cold enough, water vapor in clouds will crystallize and form snow. The crystal grows around a tiny speck of dust. Snowflakes are made up of six-sided crystals. Their shape depends on the water vapor, the temperature, and many other factors. Each snowflake is unique.

◀ *Berg* is German for mountain, from which icebergs got their name. Only one-eighth of the iceberg sticks above the surface. The hidden part of an iceberg sank the liner Titanic.

▼ Skis and skates depend on the fact that ice melts under pressure. As the ice and snow beneath them melts, friction is reduced so they slide easily along.

▲ Wet laundry on a winter clothesline can freeze solid in minutes. But the ice can still sublime (change directly to water vapor without melting to water first) on a good drying day. So the clothes become "dry" without the ice having melted.

integrated circuit

A large electronic circuit can be made by putting all the different parts on one tiny silicon wafer. The separate transistors, and the wires that join them, are all produced as one. So are all the special items such as resistors (which control the flow of electricity) and capacitors (which store it). This is known as an integrated circuit (IC). The central processing unit of a computer is a special integrated circuit no larger than your fingernail.

internal-combustion engine

Gas turbines, gasoline engines, and diesel engines all burn their fuel internally. Burning the fuel produces vast volumes of hot gas, which expand and can be made to do work. In a car, it expands in the cylinders and pushes pistons connected to the wheels. In a gas turbine, the gases are compressed by fans and the thrust is produced by a jet of escaping waste gases.

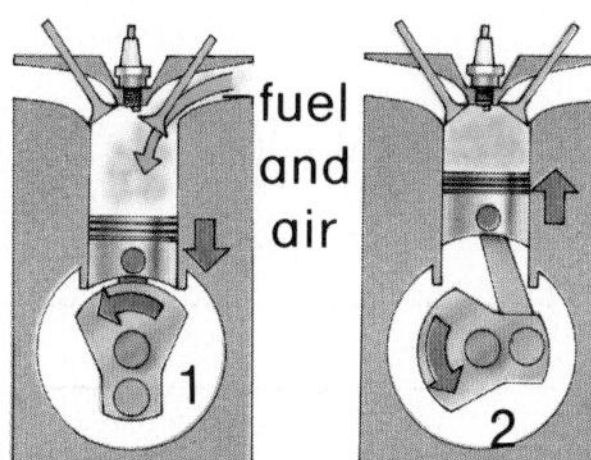

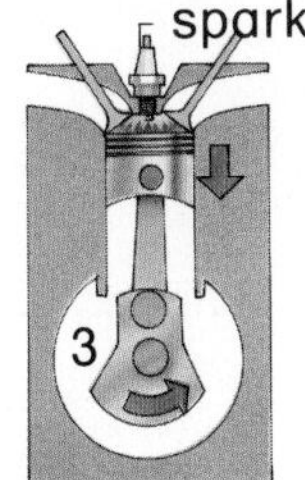

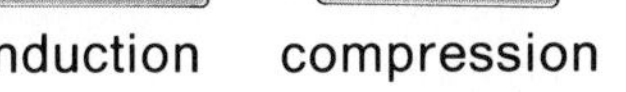

▲ Most internal-combustion engines operate in a "four stroke" cycle. The piston falls, sucking fuel and air into the cylinder. As it rises, the mixture is compressed and then ignited. The explosion drives the piston down; it then rises again to push out the exhaust gases.

inventions see **page 68**

iodine

Iodine is an element with the symbol I. It is a glistening solid which looks like a metal. Iodine dissolves in alcohol to make an antiseptic. It turns starch blue, and can be used as a test for starch (try some on a potato).

ion

An ion is an atom that has gained or lost one or more electrons. It is the same as a normal atom, but it will energetically join with other ions that can accept the extra electron or electrons.

▶ A fluorine atom has nine electrons orbiting the nucleus in two layers, or shells. The outer shell contains seven electrons. If an extra electron joins it, the atom becomes an ion.

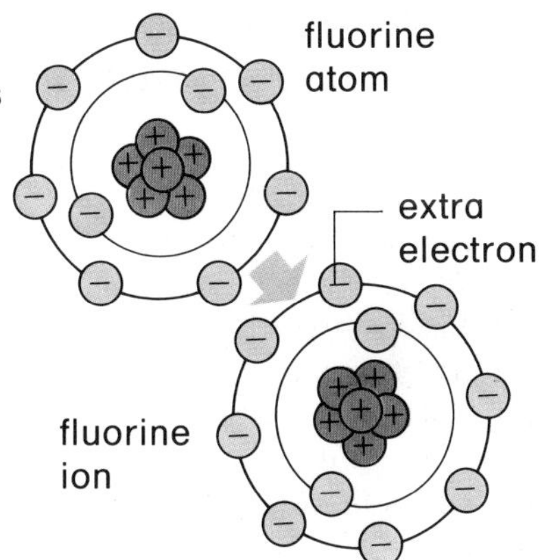

ionosphere

High in the atmosphere, the atoms are so thinly spread out that many of them break into ions because of the solar energy. This layer is the ionosphere.

iridescence

Iridescence is the name given to the shimmering rainbow effect that can sometimes be seen in bubbles, or in oil on water. It occurs because the light reflected from the bottom of the oil film interferes with the light bouncing off the top edge of the film. The white light is split into the colors of the rainbow. Some natural objects, such as the gemstone opal and the wings of a butterfly, are iridescent. They have patterns of very fine lines that reflect different colors of light. It is strange to think that the brilliant purple of a butterfly's wing is produced by scales that are really brown.

INVENTIONS

Do you know the difference between a discovery and an invention? Discoveries occur when people find out about something that already exists — such as GRAVITY, or a DRUG in a wild plant. An invention is something that people make for the first time. The WHEEL was an important invention 5,000 years ago. COMPUTERS are more recent inventions of more recent times.

DID YOU KNOW?

The microchip is one of the smallest inventions. It also has the most uses. These tiny chips control many other inventions — from a huge aircraft to a toaster.

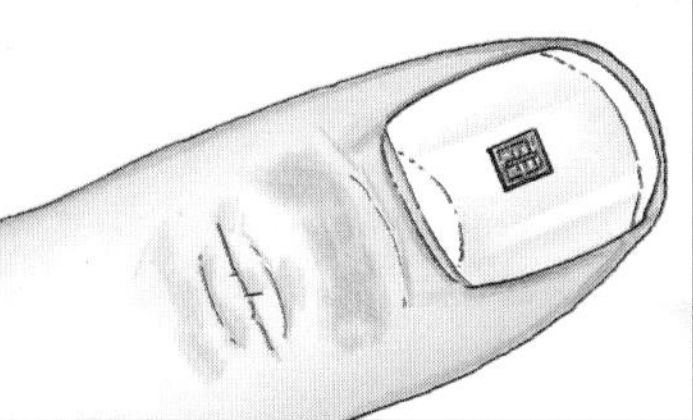

DID YOU KNOW?

John Baird is said to have invented TV in England in 1924, but Ferdinand Braun, a German scientist, had the idea for a television tube in 1897.

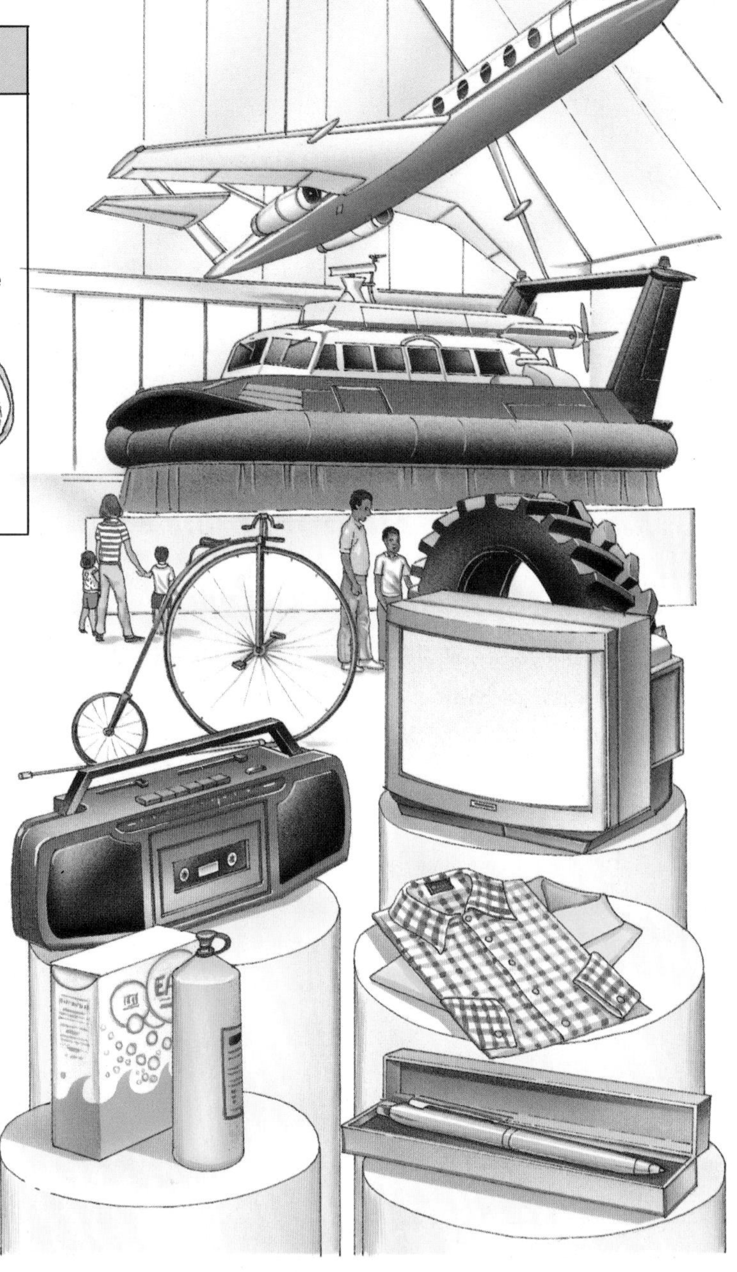

▶ Many inventions of the modern world were developed by individuals working at home. The jet engine was first designed by an engineer in his spare time. The hovercraft was designed by a boat builder as a hobby. The bicycle was invented by a Scottish blacksmith in 1839. The pneumatic tire was invented by a vet named J.B. Dunlop, and two Hungarians, Ladislao and Georg Biro, a writer and a chemist, invented the ballpoint pen in 1938.

INVENTIONS TIMETABLE

1 million years ago – stone tools (Hungary)
40,000 B.C. – bows and arrows (Africa)
10,000 B.C. – clay pots (Egypt)
8000 B.C. – copper knives (Iran)
3500 B.C. – plow (Syria)
3000 B.C. – wheel (Iraq)
2500 B.C. – paper, from papyrus reed (Egypt)
2000 B.C. – kite (China)
1500 B.C. – sundial (Persia)
1000 B.C. – iron weapons (Europe)
A.D. 100 – paper, from pulp (China)
1100 – compass (China)
1440 – printing press (Germany)
1530 – telescope (Italy)
1765 – steam engine (Great Britain)
1822 – camera (France)
1835 – computer (Great Britain)
1903 – airplane (United States)
1905 – Bakelite (United States)
1920 – helicopter (Spain)
1934 – jet engine (Great Britain, Germany)
1948 – photo-typesetting (France)
1958 – silicon chip (United States)
1960 – laser (United States)
1981 – space shuttle (United States)

▶ Iron is extracted from naturally occurring iron ore in a blast furnace. The ore is burned with limestone and coke. They react with the ore to produce iron, which collects as a liquid at the bottom of the furnace. Most of the iron is used to make steel. Steel is iron which contains carbon to make it harder.

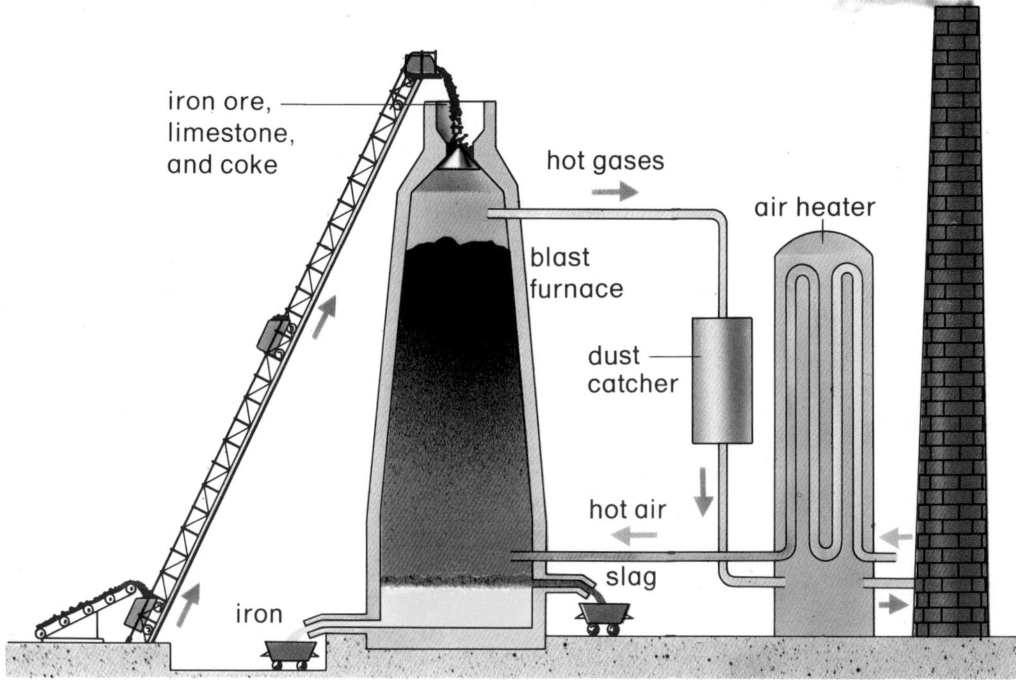

iron

Iron is the most widely used METAL in the world. Wrought iron is hammered out flat and is used for decorative work. Cast iron is poured into a mold to cool. It is so brittle that it will shatter if you drop it. Iron is also used to make STEEL. Steel is much harder than iron. It is used to build bridges and ships and to make cars. Iron and steel react with air and form RUST, so they are painted or coated with plastic or zinc to protect them. See **galvanizing**.

irrigation

Irrigation is the piping or raising of WATER to areas without enough water to grow crops. Farmers have irrigated fields in dry parts of the world for thousands of years.

isobar

Isobars are lines on a WEATHER map that run through areas of equal AIR PRESSURE. Like the contours on a MAP (which show height), isobars show how air pressure changes from one area to another.

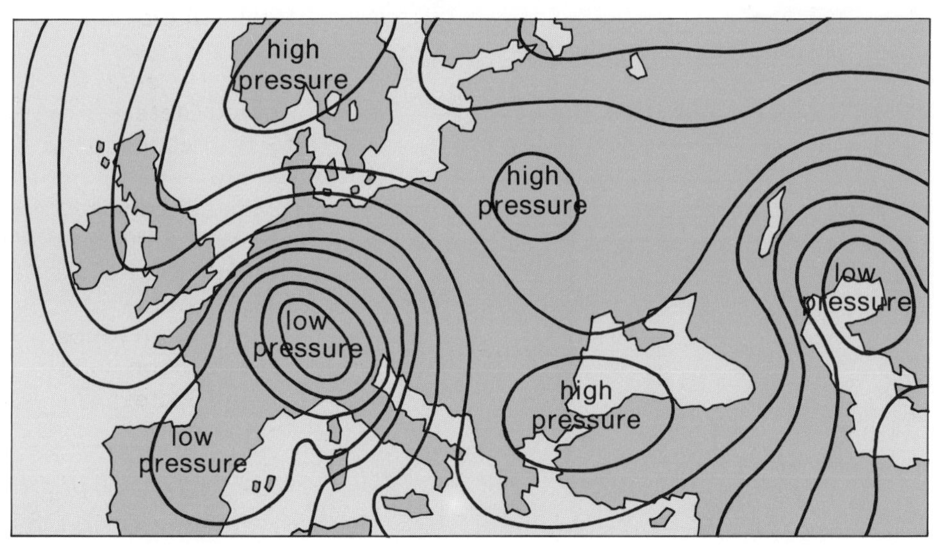

◀ The curved lines on this weather map are isobars. They link areas with the same air pressure. The pattern of high and low pressure areas enables scientists to predict the weather in the following day or two. An area of low pressure, such as the one seen here over Europe, brings rainy weather.

▲ The isotherms on this map of North America show how the sea helps to keep the land warmer in winter, when cold Arctic air moves south.

isotherm
Isotherms are lines on a CLIMATE map that join places with the same TEMPERATURE. They are important in weather forecasting.

isotope
An ELEMENT has a fixed number of PROTONS in its NUCLEUS. But the number of NEUTRONS may vary. An ATOM with a different number of neutrons from the most common atom is an isotope. Isotopes gradually break down into different ELEMENTS. See **half-life**.

▼ Hydrogen has three isotopes: hydrogen itself has one proton; deuterium has a proton and a neutron; tritium has a proton and two neutrons.

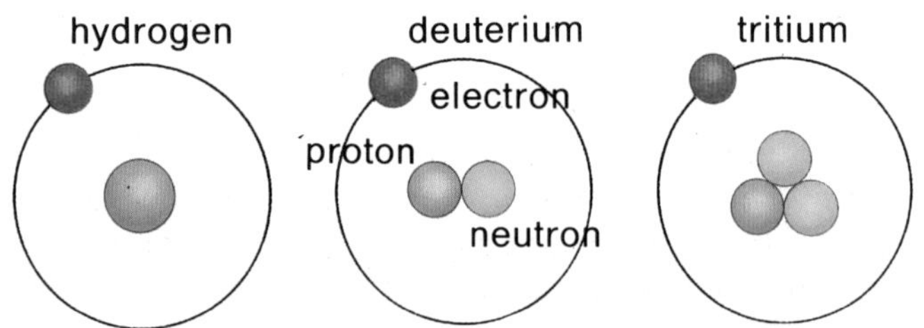

jet see turbine

jet stream
The jet stream is a region of strong WIND about 9 mi (15 km) up in the ATMOSPHERE. The wind may have a speed of about 185 mph (300 km/h) in a band up to 300 mi (500 km) wide. Aircraft can fly faster with the jet stream.

LIFE STORY

Joule
The joule is named after British physicist James Prescott Joule (1818–1889. The joule is a unit of ENERGY. Energy used to be measured in calories. One calorie equals 4.2 joules. Joule studied HEAT and ELECTRICITY. Through his experiments he showed that when heat is produced, another form of ENERGY is always lost. He therefore proved that heat itself is a form of energy.

Jupiter
Jupiter is the fifth PLANET. Its MASS is 318 times that of Earth. Clouds of frozen chemicals whirl around the surface. Jupiter's Great Red Spot is the center of a CYCLONE that is bigger than the Earth.

kerosene

Kerosene is a liquid FUEL used in many types of INTERNAL-COMBUSTION ENGINES. It is also called paraffin.

kilowatt

A kilowatt is an amount of POWER, equal to a thousand WATTS. A kilowatt converts 1,000 JOULES of ELECTRICITY into HEAT every second.

kaleidoscope

This simple device was invented in 1816 by Sir David Brewster, a British scientist. A kaleidoscope is a long tube with mirrors set at 60-degree angles. Little pieces of colored glass or plastic at one end of the kaleidoscope seem to form a continuous star-shaped design because of their REFLECTION. As the tube is turned, the pattern changes endlessly. The pattern may be nothing special. It is the reflections that look amazing.

DID YOU KNOW?

The most powerful nuclear power station in the world is at Fukushima, Japan. Its ten reactors produce 9,000 kilowatts (nine megawatts) of power. The largest single reactor is at Ignalina in Lithuania. It produces 1,500 megawatts (MW). The most powerful power station of all is hydro-electric, built at Grand Coulee, Washington, in 1942. Its output is more than 10,000 MW — enough for a city of 16 million people!

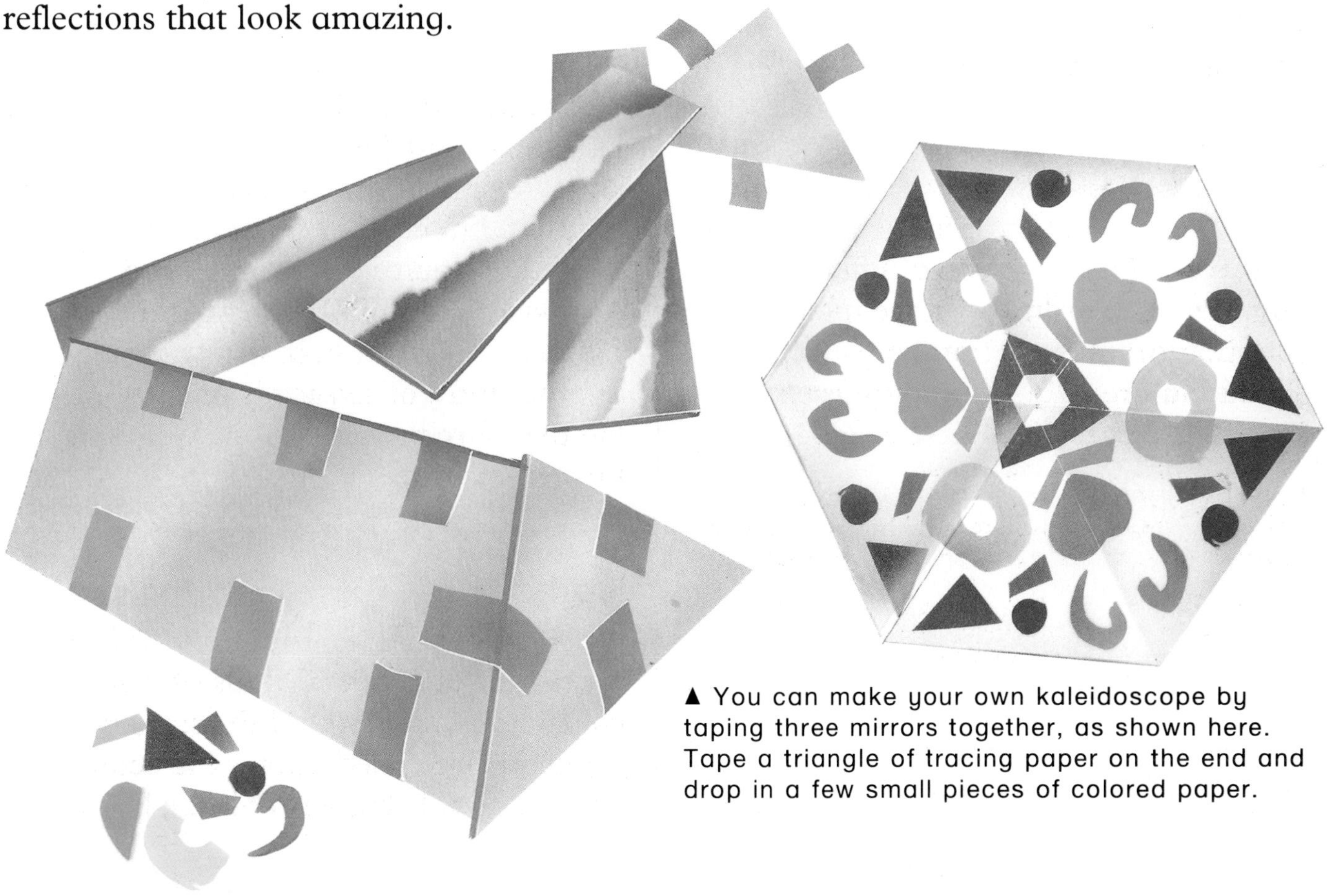

▲ You can make your own kaleidoscope by taping three mirrors together, as shown here. Tape a triangle of tracing paper on the end and drop in a few small pieces of colored paper.

L

laser see **page 73**

latent heat

Latent means hidden. Latent HEAT is the ENERGY a substance uses up (or gives out) when it goes through a CHANGE OF STATE. When a solid is heated to its MELTING point, it needs to take in extra HEAT ENERGY to change to a liquid, but its TEMPERATURE stays the same. When the liquid freezes back to a solid, this latent heat is given out again. Latent heat is also taken in when a liquid changes to a gas and is given out when a gas condenses to a liquid. This is why steam will scald you, and also explains why sweating keeps you cool. Heat from your body is taken in as latent heat by the drops of sweat and they EVAPORATE.

latitude and longitude

How do you know where you are on the EARTH'S surface? On land you read a MAP or a nearby road sign. But when you are in the middle of the ocean, you have no fixed landmarks. The Earth has only two permanent landmarks, the North and South poles. Lines of longitude are imaginary lines that run from the North Pole to the South Pole. The place everyone measures from is the Greenwich Meridian. This is the line of 0 longitude, which passes through London, England. Lines of latitude run around the Earth at right angles to longitude. Latitude is measured as degrees north or south of the equator.

▼ Any place can be identified by its latitude and longitude. New York is at 40°N 74°W, where a line 40 degrees north of the equator crosses another 74 degrees west of Greenwich.

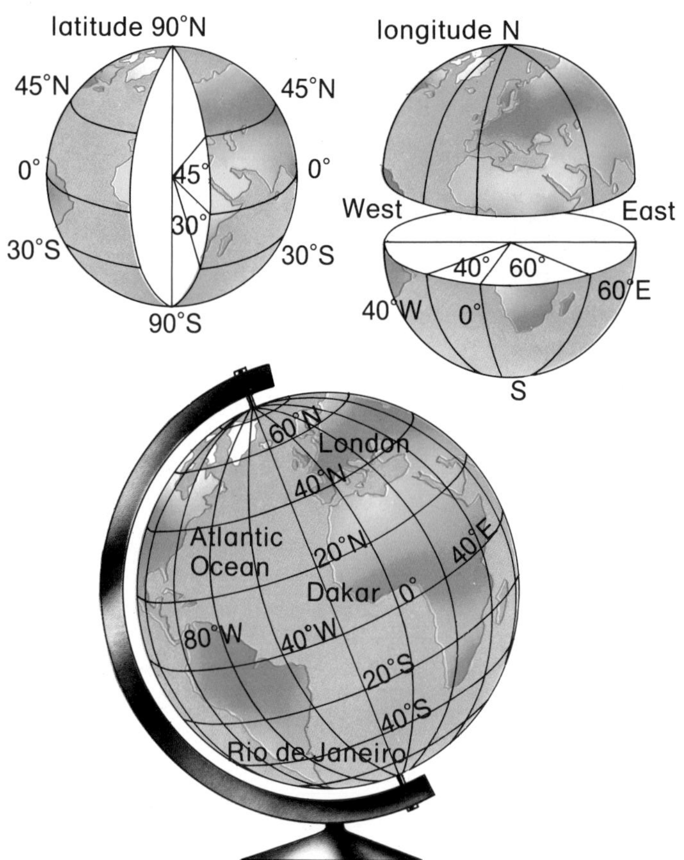

lava

Lava is hot melted ROCK from inside the EARTH that is released when a VOLCANO erupts. It is able to flow when red-hot, but it slowly hardens back to rock as it cools. Some lava is full of gas bubbles and can actually float! Pumice stone is a kind of lava you can buy at a drugstore. The longest lava flow ever recorded measured more than 37 mi (60 km), in Iceland during 1783.

LASER

Laser stands for Lightwave Amplification by Stimulated Emission of Radiation. Lasers are similar to masers, which amplify MICROWAVES rather than LIGHT. Lasers produce a beam of radiation by pumping energy into ATOMS, sometimes the atoms in a ruby CRYSTAL. As the atoms return to their normal state, the ENERGY is released as an intense beam of pure light.

▼ Laser light is a powerful form of energy. Eye surgeons often use lasers to create a tiny weld inside the eye. The weld helps the delicate eye tissues hold together while they heal.

▼ The beam of light from a laser does not spread out, like light from a common lamp. It travels in a perfectly straight line and can be used as a precise measuring tool. Builders use a laser beam to check if a long tunnel is straight. Tunnels can be bored with amazing accuracy, using a laser to help check the progress.

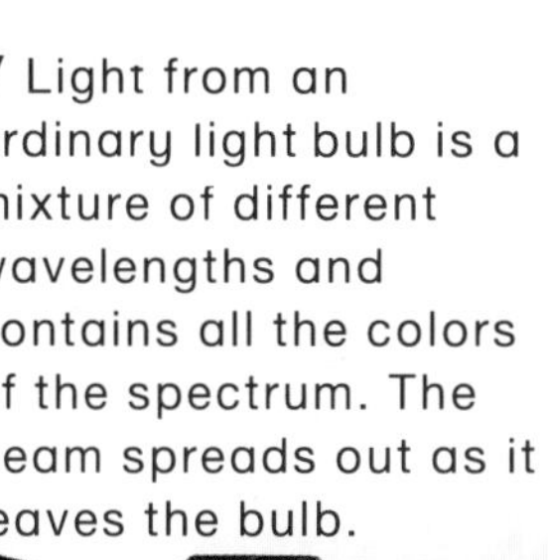

▼ Light from an ordinary light bulb is a mixture of different wavelengths and contains all the colors of the spectrum. The beam spreads out as it leaves the bulb.

ordinary light

laser light

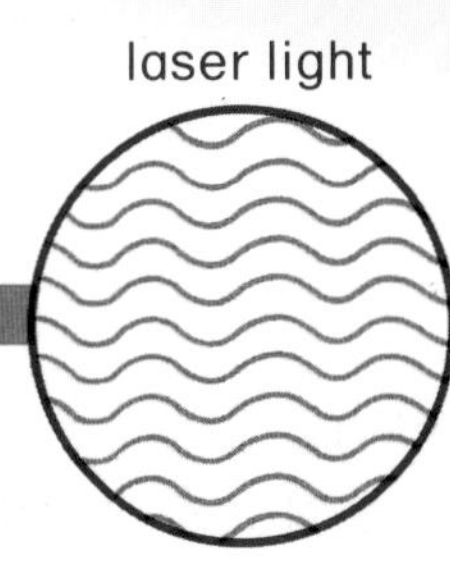

▲ Unlike ordinary light, laser light is coherent, which means it is all the same wavelength and is in perfect "step." Ruby lasers produce flashes, or pulses, of light. Gas lasers produce a continuous beam of laser light from a tube filled with gas.

▶ Lasers can be used in industry. As the laser beam hits a metal surface, the high temperatures produced allow technicians to cut solid steel. Since there is no actual "blade," it is easier to control the shape of the cut.

L

lead

Lead is a soft, heavy METAL that melts easily. Its chemical symbol is Pb, from the Latin *plumbum* — plumbers were named for the lead pipes they used. Lead prevents rust, shields things from harmful rays, and is easy to work with. It has many uses. But it can collect in body tissues and cause poisoning, so it is no longer used in water pipes or other common products.

lens

Lenses focus rays. If a lens brings the rays closer together it is positive (convex). A negative (concave) lens spreads rays out. Most lenses are made of GLASS. A positive or convex lens is thicker in the middle, and a negative or concave lens is thicker at the edge. You can use a lens to focus an image of a window on the opposite wall or on a piece of paper. Magnetic lenses can focus beams of ELECTRONS. They are used in ELECTRON MICROSCOPES and TV sets.

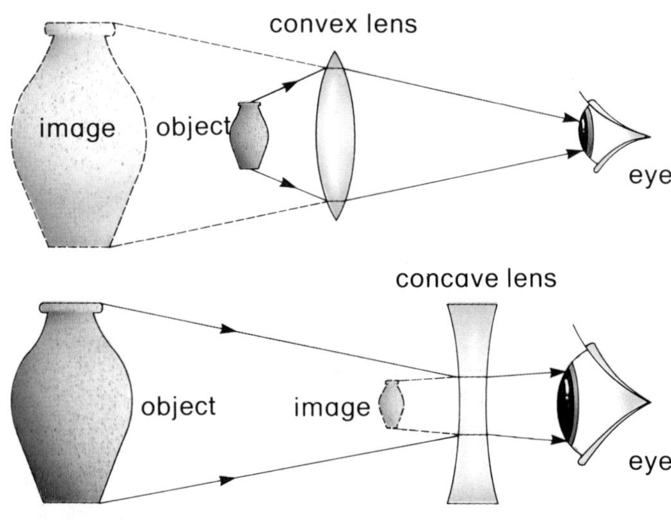

▲ A concave lens bends light rays inward, producing a small image near your eye. A convex lens bends light rays outward, so it produces a large image that appears farther away.

lever

Levers allow you to lift heavy weights more easily. Imagine a strong bar with a load on one end and someone standing at the other. This is a basic lever. Between the two is the place where the lever turns, called the fulcrum. If the fulcrum is near the load, not much downward PRESSURE, or effort, is needed to lift it. If the fulcrum is farther away, it takes more effort to lift the weight, but it can be lifted higher.

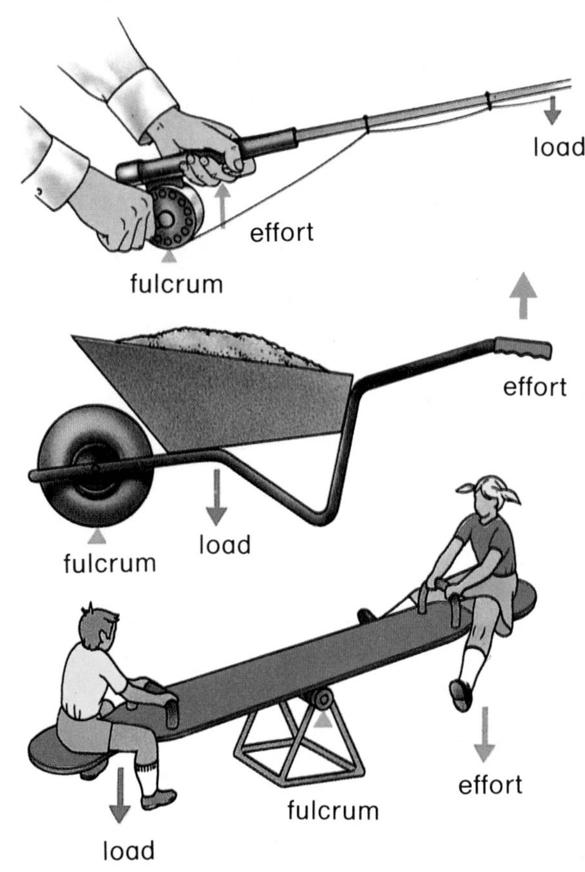

▲ There are three classes of levers. They differ in the positions of the effort, fulcrum, and load. The seesaw is a first-class lever, a wheelbarrow is second class, and a fishing rod is third class.

light

Light is the narrow band of ELECTROMAGNETIC RADIATION that we can see. We see objects when light is reflected from them. See **color**.

LIGHTING

The earliest lamps were OIL lamps. As the oil burned, the FLAME gave out light. Modern lights are powered by ELECTRICITY. Lights are not just used to help people see around them. Some are used to make light shows in discos and theaters. Many kinds of lights are used to make brightly colored advertising signs. Most lights work by heating a metal filament inside the bulb until it glows brightly. Filament lights get hot. Fluorescent lights give out cold light and use less power.

The first electric lamp was made in 1860 by Joseph Swan. He and Thomas Edison later made a lamp with a carbon filament called an "ediswan" lamp!

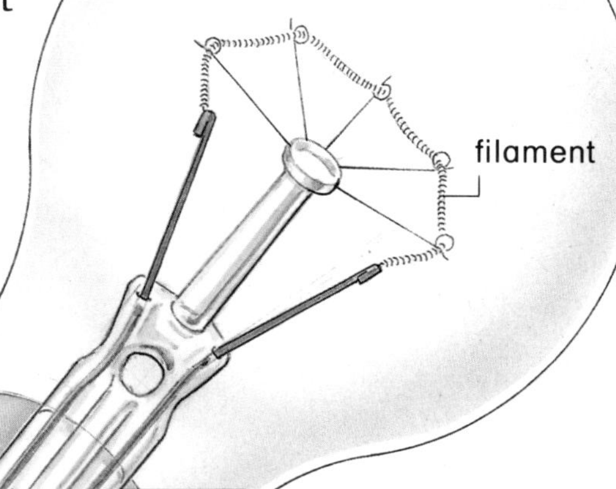

▶ Standard electric light bulbs have a coiled filament made of tungsten. The filament becomes white-hot in a fraction of a second when the light is turned on. The bulb is filled with an unreactive gas like argon to keep the filament from burning away.

◀ At the center of the light bulb is a glass column. Air is sucked out and replaced with argon.

◀ Fluorescent lights are usually made as long straight tubes for use in factories or offices, but smaller bulbs are now available. They can be used in a standard light socket at home. They take a few moments to reach full brightness, but they last far longer and use much less energy than ordinary filament light bulbs.

DID YOU KNOW?

Fluorescent lights have no filament. They contain a gas that glows when electricity passes through it. The gas may give off colored light. Neon glows red.

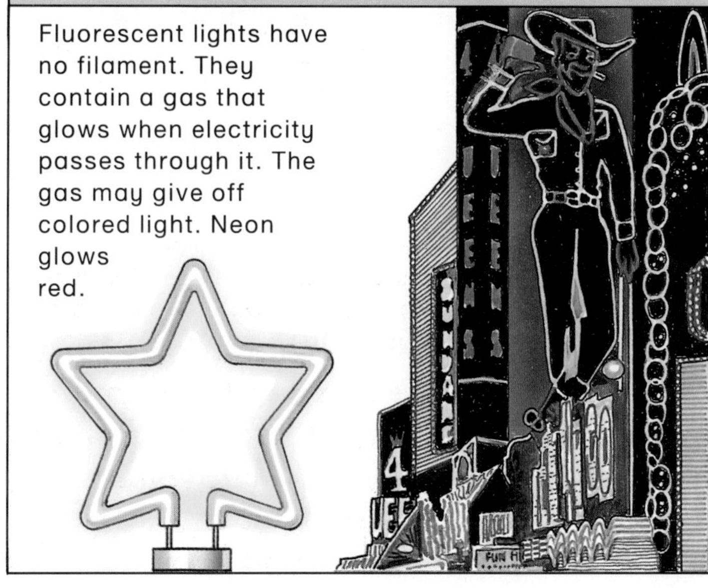

LIGHTNING

When objects move close to each other they can sometimes transfer ELECTRONS. The result is a build-up of static ELECTRICITY. The most dramatic example is lightning. Massive air currents are caused as hot air rises, often in summer. Droplets of water rise and fall in the rushing currents of air, producing huge charges of static electricity in the clouds. Eventually a massive spark flashes down to Earth or across to another cloud. The roar of thunder is heard several miles away.

DID YOU KNOW?

You can produce miniature lightning at home. Brushing long hair can cause a build-up of static. The crackling sounds are the same as thunder. In a dark room, you can even see the tiny blue sparks of electricity when you take off a synthetic-fiber sweater. But don't worry, the sparks are harmless.

▼ Lightning flashes can be 20 mi (30 km) from end to end. The central spark measures less than an inch but the whole glowing flash may be 16 ft (5 m) across.

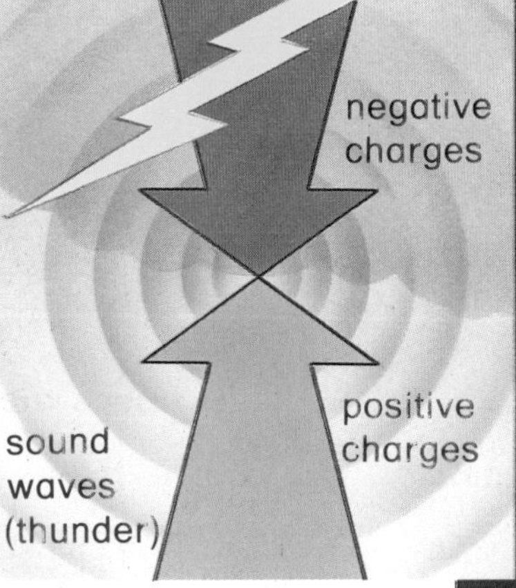

▲ Lightning produces about 100 million volts of electricity and heats the air to over 50,000°F. The rapid expansion of the heated air causes thunder.

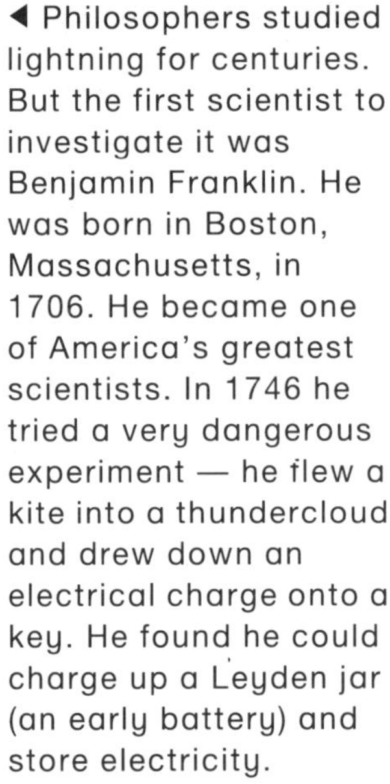

◀ Philosophers studied lightning for centuries. But the first scientist to investigate it was Benjamin Franklin. He was born in Boston, Massachusetts, in 1706. He became one of America's greatest scientists. In 1746 he tried a very dangerous experiment — he flew a kite into a thundercloud and drew down an electrical charge onto a key. He found he could charge up a Leyden jar (an early battery) and store electricity.

light-year

A light-year is not a time but a distance. It is the distance that LIGHT travels in one year, about 5.9 trillion miles.

liquid crystal see **page 78**

litmus

Litmus is an INDICATOR obtained from the juice of the lichen plant *Lecanora*. ACIDS turn litmus red and alkalis turn it blue.

logic

In philosophy, logic is a system for analyzing arguments. Logic is also a way of handling data by COMPUTERS, such as comparing the size of two numbers.

▼ A computer breaks down logic operations into a series of simple yes/no questions. This flow chart shows how the decisions a bus driver makes can be broken down in the same way.

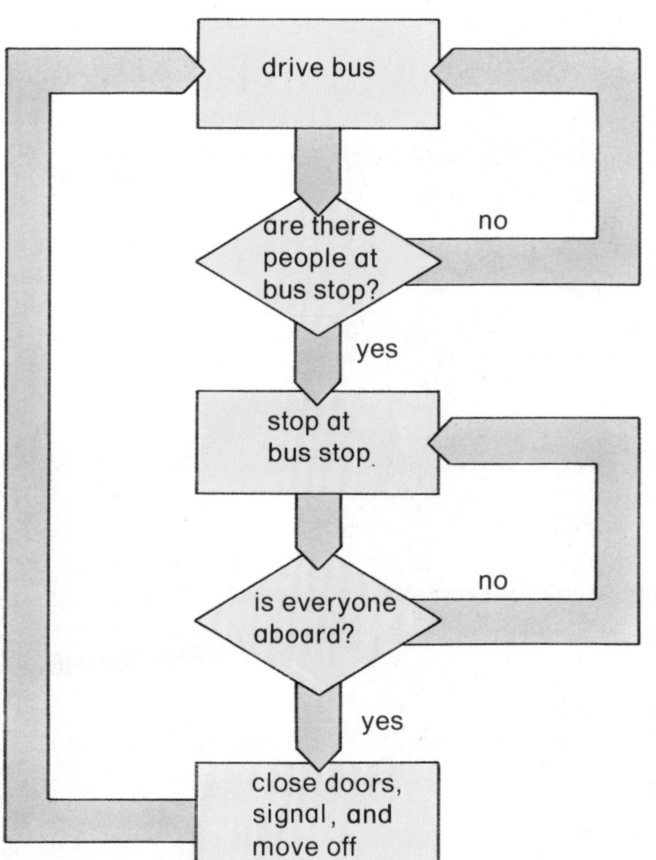

loudspeaker

A loudspeaker changes an electric CURRENT into SOUND. Inside a loudspeaker is a cone. It was traditionally made from paper, but it is now often made of plastic instead. In the middle of the cone is a wire coil around a magnet. This magnet vibrates when an electric current passes through the wire. The current increases and decreases according to the signal received from the radio, TELEVISION, or hi-fi system. As a result, the cone creates a copy of the original sound, sending out vibrations which our ears hear as sound.

DID YOU KNOW?

Some hi-fis have several speakers, to reproduce sounds of different frequencies. The result is a higher quality of sound than a single speaker could produce. The *tweeter* produces high-pitched sounds, and the *squawker* produces sounds in the middle of the range. Low-pitched sounds are produced by the *woofer*.

lubricant

When two materials rub together they produce FRICTION. Oiling the surfaces can help them slide smoothly, because OIL is a lubricant. Graphite (a form of CARBON) and talc are solid lubricants.

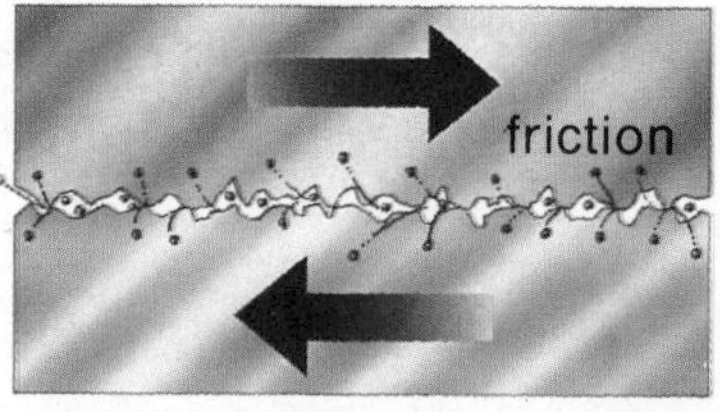

◀ When surfaces rub together, microscopic roughnesses catch on each other and produce friction.

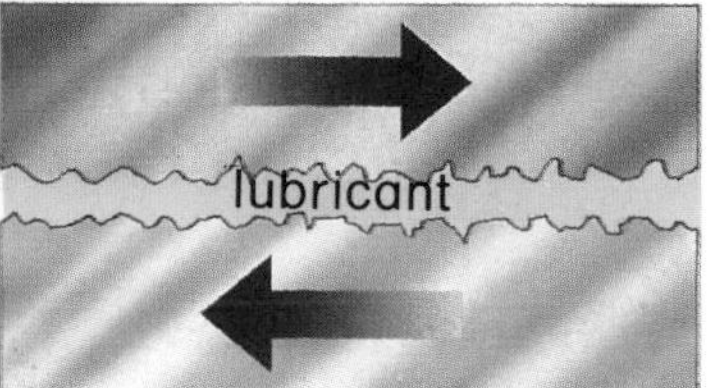

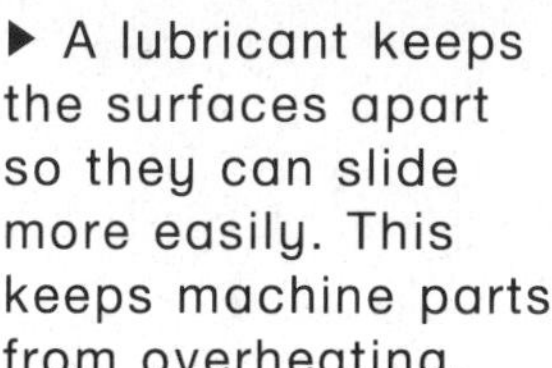

▶ A lubricant keeps the surfaces apart so they can slide more easily. This keeps machine parts from overheating.

LIQUID CRYSTAL

Liquid crystals have MOLECULES that line up with each other. The result is not a solid, but something with a consistency rather like molasses. Because of the lines of molecules, light that passes through a liquid crystal may be POLARIZED. But the effect changes depending on the TEMPERATURE of the liquid crystal and whether it carries an electric charge.

vertically polarized light

crystals arranged horizontally

polarizer

POLARIZED LIGHT

Light rays normally vibrate in all directions. But polarized light vibrates in only one plane. If a light beam hits a liquid crystal where the molecules are arranged vertically, only the light that vibrates vertically can pass through. A liquid crystal with molecules arranged horizontally will then stop the rest of the light. The crystal looks dark. This effect appears and disappears as an electric charge is switched on and off.

▶ If you look very closely at a calculator, you may be able to catch sight of the microcircuit which carries charges of electricity to the display panel. When a liquid crystal panel is switched on, it becomes dark so you can see it. The seven bars on a digital display are enough to make up the ten numbers from zero to nine.

front electrode

liquid crystal layer

polarizer

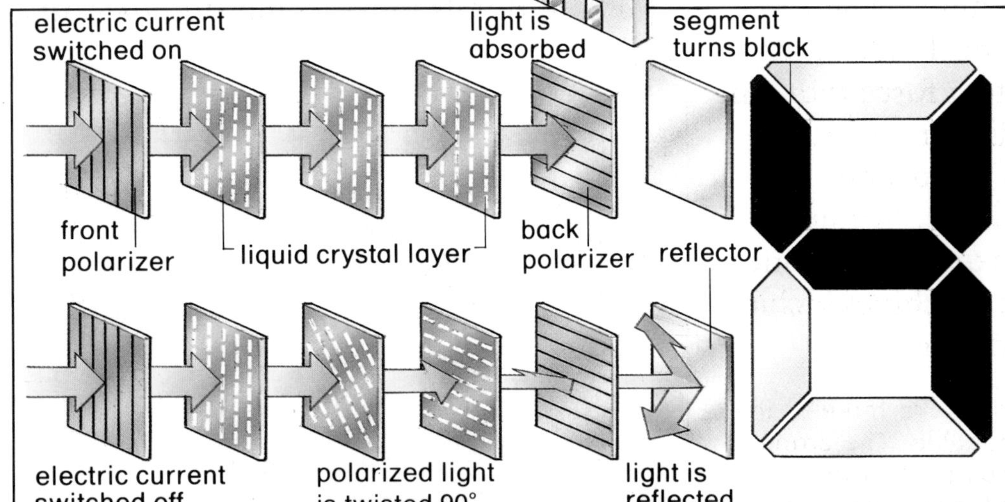

LIQUID CRYSTAL DISPLAY

A liquid crystal display has two polarizing filters, with liquid crystals in between. When the current is off, the crystals turn the light 90 degrees. The light can then pass through the second filter to a reflector and bounce back. When the current is applied, the crystals line up and the light cannot escape. This turns the segment black.

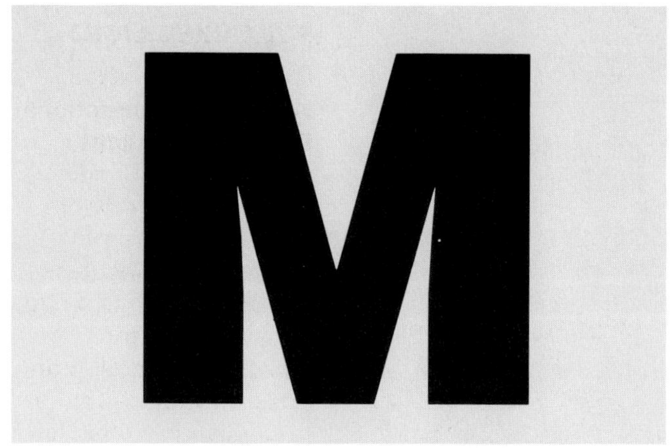

Mach

The Mach number compares the speed of a moving object (like an AIRCRAFT) in any medium (such as AIR) with the speed of SOUND in that medium. The speed of sound is Mach 1. Sound travels at different speeds in air, depending on height and temperature. Mach 1 is about 750 mph (1,200 km/h) on a cold day at sea level and 660 mph (1,060 km/h) at the height of airliner flight. Subsonic travel is below the speed of sound (less than Mach 1). Travel at Mach 1 or above is supersonic.

machine

Machines are devices that change ENERGY from one form into a more useful form. Scissors are simple machines. They change the energy of your food, which powers your fingers, into a force that can cut paper, which your fingers alone cannot do efficiently. The earliest machine was an ax. Cranes, farming equipment, and staplers are all machines. Commonly used simple machines include a car jack and a screwdriver.

▶ A crane, ax, and screwdriver are three of the six basic types of simple machine. The crane uses a pulley, the ax is a wedge, and the screwdriver is an example of a screw machine.

magnesium

Magnesium is a very light silvery METAL. It burns in air with a brilliant white light (it gives off a lot of ULTRAVIOLET too). Magnesium powder is used in FIREWORKS. ALLOYS of magnesium are used to make light parts for AIRCRAFT and high-performance cars.

magnet see **page 80**

magnification

Magnification is the measure of how much bigger an object is made to look by a LENS or a curved MIRROR.

map see **page 82**

Mars

Mars is the planet nearest the EARTH. It is half as wide as the Earth and has only one tenth of Earth's MASS.

mass

Mass is the amount of MATTER in an object. A kilogram of LEAD has a mass of one kilogram. On the MOON it would weigh only one sixth as much because the Moon's GRAVITY is only one sixth as strong as EARTH's. But its mass would stay the same.

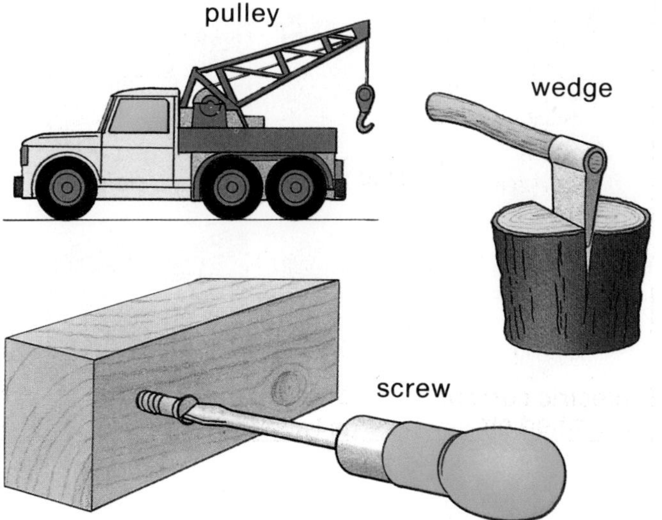

MAGNETISM

In ancient times, people found rough sticks of iron ORE that would attract other IRON objects. When hung on a thread, these natural magnets (called lodestones) would point north/south, and were used to navigate. Iron is the only element that can be magnetized. All the ATOMS in the bar can be lined up so that they point the same way.

DID YOU KNOW?

The center of the Earth is a huge, weak magnet. A compass needle is a magnet, too. The compass needle lines up with the Earth's magnetic field. It points north.

The north magnetic pole is not exactly at the real North Pole. It moves a few miles each year. At the present time it is between Canada and Greenland.

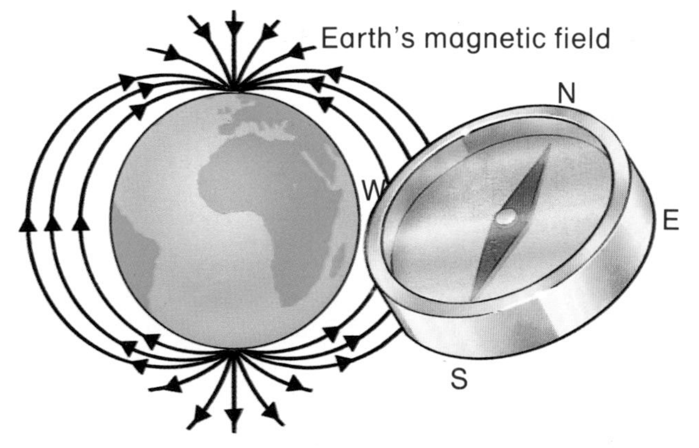

▼ Both the north and south poles of a horseshoe magnet can be used to pick up an object. The invisible lines of magnetic force stretch out between the two poles.

N

magnetic field of a horseshoe magnet

S

▲ Magnets are used as door catches. The steel magnet is fixed to the frame and attracts a small iron bar on the edge of the door.

◀ A coil of wire around a large iron core can carry a current of electricity. When this is switched on, the iron becomes a strong electromagnet. The magnetism vanishes when the current is turned off. Electromagnets can pick up lumps of iron and steel.

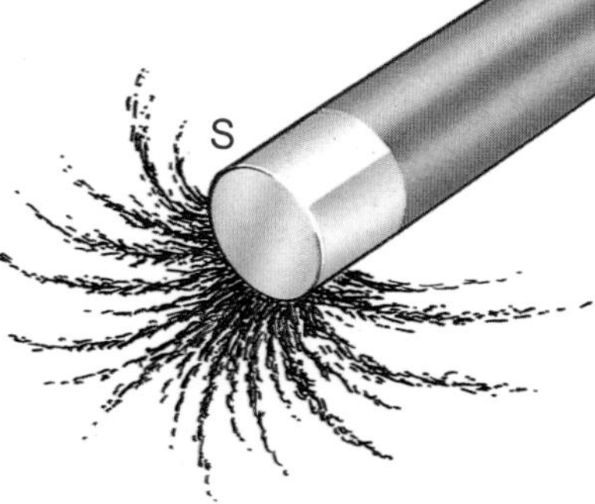

▲ If you lay a piece of paper on top of a bar magnet and scatter iron filings over it, you can see the directions of the lines of force.

mathematics

Mathematics is the science of NUMBERS. Addition means putting numbers together: $4 + 5 = 9$. Subtraction is done by taking one number from another: $9 - 5 = 4$. In multiplication, an amount is repeated a certain number of times to give the total: $3 \times 3 = 9$. And division takes place when you split up a number into equal parts: $18 \div 2 = 9$. Algebra is a form of mathematics in which you use letters as symbols for unknown quantities, and GEOMETRY is the study of shapes. Trigonometry is used to work out angles and the measurement of triangles. It is important in surveying and navigation. Probability deals with chance. Suppose you have tossed a coin ten times and it has come down heads each time. What is the probability that it will be heads next throw? Ten to one? No! The chances are still equal. Without mathematics, many other sciences could not have developed. Physicists, engineers, and computer scientists all use mathematics.

matter

Matter is the term used to describe any substance. Air is matter; so is a book. Matter is what the UNIVERSE is made of.

measurements

People have used measurements since ancient times. Many of the oldest units of measurement were based on parts of the body. A foot was taken from the length of a man's foot and did not have an exact number of inches. People still talk of the height of a horse in hands (one hand equals four inches). Metric measurements were first introduced by scientists in France in the 18th century. A METER was originally taken to be one ten-millionth of the distance from the North POLE to the Equator. See **SI units**.

melting

Melting is the CHANGE OF STATE from solid to liquid. The temperature at which this occurs is the melting point. See **ice and snow, water**.

▼ These devices are used to measure different quantities. Most countries use metric measurements, but some still use the system of gallons, feet, and pounds.

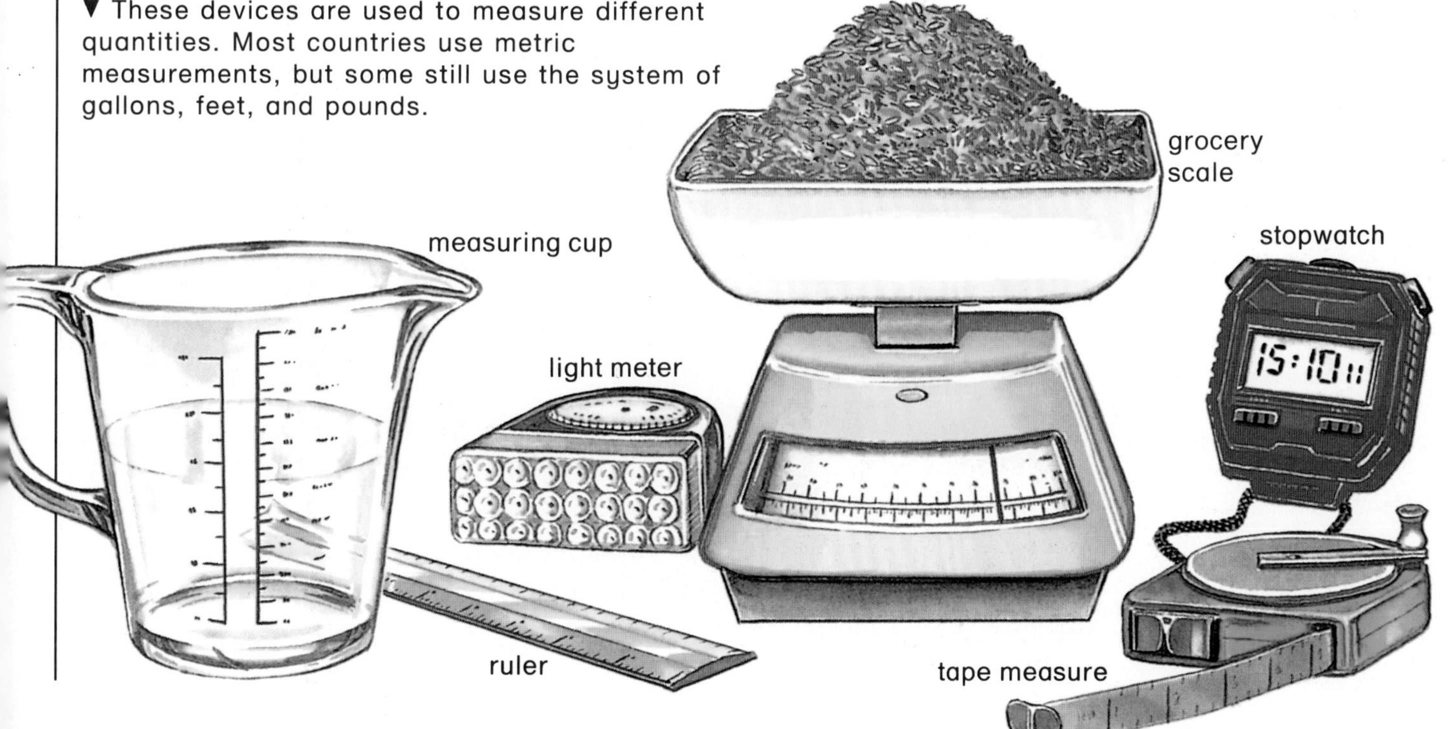

MAPS

A map is a scale drawing of an area that shows features of interest. Maps usually show parts of the world, but there are brain maps and star maps, too. Road maps show you how to find your way around. Other maps allow scientists to work out the best place to drill for OIL or GAS. Maps today include computer photos produced from SATELLITE data.

◀ This is how Europeans saw the world 2,500 years ago. In the middle was the Mediterranean Sea. Two thousand years later, maps began to show the Western Hemisphere. This map was published in 1545.

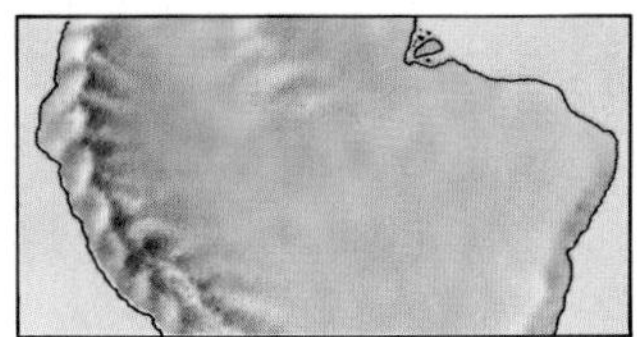

relief map

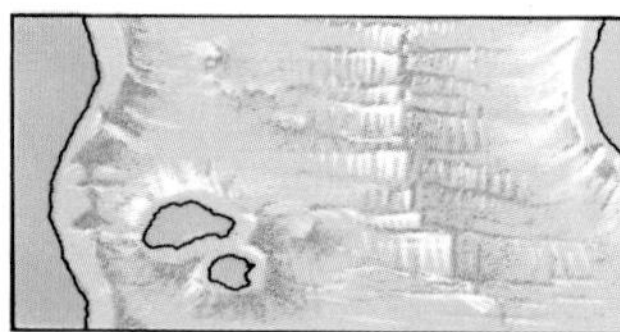

sea map

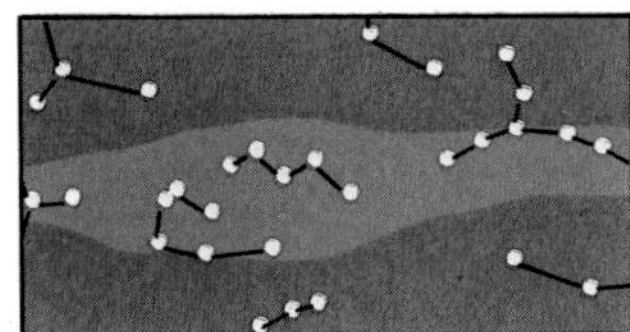

star map

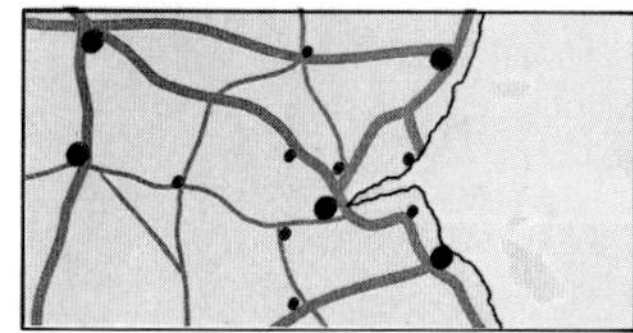

road map

◀ Relief maps show the surface of the land. Maps of the seafloor are important for plotting a ship's course or searching for minerals. Star maps help navigators and are valuable when a new star appears in the sky. The commonest maps are road maps.

▶ Try making a map of your own area. You can draw the roads and mark down the school and the names of people you know. Trees and side roads are important, too. In a few years, much will be altered. Your map will be a record of how things used to be.

MAP PROJECTIONS

Maps of the world are always inaccurate! If you imagine the globe inside a grid, you can see how it becomes altered as the grid is opened out. These are the two most commonly used map projections.

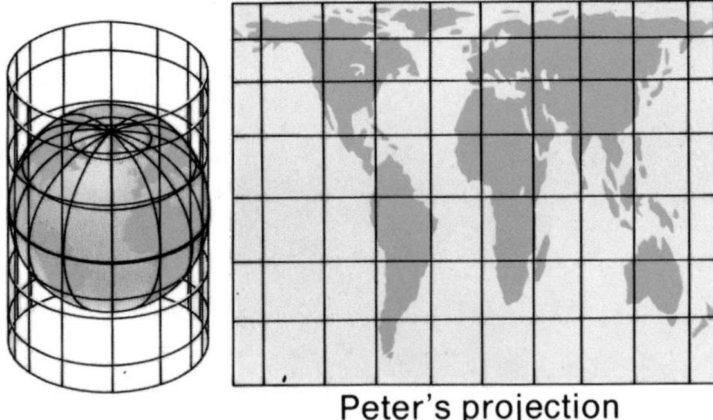

Peter's projection

Mercator projection

M

meniscus

In a liquid, the pull between the molecules causes SURFACE TENSION. It is almost as though the liquid had a skin. If you fill a narrow tube with WATER, the water curves up at the sides of the tube. This is the meniscus.

▶ The shape of a liquid's meniscus depends on the strength of the liquid's surface tension. Water curves upward where it meets the wall of a container. Mercury, which has a much stronger surface tension than water, has a downward curving meniscus.

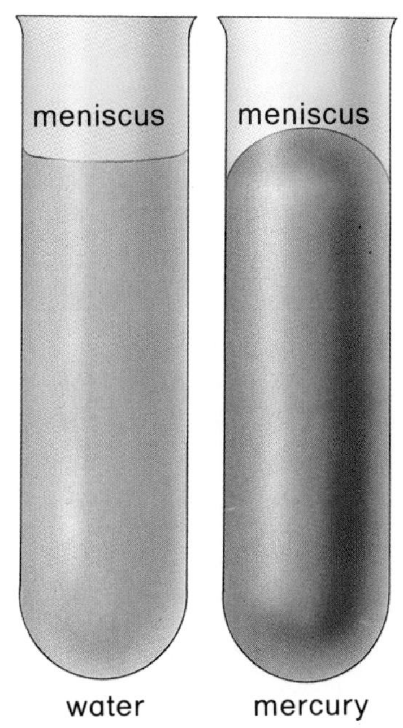

mercury

Mercury is the only METAL that is liquid at room temperatures. It is used in THERMOMETERS because it is easy to see.

Mercury

Mercury is the name of the PLANET nearest to the SUN in our SOLAR SYSTEM. It is not much larger than the MOON.

metals see **page 84**

meteor

Meteors are shooting stars. They appear as streaks of light across the night sky. They are small pieces of ROCK that hurtle through space until they hit the thick layer of AIR around the EARTH and burn up in a streak of light.

▲ Meteor showers occur when the Earth passes through a stream of dust left behind by a comet. The best showers occur around January 4, July 29, August 12, October 21, and December 14.

meteorite

Meteorites are METEORS that are big enough to reach the ground without completely burning away. Usually they are the size of a brick, but some are huge enough to make large craters.

▼ A meteorite about 300 ft (100 m) across and composed mostly of iron produced this crater in Arizona. It hit the Earth about 50,000 years ago.

M

METALS

Metals are shiny, hard ELEMENTS that can be melted. They conduct HEAT and ELECTRICITY. Metals have many important uses.

Aluminum is a soft, very light, bluish silver element. It melts at 1,220°F (660°C). Aluminum products include foil, drink cans, and TV antennas.

Electrical wiring is usually made with **copper**. It is also used to make coins and gives fireworks a blue-green color. Copper is often used in alloys.

Gold is a beautiful yellow metal. It is never affected by corrosion and resists acids. It is used in jewelry, in electronic circuits, and to protect spacecraft.

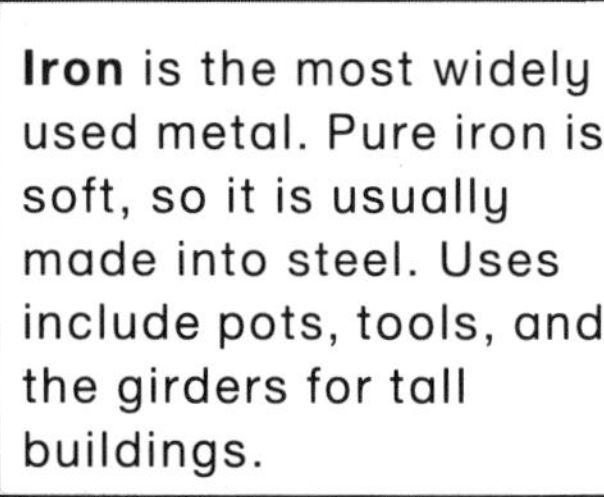

Iron is the most widely used metal. Pure iron is soft, so it is usually made into steel. Uses include pots, tools, and the girders for tall buildings.

Zinc is made into many alloys. It has long been used for the cases of batteries. Steel dipped in molten zinc is said to be galvanized. It resists rusting.

Lead is a soft, heavy metal which melts at 621°F (327°C). Solder is an alloy of lead. Lead is used in roofing and to make the plates in car batteries.

Sodium is so reactive it is hardly ever used in the pure state. It can carry the heat in a nuclear reactor, and it glows a brilliant yellow in sodium lamps.

Calcium is very reactive. It is important for life. Calcium is found in dairy products and also in vegetables such as spinach and rhubarb.

Titanium is very light, but not quite as light as aluminum. It does not melt until it reaches 3,300°F (1800°C) and is very hard. It is used in steel.

Tin cans are actually made of steel. They are covered with a layer of tin to keep them from rusting. Pewter is an alloy of tin, used for decorative objects.

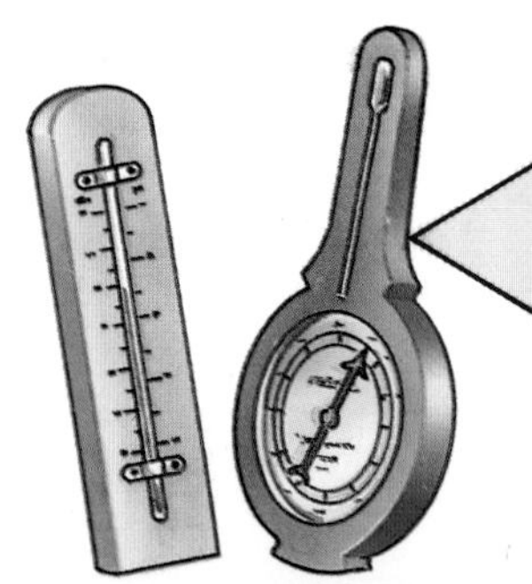

Mercury is the only liquid metal. It freezes solid at −38.2°F (−39°C). Mercury is heavier than lead. It is used in barometers and thermometers.

meteorology

Meteorology is the science of studying the weather. Around the POLES lie bands of cold air. Nearer the equator the air is hotter. Temperate countries lie between the polar and equatorial bands of air. Warm and cold air masses move across the land and sea. Where they meet they form areas of low pressure, called CYCLONES, and belts of rain, called fronts.

▼ The main factors that affect the weather are air pressure, air temperature, and the speed and direction of the wind. Meteorologists record these conditions to prepare a weather forecast.

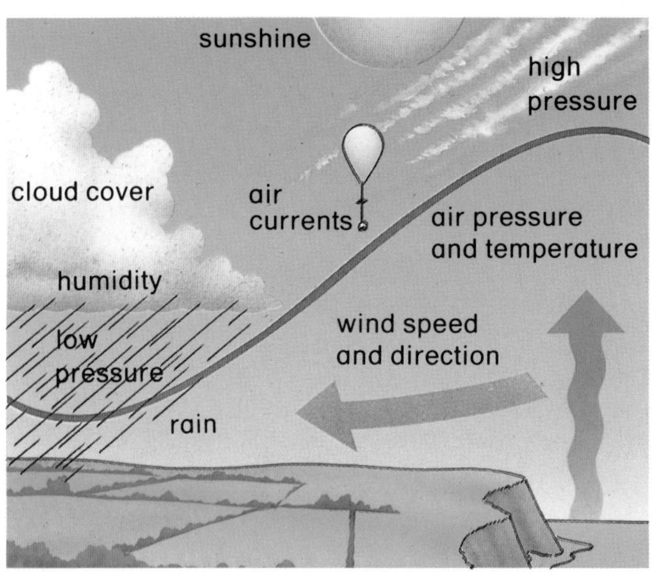

methane

Methane is a flammable gas containing hydrogen and carbon. Its formula is CH_4. Methane forms mostly from decaying organic MATTER underground and is found in natural gas. See **recycling**.

meter

The meter (1 m) was originally defined as 1/10,000,000 of the Earth's longitude from the North Pole to the Equator through Paris. It is now precise: the distance light travels in a vacuum in 1/299,792,458 of a second.

metric system

Metric MEASUREMENT is built on seven base units in a system of tens. The meter is the base unit for length, the kilogram for mass. Each unit is divided, or multiplied, into further units which are ten times smaller or larger. The prefix of each unit tells you how it relates to the base unit. For example, a *centi*meter means one hundredth of a meter. A *milli*meter is a thousandth of a meter. The metric system is the system of measuring used in science throughout the world.

microchip

A microchip is the complex system of TRANSISTORS, CIRCUITS, and other components on a single wafer of SILICON. This INTEGRATED CIRCUIT is then mounted in a plastic block. See **microprocessor**.

micrometer (1)

A micrometer is a screw gauge used by engineers for accurately measuring the diameter or thickness of small objects.

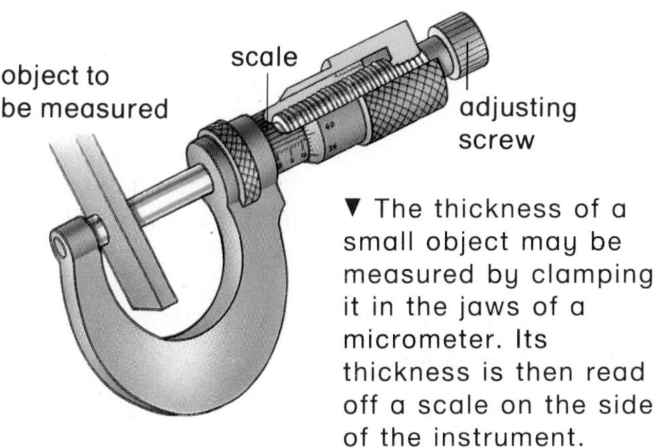

▼ The thickness of a small object may be measured by clamping it in the jaws of a micrometer. Its thickness is then read off a scale on the side of the instrument.

micrometer (2)

Microscopic objects are measured in micrometers, or millionths of a meter.

M

microphone
A microphone converts sound waves into ELECTRICAL signals. Inside a microphone is a diaphragm, a thin sheet of paper or plastic, which is vibrated by sounds. The diaphragm is connected to a MAGNET. When the diaphragm vibrates, the magnet's movements produce ELECTRICITY in a nearby coil. The pattern of electrical signals represents the original sounds. A LOUDSPEAKER can convert these electrical signals back to SOUND.

microprocessor
A microprocessor is an INTEGRATED CIRCUIT or MICROCHIP that processes data in a COMPUTER. The central processing units in early computers had TRANSISTORS and other components soldered together, and they were very large. Now they are made by projecting a reduced image of a template onto a tiny light-sensitive silicon chip. The entire central processing unit can fit onto a chip the size of your fingernail. The chip is held in a plastic mount.

microscope
How do you look at something very small? You bring it closer to your eye. The trouble is that if you bring the object too close your eye can no longer focus on it. A microscope allows you to study tiny objects that your eye cannot make out. The LENS is the important part of a microscope. It bends LIGHT shining through the object before it reaches your eye, so the object appears larger than it really is. The simple microscope has just one lens which MAGNIFIES specimens. But even a simple microscope allows you to see bacteria. Compound microscopes have several lenses, to make the picture even sharper. Simple microscopes can magnify up to 500 times, compound microscopes about 2,000 times. An ELECTRON MICROSCOPE uses a beam of electrons to magnify dry objects in a VACUUM. Electron microscopes can magnify hundreds of thousands of times. Scanning electron microscopes show surface features, and a tunneling microscope can reveal details of the position of ATOMS. Other microscopes use X-RAYS and ULTRAVIOLET rays.

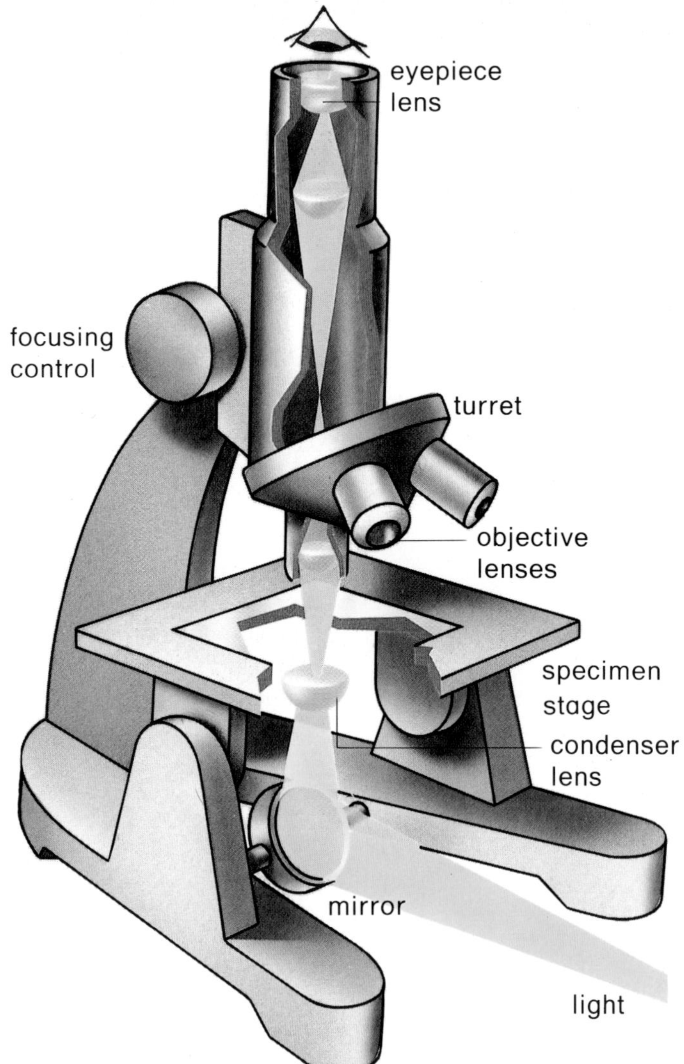

▲ A thin, transparent specimen placed on the specimen table of a light microscope is magnified by the objective lens and viewed through the eyepiece lens. A selection of objective lenses give different magnifications.

MICROWAVES

Microwaves are a form of RADIATION. Their wavelengths start at the shortest RADIO waves and continue to the INFRARED. Like radio waves, they can travel long distances. But, like infrared, they can produce HEAT. They are reflected by metal surfaces and cannot penetrate deeply through softer substances. But when they do penetrate, they release ENERGY as heat.

RADAR

Microwaves are used in radar. They are sent out by an antenna and are reflected by aircraft in the area. The reflections are displayed on a computer screen.

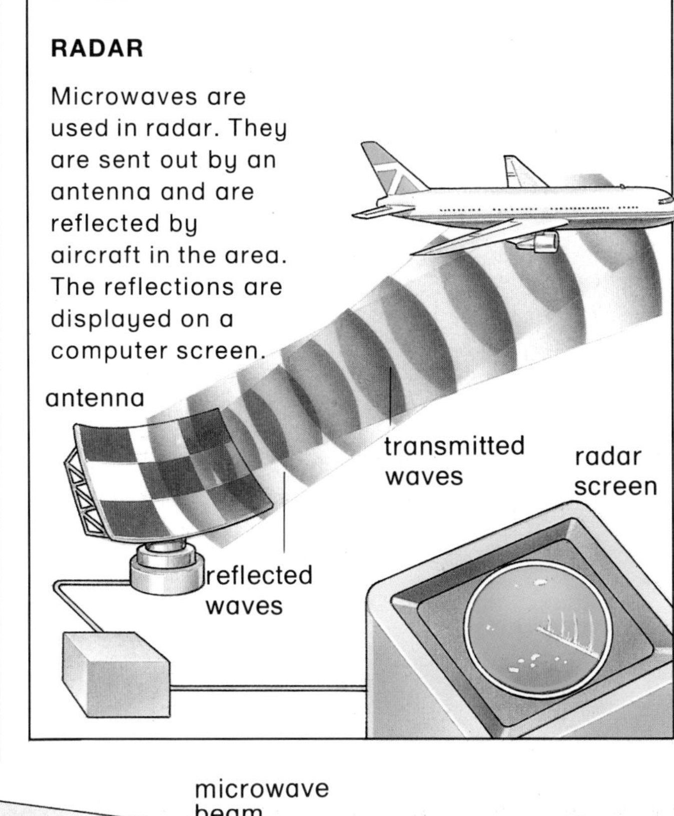

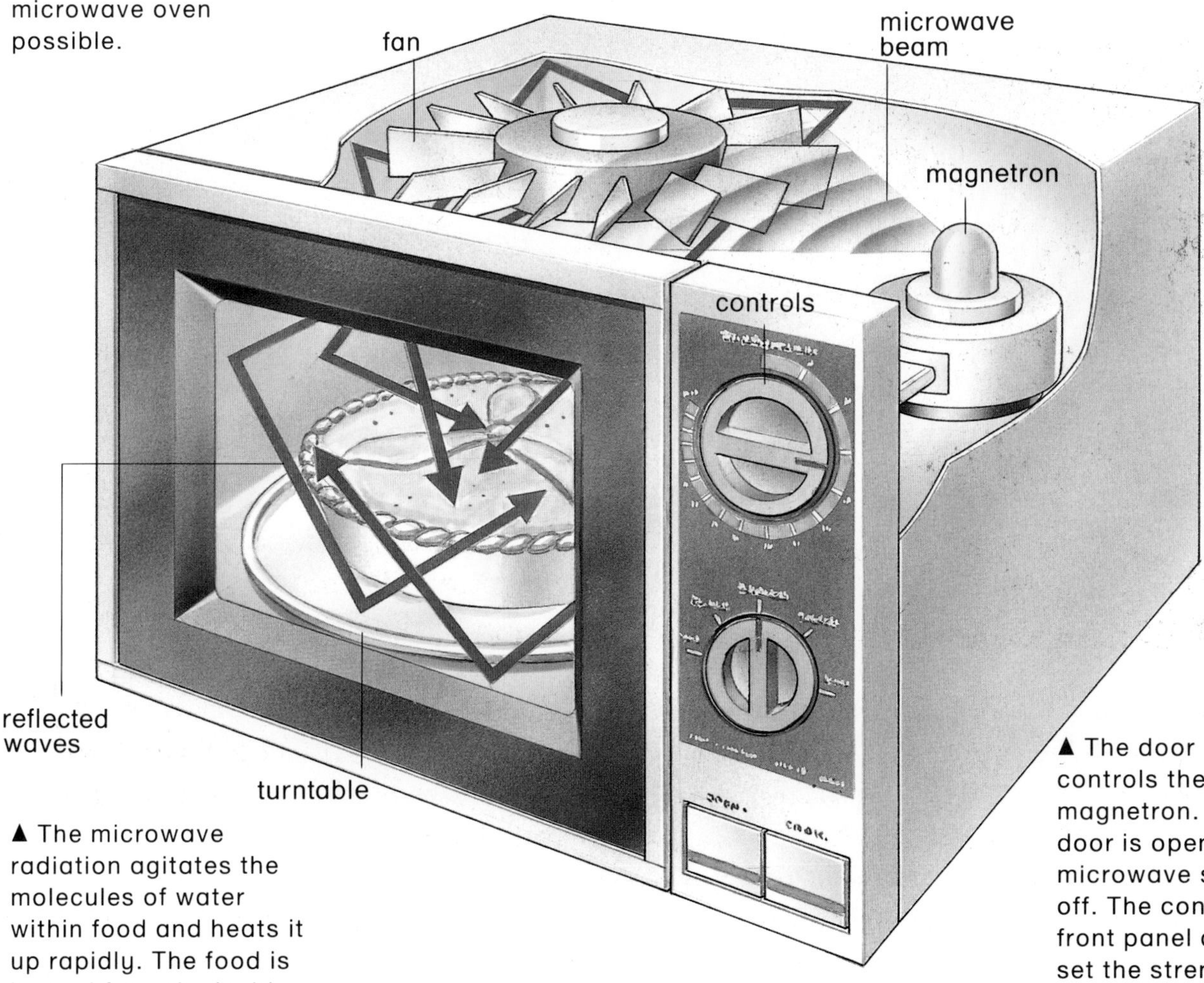

▼ Microwaves are produced by a special generator known as a magnetron. The invention of small magnetrons made the microwave oven possible.

▼ A rotating microwave reflector and a turntable plate help spread the radiation so the food is cooked evenly.

fan

microwave beam

magnetron

controls

reflected waves

turntable

▲ The microwave radiation agitates the molecules of water within food and heats it up rapidly. The food is heated from the inside.

▲ The door catch controls the magnetron. When the door is opened, the microwave switches off. The controls on the front panel allow you to set the strength of radiation and the time.

M

Milky Way

The EARTH and the rest of the SOLAR SYSTEM are part of the GALAXY that we call the Milky Way. If you look up in the sky at night through the thin part of the galaxy, you see the darkness of space beyond our galaxy most clearly. But if you turn to look through the thickness of the galaxy, you see millions of other STARS. They are our neighbors in the galaxy. There are so many that this portion of the sky looks "milky." The Milky Way is a spiral galaxy that is 100,000 LIGHT-YEARS across and 1,000 light-years thick. It contains about 100 trillion stars. Our Solar System is near the edge of the galaxy, which is why we get such a good view of the rest of space.

▲ Every star visible in the night sky belongs to the Milky Way galaxy.

minerals

Minerals are natural ELEMENTS or COMPOUNDS which make up ROCKS. They often form beautiful CRYSTALS. GEMS, metal ORES, SAND, SALTS, and even talc are different kinds of minerals.

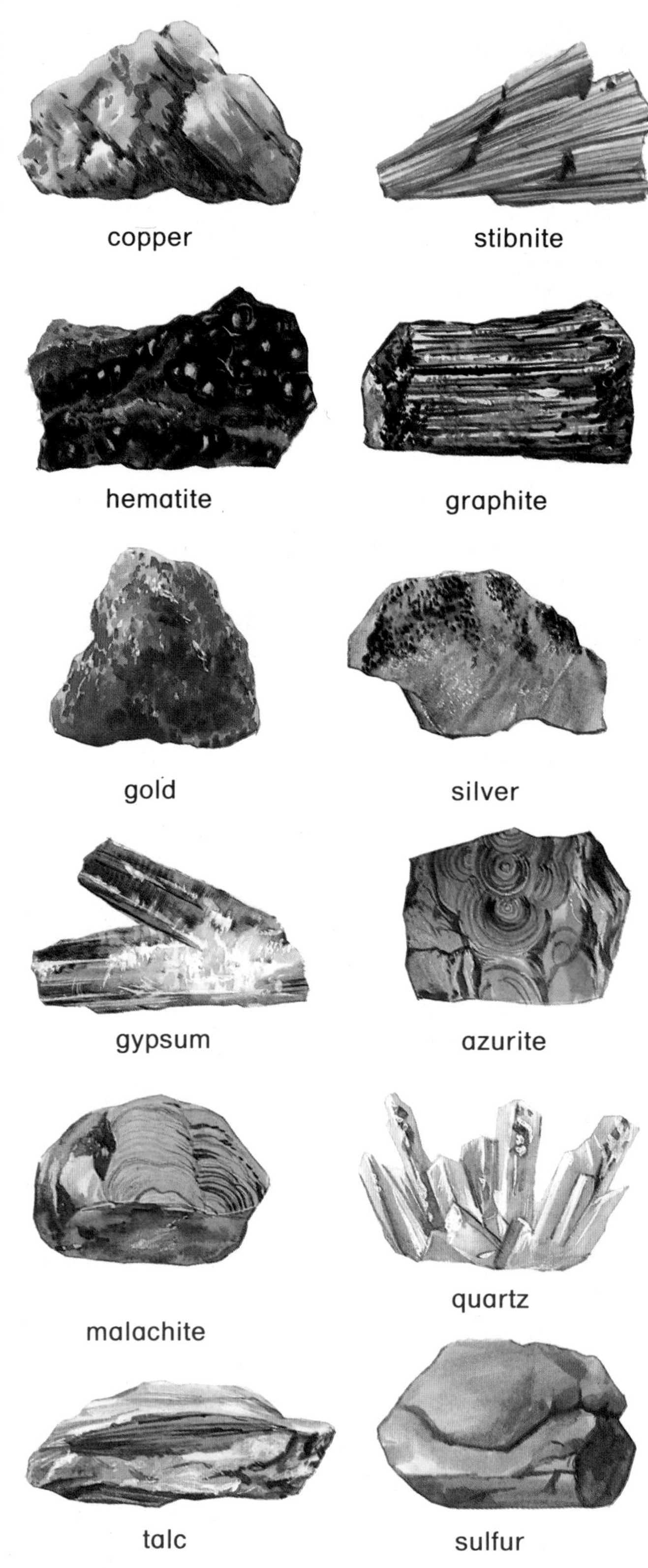

▲ Minerals exist in many different forms. Some are glassy crystals, others are brightly colored rocks. Minerals may be elements, such as gold or sulfur, or compounds such as metal ores. Many minerals are used for jewelry.

M

mirage

A mirage sometimes appears when layers of AIR near the ground become hot. The hot air can act as a LENS, bending rays of light. You may see an image of the sky reflected onto the ground by the hot air. It looks as if there is water ahead. This is called a mirage. You can see this effect on roads during a hot summer.

mirror

Smooth and polished surfaces reflect LIGHT. They act as mirrors. A flat mirror shows an opposite image — your left side appears on your right in the mirror. A curved mirror can act like a LENS by bending light rays to form a magnified image. The wavy mirrors at a fair distort light rays to make you look weird.

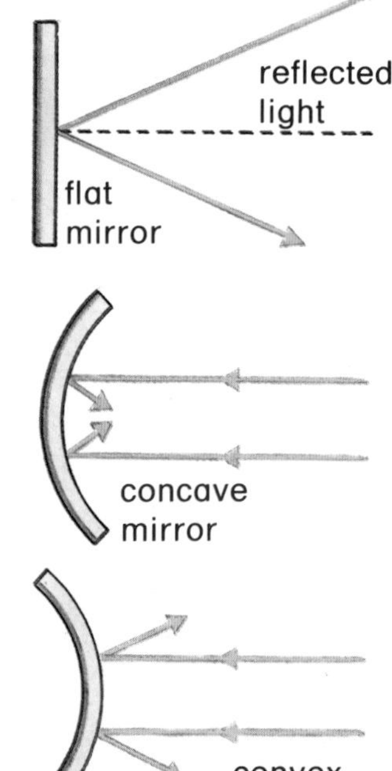

▶ The shape of a mirror affects the image it produces. A flat mirror reflects light at the same angle at which it hits the mirror, producing an undistorted image.

▶ Concave mirrors reflect light inward and magnify the image.

▶ Convex mirrors reflect light outward and produce a smaller image.

missile

A missile is something that is thrown. A spear is a missile; so is a stone that breaks a window. Weapons that are sent up by ROCKET and guided to their targets are missiles too.

modem

DIGITAL information in BINARY form can be changed to an ANALOG sound signal and sent along a TELEPHONE wire to a COMPUTER or FAX machine. The device that changes the signal is a modem. The name comes from the words MOdulator and DEModulator.

molecule

A molecule is the smallest particle of a COMPOUND or ELEMENT that can exist on its own. It is a group of ATOMS joined together by forces called bonds.

▲ If a car stops suddenly, the momentum of the driver and passengers keeps them moving. They are stopped by applying a force in the opposite direction. This is provided by a seat belt.

momentum

A moving body tends to keep moving unless an outside FORCE stops it. This is the principle of INERTIA. The amount of ENERGY the body has depends on its MASS and its VELOCITY. Momentum is measured by multiplying mass by velocity. If a car stops suddenly, the passengers' momentum carries them on until they hit the inside of the car, unless they are stopped by a seat belt or an air bag.

M

monorail

A train which runs on a single rail is a monorail (*mono* is Greek for "one"). Some monorail trains are raised by MAGNETS and glide along on a cushion of air. This is known as magnetic levitation (Maglev for short).

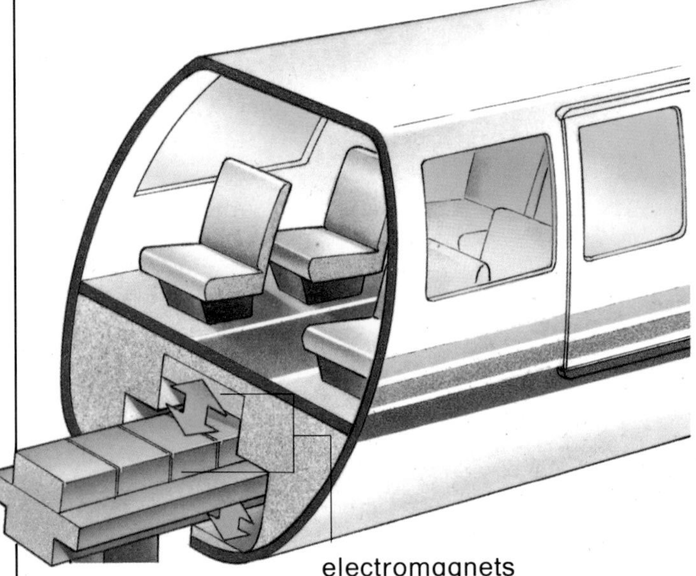

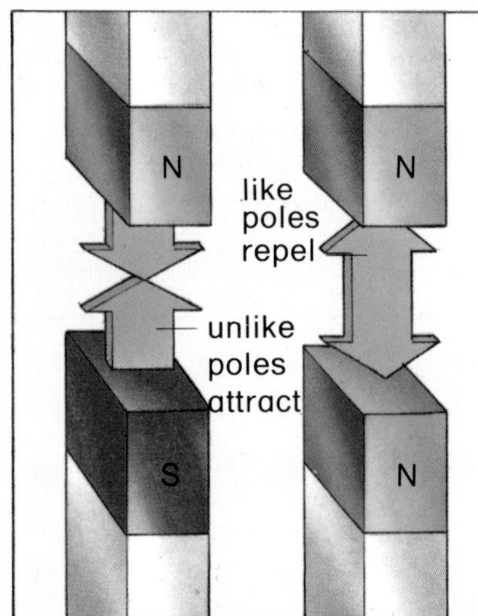

▲ Like poles of a magnet push each other away, or repel. This force is used to support a Maglev train. Electromagnets on the track and the underside of the train repel each other, lifting the train off the track.

monsoon

The monsoon season is caused when bands of hot and cold AIR meet in the tropics. A monsoon is a tropical wind that occurs at a particular time of year and blows constantly in one direction. It brings heavy rains. See **meteorology**.

▲ The heavily cratered Moon always shows the same face as it orbits the Earth.

moon

The Moon is our nearest neighbor in space, about 238,860 mi (384,400 km) from Earth. It probably formed from fragments around the young Earth. It is 2,160 mi (3,476 km) in diameter, and its MASS is only about one-hundredth of the Earth's mass. The Moon orbits the Earth once every 27.32 days, but because the Earth is also moving, the time from one New Moon to the next is 29.53 days.

▼ Sunshine lights up half of the Moon, but we cannot always see all of the lit half from Earth. The result is that the Moon goes through a 29-day cycle, the Phases of the Moon.

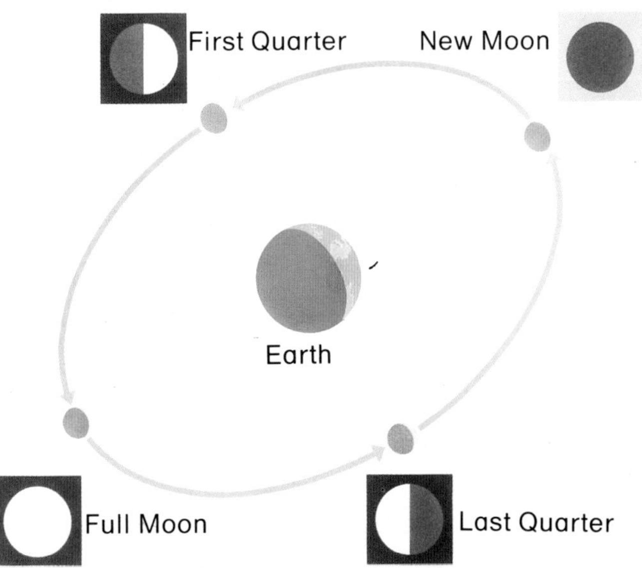

motion pictures see **cinema**

motor

A motor is a device which turns ENERGY into MOVEMENT. An ELECTRIC current passing through a coil in a MAGNETIC field will make the coil move. This is the idea behind an electric motor.

▼ In this simple electric motor, a battery supplies electric current to a wire coil in a magnetic field. This makes the coil rotate.

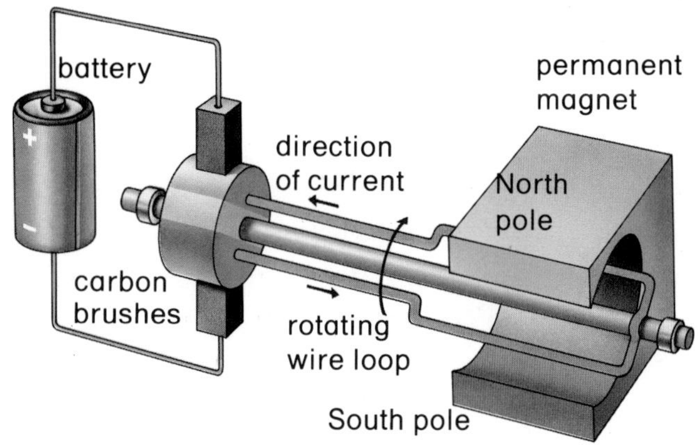

mountain

Mountains are high hills with steep slopes. Most mountain ranges are found where huge land masses have crashed into each other, pushing the layers of rock upward over millions of years. Others are formed by the folding of rocks as plates shift in the Earth's crust. The highest mountain ranges are also the youngest. The oldest mountains, such as the Appalachians, have been gradually worn down by the forces of EROSION. See **plate tectonics**.

DID YOU KNOW?

Millions of years ago, as the continents drifted toward their present positions, India crashed into Asia. As a result of this great collision the Himalayan mountains were formed. The rocks between the two land masses were forced upward, and the ancient seafloor ended up at the top of the Himalayas.

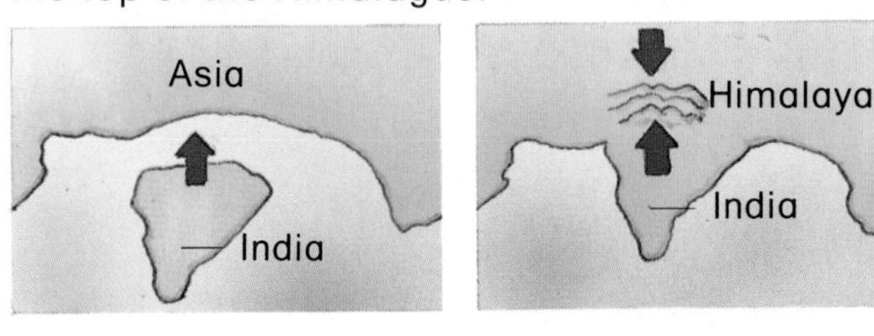

▼ When plates of land push against one another, some of the rocks may be thrust upward to form mountains. The land may fold or it may break and push up large blocks of rock.

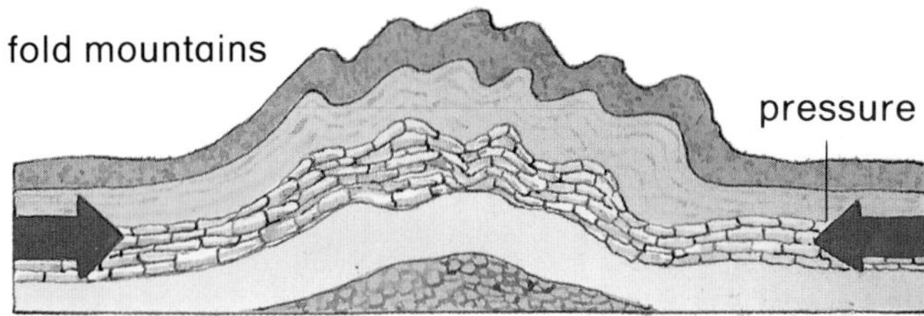

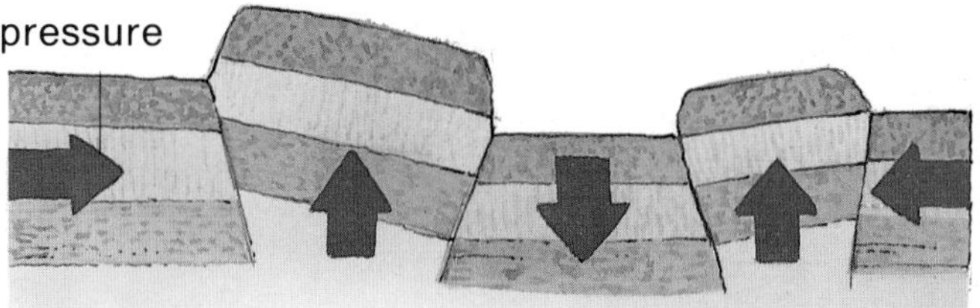

movement

Movement is a change of position in an object, like the movement of the hands of a clock. Motion is when an object goes to a different place. A car along a road is in motion; its pistons are in movement.

▼ Because a snake has no legs it moves either by pushing out sideways and to the rear in a zig-zag movement or by sending a rippling (concertina) movement straight along its body.

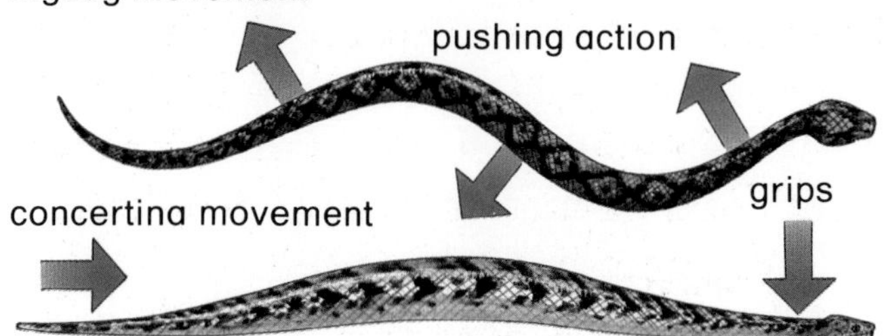

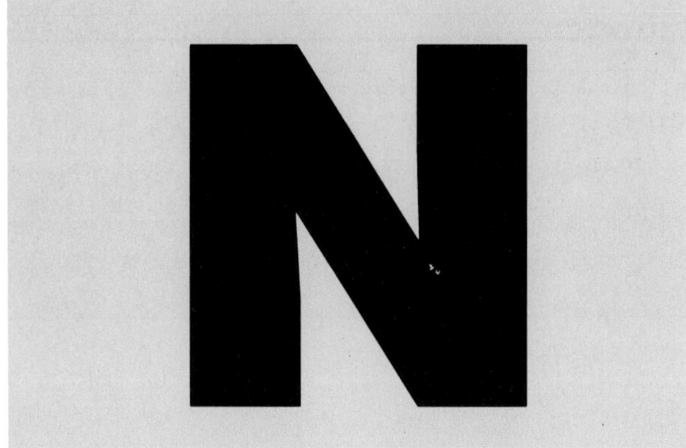

natural gas see **methane**

nebula

The word "nebula" was first used by ancient astronomers to describe a luminous cloud in the sky. TELESCOPES showed there are also many dark nebulae. Nebulae are great clouds of fine dust and gas that give rise to new STARS or that are thrown out when a star dies.

▼ Newborn stars shine brightly in the center of the Orion nebula. A dark horsehead-shaped cloud stands out against the bright gas behind.

neon

Neon is one of the inert gases. This means that it hardly ever forms COMPOUNDS because its ATOMS will not react with other atoms. But neon still has a use. If you put a strong charge of ELECTRICITY across a tube containing some neon, then the neon glows bright red. Neon lights are used to make colorful advertising signs. See **lighting**.

Neptune

Neptune is the eighth of the nine known planets of the SOLAR SYSTEM. It is 31,000 mi (50,000 km) across, and it takes 164.82 Earth years to orbit the SUN. The Voyager space probe passed Neptune in 1989 and revealed that it has faint rings and at least eight moons. The surface temperature of Neptune is −350°F (−210°C), with winds of up to 1,200 mph (2,000 km/h) whipping across it.

neutron

A neutron is one of the particles in the nucleus of an ATOM. It is similar to a PROTON, but has no electric charge. When an atom is broken apart in a nuclear reaction, neutrons can make nearby atoms split, starting a chain reaction. A neutron bomb is an atomic weapon which gives out large amounts of neutrons. It could kill human and other life but would not damage buildings.

neutron star

Neutron stars are the smallest and heaviest STARS. They are formed when a SUPERNOVA collapses. Geninga is a neutron star only 12–19 mi (20–30 km) in diameter, yet it is heavier than the SUN. Neutron stars that flash are PULSARS.

LIFE STORY

Newton

Sir Isaac Newton (1643–1727) was the English philosopher who worked out the laws of GRAVITY. He also studied LIGHT rays and MATHEMATICS. When there was an outbreak of Black Death (the plague) in 1665 he left Cambridge University and went to stay with his parents in the Lincolnshire village where he was born. This gave him time to work out some of his best ideas. He returned to Cambridge in 1667.

nickel

Nickel is a silvery METAL which does not easily CORRODE or go dull. It is often used to make electrical connections in COMPUTERS and instruments in operating rooms. It is commonly made into coins, too (which is why our five-cent coin is called a nickel).

nicotine

Nicotiana is the tobacco plant, and nicotine is a poisonous chemical found in the leaves, which are used to make cigars and cigarettes. Nicotine has also been used as an insect spray by gardeners.

nitrates

Nitrates are COMPOUNDS of nitric ACID. Nitrates all contain NITROGEN. Some explode violently and are used to make weapons. Other nitrates are used to make fertilizers for the soil, because all living things need nitrogen to grow. If too much fertilizer is used, it can be washed into waterways. The nitrates fertilize weeds and algae in the rivers and lakes, which then become clogged.

nitrogen

Nitrogen forms 80 percent of the atmosphere. Its CHEMICAL symbol is N. Nitrogen COMPOUNDS are vital to all living things. They are needed for growth.

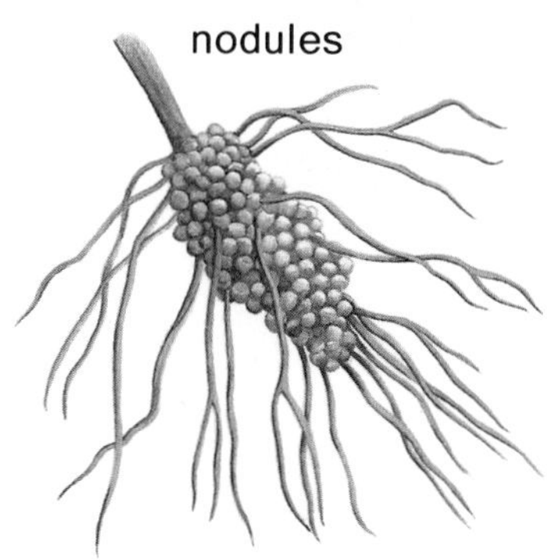

◀ Plants need nitrogen, but they cannot absorb it from the air. Some plants have nodules on their roots containing bacteria. The bacteria change nitrogen from the air into nitrates, which plants can absorb.

nitroglycerine

Nitroglycerine is an oily liquid that burns if it is spilled but explodes violently if suddenly struck or heated. To be used safely, it is soaked into sawdust or clay to make dynamite. Dynamite was invented by a Swedish industrialist, Alfred Nobel. He used the profits it brought him for Nobel Prizes, which are given for discoveries that benefit humanity.

noise

Noise is the kind of SOUND that annoys people. Electrical noise is the "hiss" behind a signal in systems like TELEVISION.

nuclear power see **page 94**

numbers see **page 95**

nylon

Nylon is a PLASTIC made up of very long thin MOLECULES. Nylon FIBERS are used to make clothes and brush bristles. Nylon is also made into machine parts and is used in surgery.

N

NUCLEAR POWER

The nucleus of an ATOM can be broken apart to produce ENERGY. Einstein's theory of RELATIVITY showed that a small MASS can be changed into a huge amount of energy. In a nuclear reactor, NEUTRONS are fired into the nuclei at very high speed. As the nuclei are hit, they break apart and shoot out still more neutrons. This can start a chain reaction, producing vast amounts of energy.

▼ The breaking of atoms to release energy is called nuclear fission. The fuel used in nuclear reactors is an isotope of uranium. Some nations make most of their electricity this way.

▼ Radioactive waste is the problem with nuclear power. But coal power stations release waste gases. Both damage the environment.

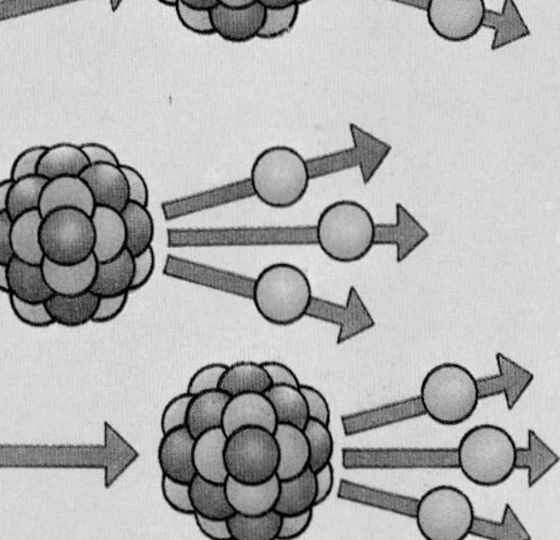

A NUCLEAR POWER STATION

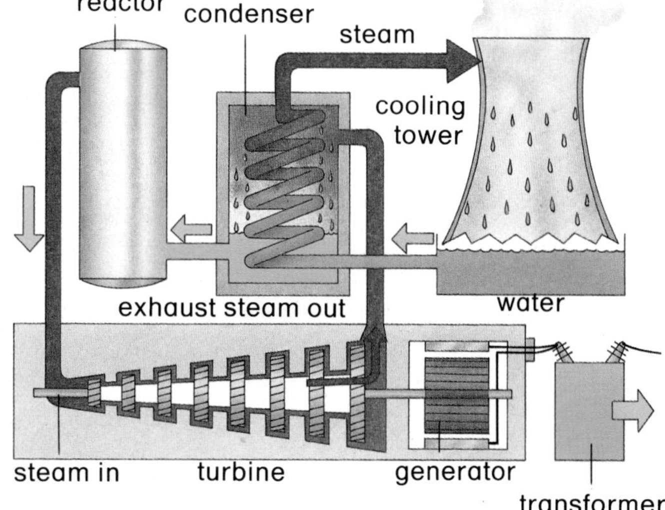

Nuclear power stations do not make electricity out of radioactivity. They use the heat energy released during nuclear fission to produce steam. The pressure of the steam drives an electric generator. Nuclear power produces no greenhouse gases, but many people worry about the risk of accidents.

▼ The nuclear reaction is controlled by sliding graphite rods in and out of the reactor core. Graphite absorbs neutrons, so the chain reaction is slowed.

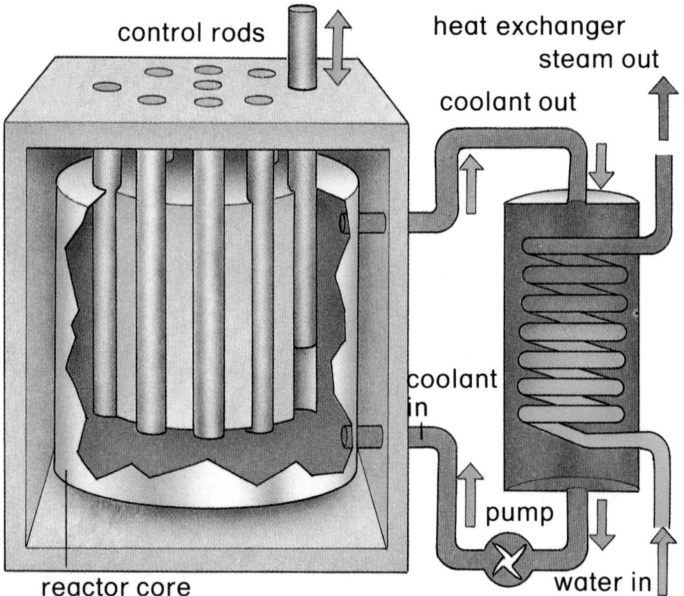

NUMBERS

Numbers can be read in any language. You would not find it easy to read a text in a different language, but numbers are a universal language. The system we use now is based on Arabic numerals, but many other systems have been used in the past. The Romans used a series of lines — I, II, III, IV, V, and so on — because they were easier to carve on stone.

NUMBER GAMES

The number 142,857 has almost magical properties. It is a "circular number." Multiply it by numbers up to 7: 1 x 142,857 = 142,857; 2 x 142,857 = 285,714; 3 x 142,857 = 428,571; 4 x 142,857 = 571,428; 5 x 142,857 = 714,285; 6 x 142,857 = 857,142. Each answer is the same series of numbers (starting at a different place each time). For higher numbers it doesn't work: 7 x 142,857 = 999,999. But divide 1 by 7 on your calculator and see what number you get!

Try this one. Ask a friend to write his or her age three times in a row. Study the number for a moment and then predict that it can be divided by seven. This works for all numbers between 10 and 99.

◀ Numbers increase hugely if you keep doubling the sum. The series goes: 1, 2, 4, 8, 16, 32, 64, 128, and so on. This is a geometrical progression. Adding the same number at each stage gives a far lower rate of increase. This is known as an arithmetical progression.

Roman

I	II	III	IV	V	VI	VII	VIII	IX	X
1	2	3	4	5	6	7	8	9	10

Mayan

•	••	•••	••••	—	• —	•• —	••• —	•••• —	— —
1	2	3	4	5	6	7	8	9	10

Chinese

一	二	三	四	五	六	七	八	九	十	十五	五十
1	2	3	4	5	6	7	8	9	10	15	50

Hindi

१	२	३	४	५	६	७	८	९	१०
1	2	3	4	5	6	7	8	9	10

▲ Most ancient number systems did not use the number zero. Zero was invented by Hindu mathematicians about A.D. 600.

▶ Calculators are invaluable for performing calculations with large numbers. They use microchips to carry out difficult operations in a fraction of a second.

▼ The numbers on a watch are usually Arabic, but some have Roman numerals. The numbers on a digital watch face are made up from seven segments.

Arabic numbers

Roman numbers

digital display

ocean

The oceans cover over two thirds of the Earth. The largest and the oldest is the Pacific Ocean. The average depth of the oceans is about 2.5 mi (4 km); their average TEMPERATURE is 39°F (4°C). The five oceans are: the Atlantic, the Pacific, the Indian, the Arctic, and the Antarctic.

octane

Octane is a liquid PETROCHEMICAL produced from crude OIL. Octane burns easily. Samples of other types of fuel are compared with octane to see how well they burn in an engine.

▼ The word *octane* comes from the Greek *oct* for "eight." The octane molecule has eight carbon atoms linked to 18 hydrogen atoms. Materials made from hydrogen and carbon are called hydrocarbons.

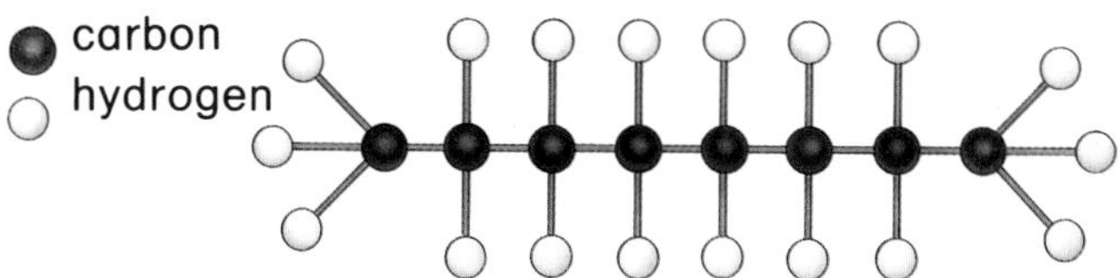

▼ Two thirds of the Earth's surface is covered by five major oceans. Water constantly evaporates from the oceans into the atmosphere and eventually falls back to Earth as rain.

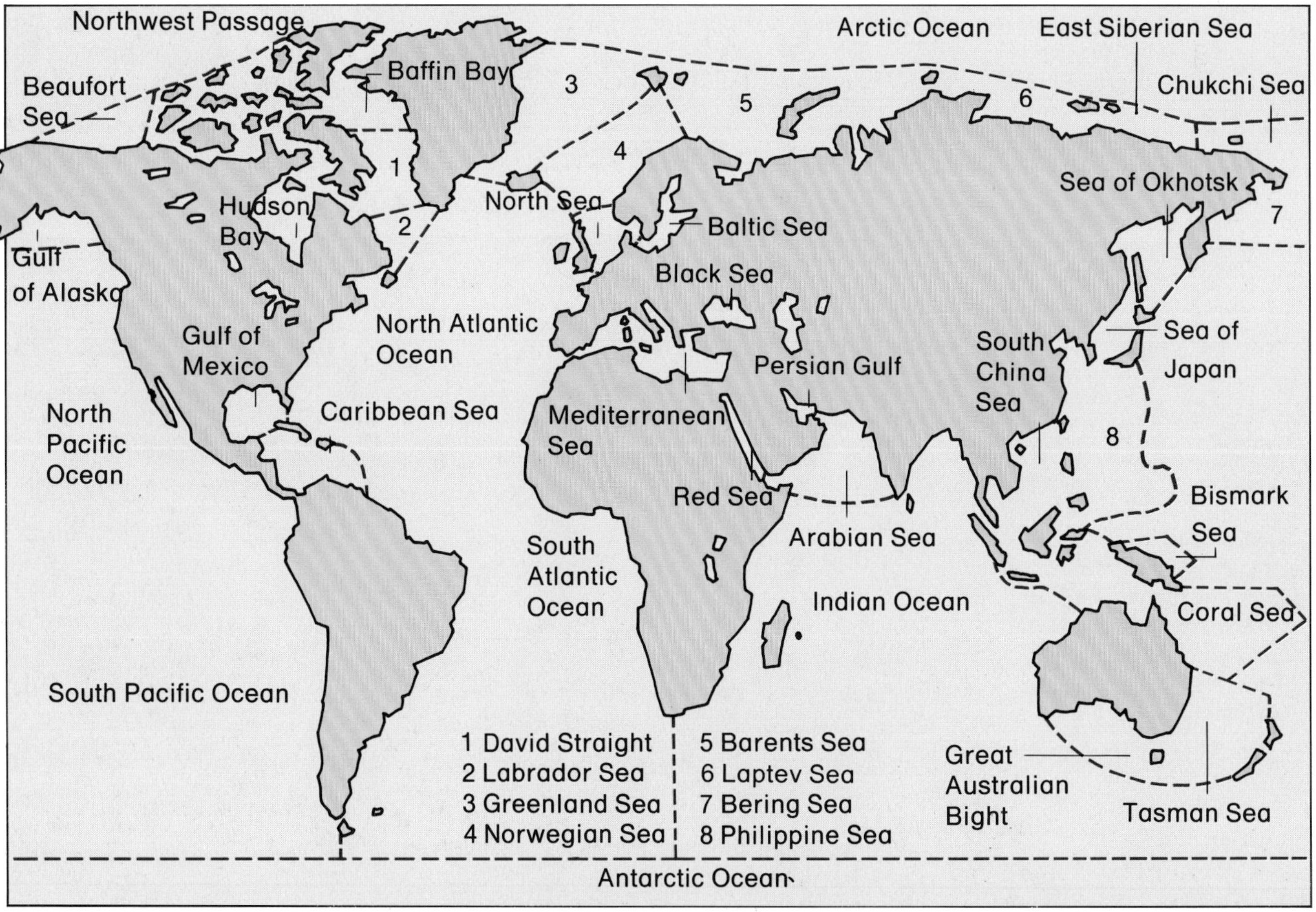

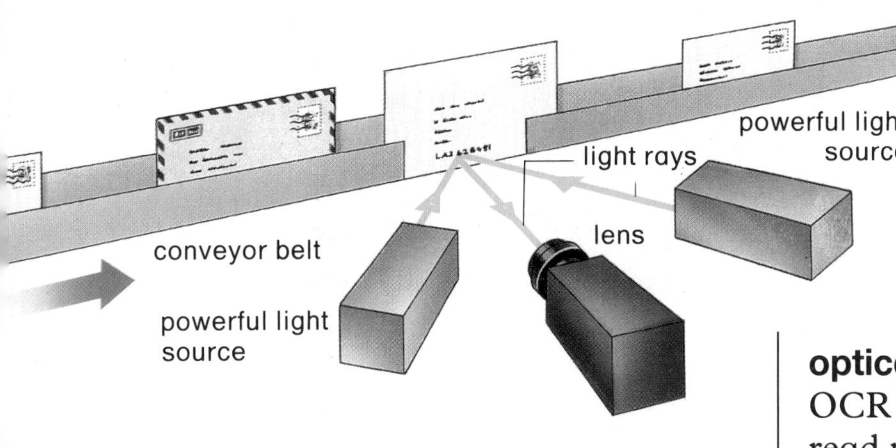

◀ Machines using optical character recognition systems can sort letters automatically by reading the zip codes printed on the envelopes.

oil

An oil is a slippery liquid which does not mix with water. Oils are often produced by living cells as an energy store. Oil from fossil plants can be collected by drilling oil wells. This is crude oil. Crude oil contains hydrocarbons — compounds made up only of HYDROGEN and CARBON. Because oils are rich in energy they make good FUELS. And because they are slippery they are used as LUBRICANTS.

▲ Oil and natural gas are found far underground. To reach the oil, a well is drilled from an oil rig down through the layers of rock. Pipelines carry the crude oil to a refinery where it is treated.

optical character recognition (OCR)

OCR is a system that allows COMPUTERS to read printed type. A scanner recognizes the shape of the characters and sends the information to the computer. A special kind of type has been developed that is easier for computers to read. The letters are made up of thick and thin lines, so they are easy to recognize.

optical fiber

An optical fiber is a hair-thin thread of glass. LIGHT shone into an optical fiber is reflected back from the outside surface of the glass, and so it cannot escape. If the glass is of high quality and very clear, the light can travel for great distances. Pulses of light from a LASER can be used to carry DIGITAL information. This is faster than sending electricity along a wire. In hospitals, optical fiber systems are used to look inside patients' bodies.

▼ Optical fibers carry information in the form of light beams bouncing between the glass walls.

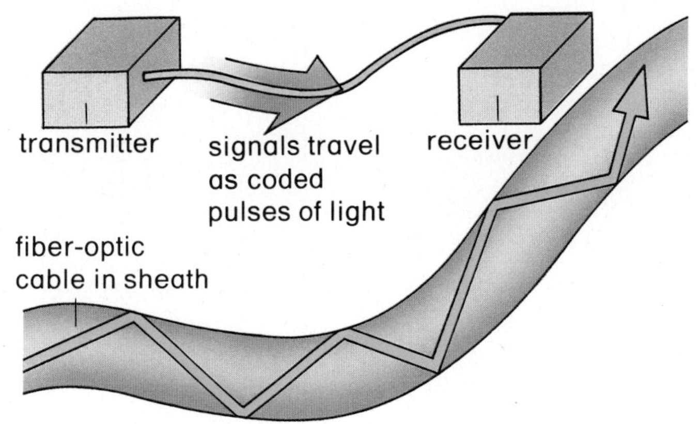

O

optical illusions
The eye picks out certain items of information in a picture, and your brain uses this to work out what you are looking at. If your eye transmits information that you do not expect, your brain can play tricks with your sight. Circles can become ovals, and straight lines can look curved.

▲ ▼ The figure on the right appears taller than the others, but they are all the same height. The vertical lines appear to bend, but they are straight. The backgrounds trick the brain.

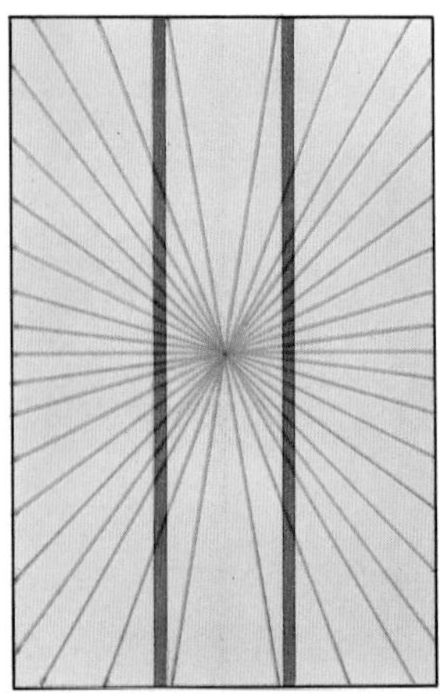

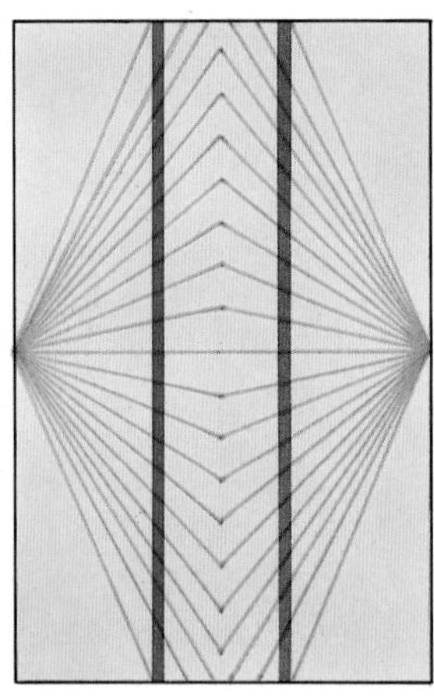

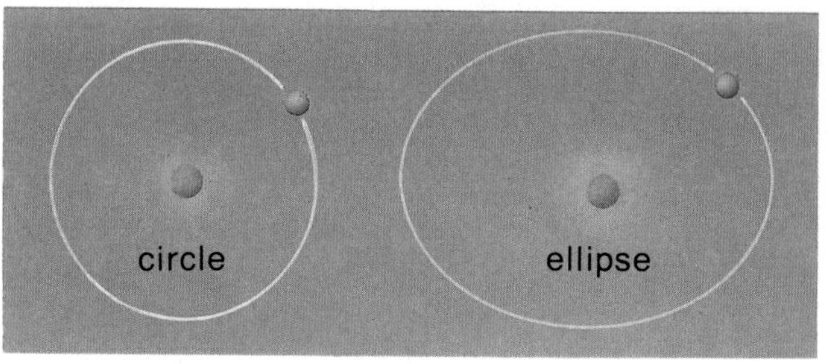

▲ Although we often talk about planets circling the Sun, the orbits of the planets are actually "flattened" circles called ellipses.

orbit
Bodies that move around each other in space are in orbit. The MOON orbits the EARTH in this way. GRAVITY keeps pulling the Moon and Earth together, but their MOTION keeps them apart. See **Solar System, spacecraft**.

ore
Ores are MINERALS that are rich in COMPOUNDS of METALS. They can be crushed and treated in order to extract the metal. Some ores (like malachite, an ore of COPPER) are beautifully colored.

oxide
Oxides are COMPOUNDS formed when an ELEMENT reacts with OXYGEN. Rust is an iron oxide; water is a HYDROGEN oxide.

oxygen
Oxygen is the second most common ELEMENT in AIR. Its chemical symbol is O. Oxygen will combine actively with many other elements. Large amounts of ENERGY may be released when this occurs. Many substances burn when they react with oxygen, like the COMBUSTION of wood in a fire. CHEMICALS inside your body react with oxygen too, which releases your energy.

ozone

ATOMS of OXYGEN usually join together in pairs, and oxygen gas has the formula O_2. With extra ENERGY they can join in threes, and this is the gas known as ozone (O_3). It is responsible for the "electrical odor" of electronic apparatus. Ozone is poisonous. The ozone layer forms in the STRATOSPHERE about 15 mi (25 km) above the Earth. The ozone MOLECULES filter out the dangerous ULTRAVIOLET rays from the SUN and protect us from their effects. Some AEROSOLS and REFRIGERATORS contain CHLOROFLUOROCARBONS (CFCs), which can damage the ozone layer. The use of CFCs is strictly controlled in many countries.

▼ The ozone layer, at a height of 12–19 mi (15–30 km) in the atmosphere, protects us from the harmful effects of ultraviolet radiation from the Sun.

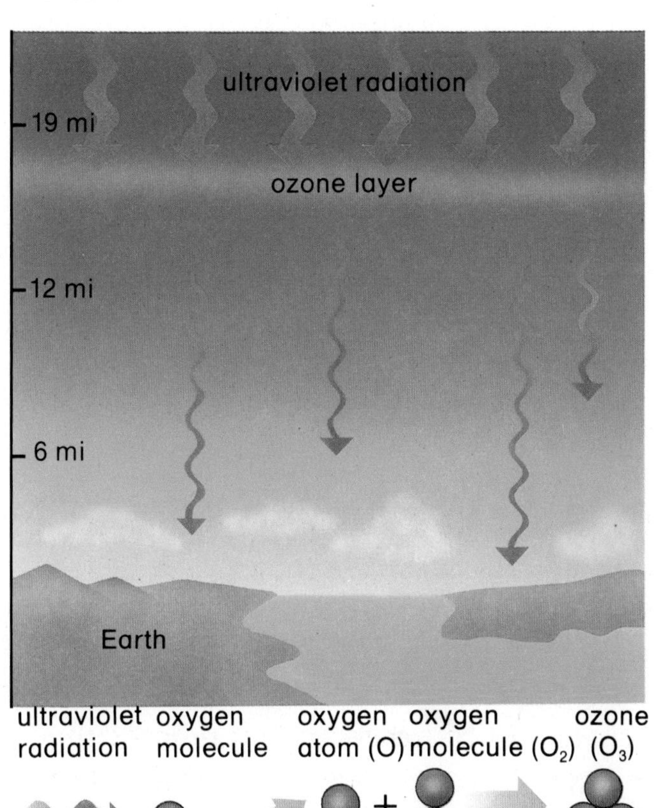

P

paleontology

Paleontology is the science of FOSSILS. When living things die they are sometimes buried in a layer of mud. After millions of years the mud turns to solid ROCK and the remains are preserved as fossils. Each layer of rock can be dated, and this tells us the age of the fossils in that layer. By studying fossils, paleontologists have discovered much about life forms that died out millions of years ago. Most exciting are the fossils of dinosaurs, some of which were as large as a bus. Paleontologists know not only what the dinosaurs looked like but also how they lived and what they ate.

▼ When paleontologists find fossils, they carefully dig up the remains and take them to a laboratory to be cleaned and identified.

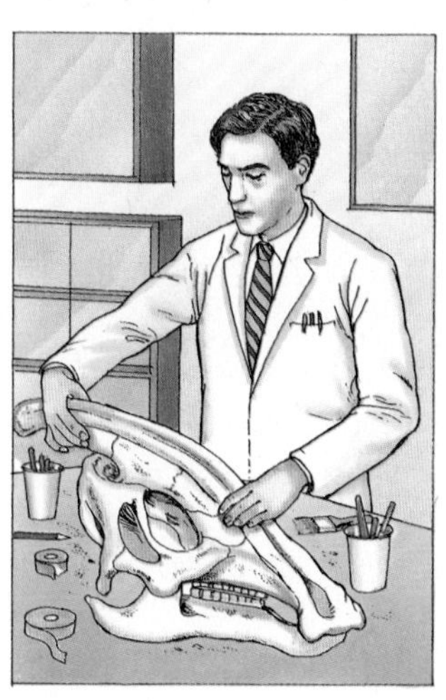

▶ Paper is made mostly from trees. Logs are ground into wood pulp, and mixed with water. The mixture passes onto a wire mesh which traps the wood fibers and forms a web of paper. The paper is then rolled and dried.

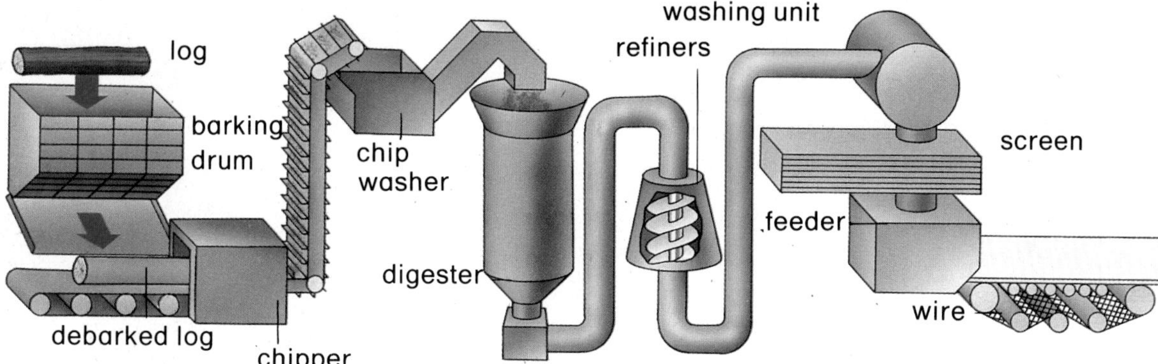

paper

In ancient times, people used to write on animal skin or thin layers of plant material, like papyrus. But about two thousand years ago the Chinese found out how to make a thin paste of vegetable fibers and let it dry out in a sheet. This was how paper was first made. Most paper is made from wood, but RECYCLED paper is made from paper waste.

parachute

A parachute is a large "umbrella" of light cloth. Its large area creates high AIR resistance so people can float safely down to the ground. Parachutes are also used to slow down race cars or planes at the end of their run.

parsec

A parsec is a measurement used in ASTRONOMY. It is the distance you would have to travel for the SUN and Earth to look as if they were almost touching (one degree second of an arc apart) in space. A parsec equals 3.26 LIGHT-YEARS, or 19.17 trillion mi (30.86 trillion km).

particle

Particles are tiny objects. Some particles are visible, such as sand grains. Others, such as PROTONS, are tinier than an ATOM.

pendulum

Any object that swings freely back and forth at the end of a rod or string is a pendulum. The number of swings it makes each minute depends only on the length of the pendulum, and not (as you might think) on the weight of the object at the end. See **Foucault**.

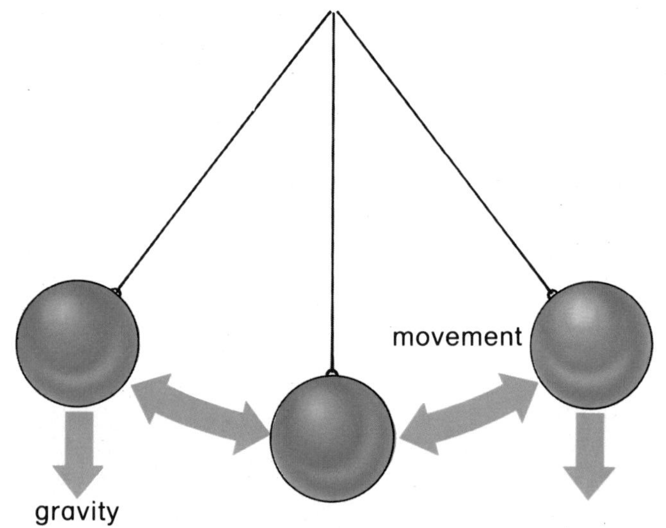

▲ A pendulum is a weight on the end of a string. When the weight, called a bob, swings out to one side, gravity pulls it back. If left to swing, air resistance eventually slows it down to a halt.

periscope

A periscope is a tube with peephole at one end and an angled mirror at both ends. It allows you to see higher or lower than normal or around a corner. The mirrors reflect light from the object toward your

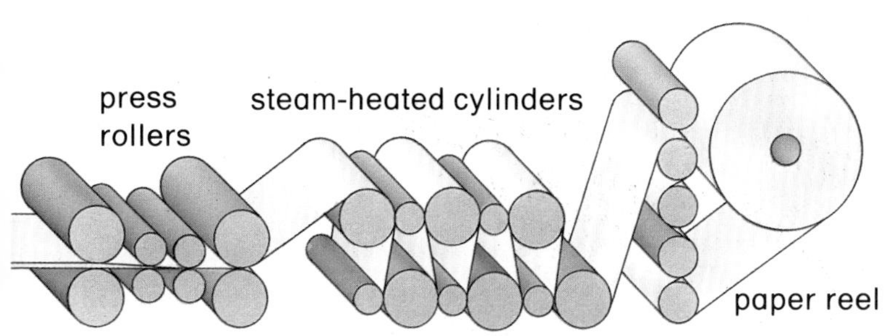

eyes, so you can see around obstacles. Periscopes are used in submarines to look above the surface of the sea. Scientists have used them to look inside nuclear reactors.

perpetual motion

For many years inventors tried to make a machine that would work without using ENERGY. It would then keep turning forever, by perpetual motion. But nothing can work without using some energy, so perpetual motion is impossible. Many different machines were tried out, but all of them were bound to fail.

▲ In this perpetual motion machine the ball bearings were supposed to turn the wheel, which would drive the screw around and lift the balls back to the top. However, energy is lost as friction, so the machine could never work.

petrochemicals

Petrochemicals are CHEMICALS made from crude OIL (petroleum) and NATURAL GAS. They include GASOLINE and kerosene. They are used to make PLASTICS, synthetic fabrics, DRUGS, and many other products.

▼ A wide range of household products, plastics, artificial rubber, soap, cosmetics, and animal food are made from petrochemicals.

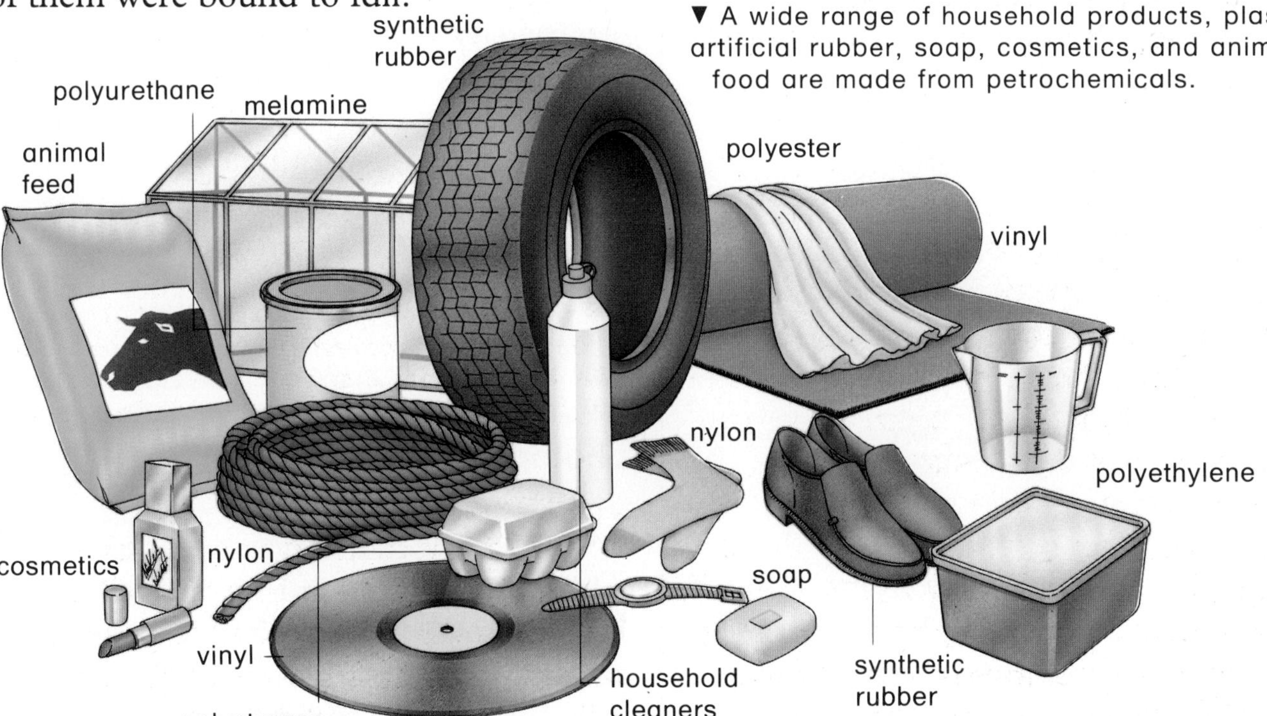

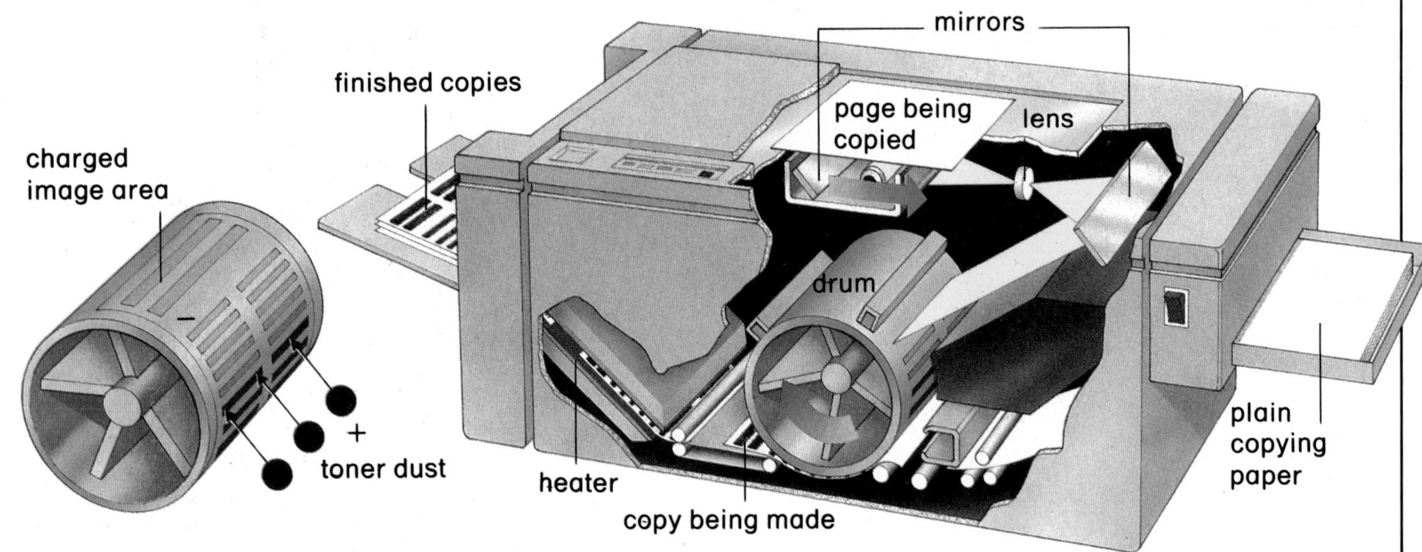

▲ A photocopier works by making a powdered pigment, called toner, stick to a blank sheet of paper in a pattern that exactly matches the ink on the original page.

pharmacology

Pharmacology is the study of DRUGS and how they work. Pharmacologists aim to develop better, safer drugs to treat disease.

phosphorus

We all contain small amounts of phosphorus. It is found in bones, blood, and teeth. Pure phosphorus is a very active ELEMENT. It burns easily, and it is used to make match heads. The symbol for phosphorus is P.

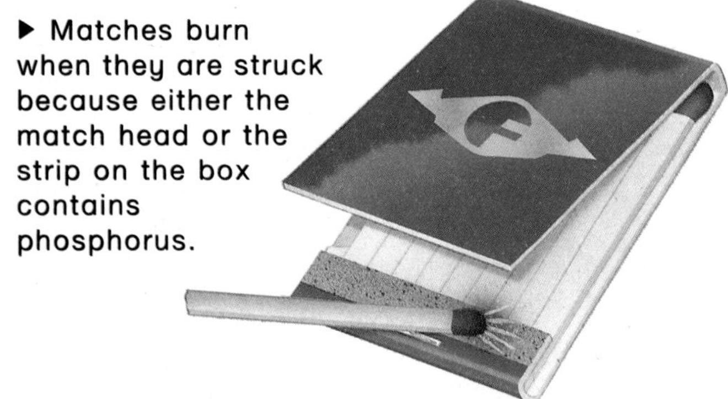

▶ Matches burn when they are struck because either the match head or the strip on the box contains phosphorus.

photocopier

It is hard to imagine modern life without photocopiers. A photocopier produces an exact copy of the image on a page. At one time, the best way to copy a document was to type it all out by hand. An American lawyer, Chester Carlson, became so tired of this work he decided to find a better way. This is how the idea of photocopying was born. When you photocopy something, an image of the page is projected onto a drum and a static electric charge is transferred to the drum wherever the image is dark, whether it is words or pictures. The electric charge attracts toner dust onto the drum, which it then transfers to a blank sheet of paper. A heater fixes the toner to the paper and the result is a copy that matches the original. The first photocopier went on sale in 1950.

photography see **page 103**

photon

The photon is a unit of LIGHT ENERGY. It has no MASS when it is at rest, but scientists can measure its MOMENTUM when it is traveling at the speed of light.

PHOTOGRAPHY

Photography means "drawing a picture with light." The scene is focused onto film by a lens. Behind the lens a shutter keeps out the light. At the moment the button is pressed, the shutter opens for a split second to allow a certain amount of light onto the film. The light strikes the chemicals in the film and produces a permanent image.

▶ Color film is made up of six layers. Separate layers absorb blue, green, and red light. In this way the whole picture is recorded. A plastic base supports the film, and a dark backing absorbs any remaining light.

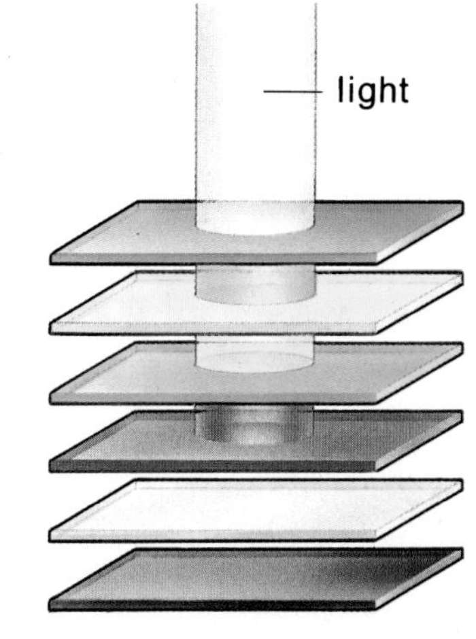

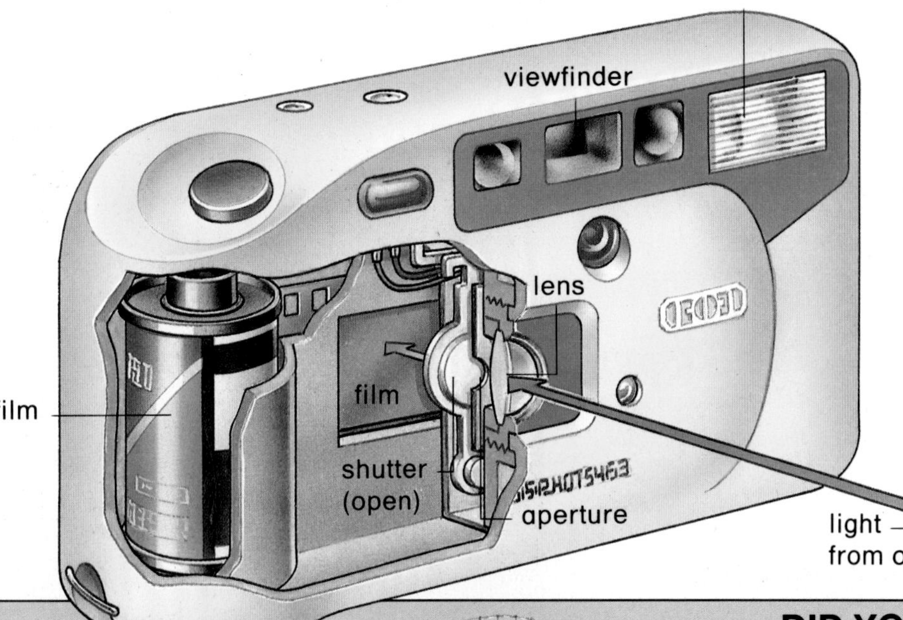

◀ The size of the shutter hole is the aperture. The length of time the shutter is open is called the exposure time. Automatic cameras have a small light sensor. This sets the exposure for a longer time if the light is dull. When the picture has been taken, the film winds on, ready for the next shot.

DID YOU KNOW?

Vacation snapshots often show the people too far away. All you see is a few stone columns and some tiny figures. This does not make an interesting photograph.

Remember to keep the buildings at a distance. This way you can get most of them into the picture. But do the opposite with the people: keep them near the camera (about 10 ft (3 m)). You can still see the building in the background. But take care not to slant the camera or the Leaning Tower of Pisa may end up looking perfectly upright.

P

physics

Physics is the science of studying MATTER and ENERGY. This includes LIGHT, SOUND, ELECTRICITY, MAGNETISM, RADIATION, and moving objects. Nuclear physics studies the PARTICLES inside the ATOM and the energy they contain. This led to the development of nuclear energy and weapons in the first half of this century. Many physicists are trying to find energy sources which do not cause pollution.

piezoelectricity

Some crystals (such as QUARTZ) will change mechanical ENERGY into ELECTRICITY if you squeeze them. Gas heaters often work like this, creating a spark when you squeeze a trigger. It works the other way around, too. An electrical charge on a piezoelectric crystal produces movement. This is how a quartz watch works.

▼ Some gas heaters have a piezoelectric igniter. Pushing the button bends a piezoelectric crystal and creates a spark, which lights the gas.

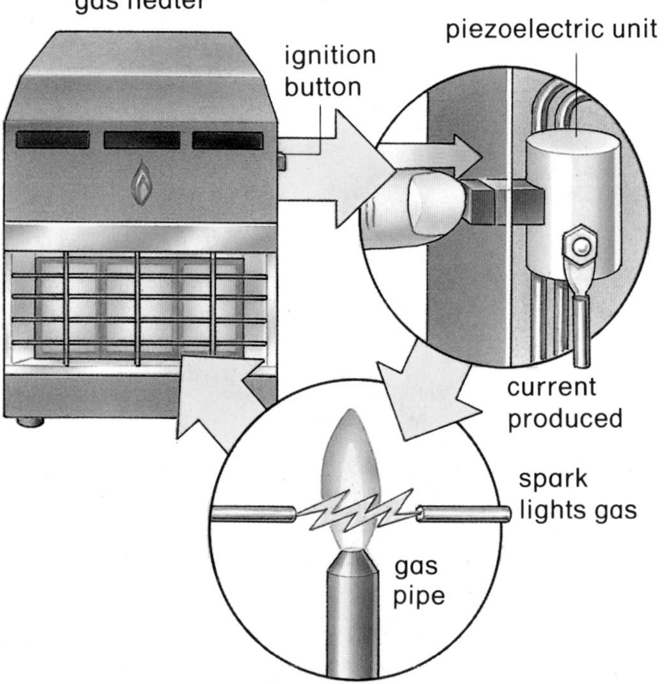

planet

A planet is a large body that orbits a STAR. Our SUN, like other stars, is hot and gives out light, which illuminates its planets. There are nine known planets in our SOLAR SYSTEM. Some, like the Earth, are made of rock and metal, but the huge planets like JUPITER are mostly gas.

▲ The planets grew out of the spinning ring of gas and dust left over from the formation of the Sun. Solid particles stuck together, forming larger bodies which eventually became the planets. The Sun's gravity holds them in orbit.

PLASTICS

Plastics are made by joining MOLECULES together in chains. Plastics are polymers (*poly* means "lots," and *merus* means "parts"). They are synthetic. In nature, things like cotton and fingernails are the closest to man-made plastics. There are lots of kinds of plastic, such as PVC, Plexiglas, and polyethylene, all with different properties. Look around and you will see how much plastic there is.

DID YOU KNOW?

Many plastics, such as polystyrene and polyethylene melt when they are heated. They can then be molded into shape and are used to make household objects. If they become hot, they will melt again. These are thermoplastics.

A second group of plastics sets hard when heated. These are thermosetting plastics. Bakelite is one example, and so is glue made from plastic resin.

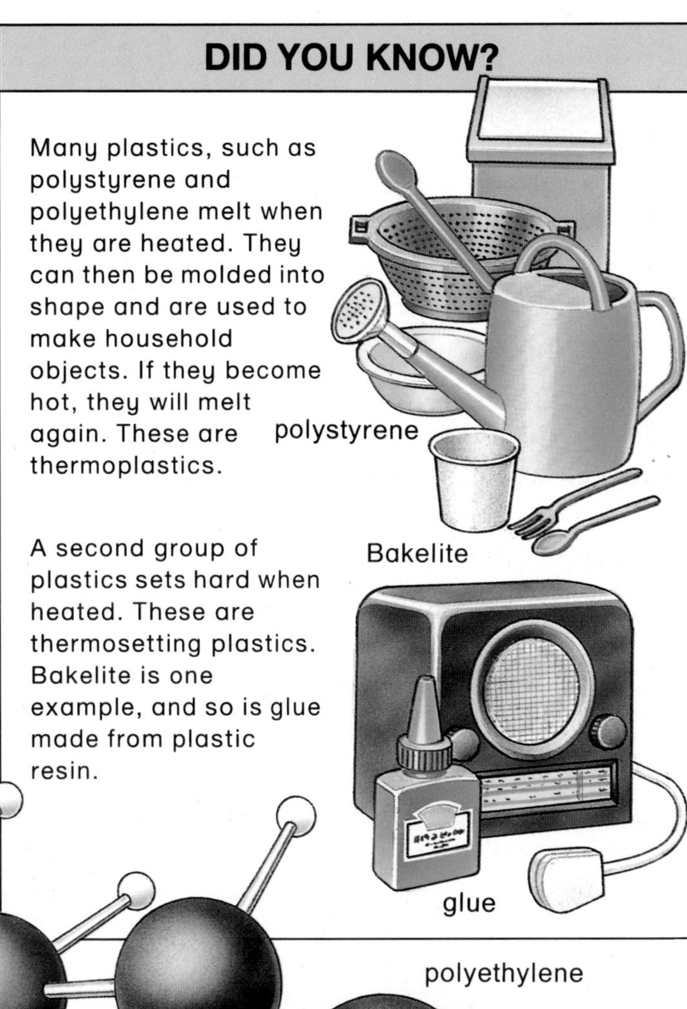

▼ Molecules of ethylene, a gas, contain two carbon atoms and four hydrogen atoms. There are two bonds between the carbons.

▼ As only one bond is needed to hold the carbon atoms together, the ethylene molecules can be joined together. This forms polyethylene.

ethylene

double bond

carbon

hydrogen

single bond

polyethylene

▶▼ Most plastics are not biodegradable. There are no microbes that can use them as food when they are dumped as waste. This can be useful — you don't want biodegradable plastic water pipes. But the plastic packaging on many objects is not biodegradable and causes pollution.

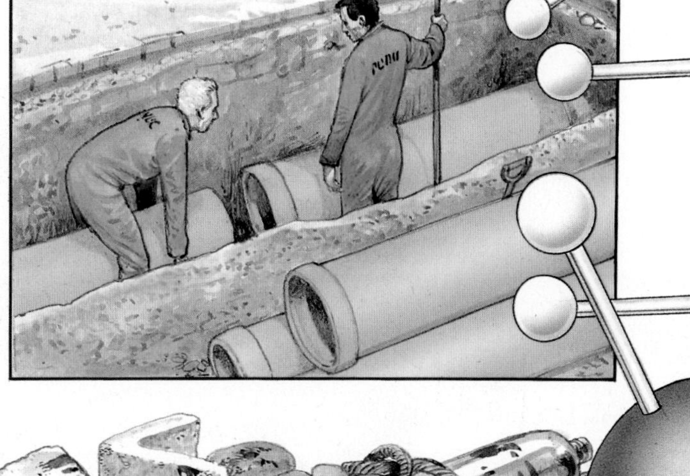

PLATE TECTONICS

Have you ever noticed how the coastlines of America and Africa fit together? It looks as if they have been torn apart. Alfred Wegener, a German geologist, noticed this, and published a theory that the continents were drifting. Plate tectonics explains how they move. The Earth's crust is made up of huge plates of rock. The movements of these plates causes the continents to drift around the Earth's surface.

▼ Three hundred million years ago there was a single mass of land. It is given the name Pangaea. As time went by, this ''super-continent'' broke up.

▼ One large mass of land drifted off to eventually become Asia, and North and South America drifted off to the west. Africa can be seen near the middle.

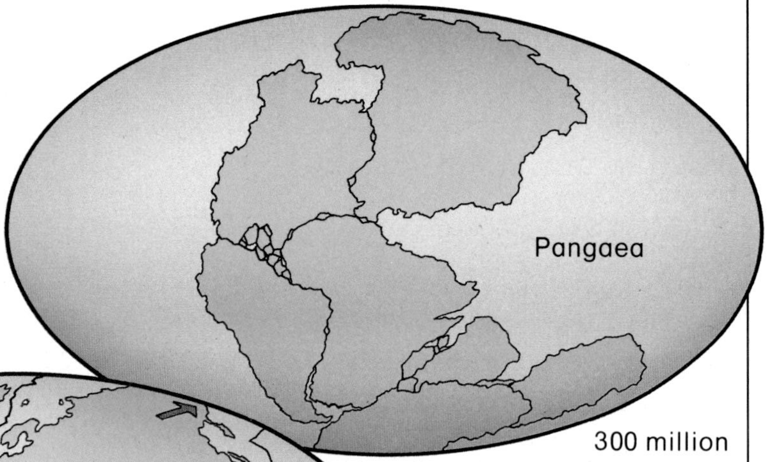

300 million years ago

▶ The present-day continents are the parts of huge plates of the Earth's crust which are higher than the sea. They are all moving very slowly. South Africa and America are drifting apart. They are moving at the same speed at which your fingernails are growing.

today

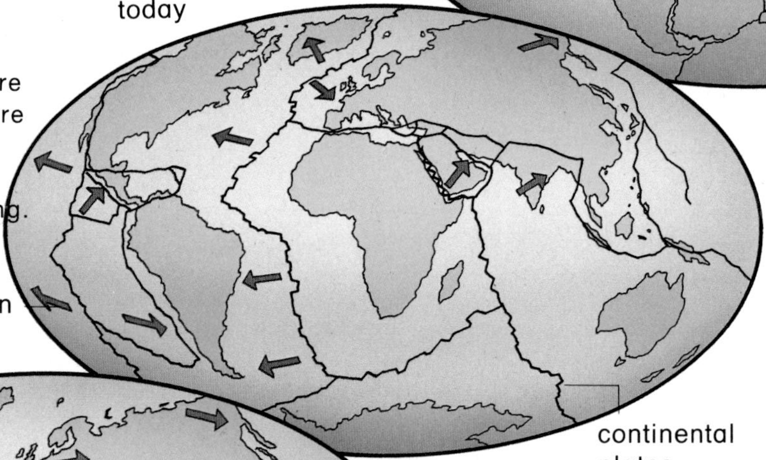

direction of drift

continental plates

▼ Where the plates meet, the ocean floor sinks down toward deeper layers of the Earth. This area is the subduction zone. Volcanoes are common near the edges of plates like these.

future

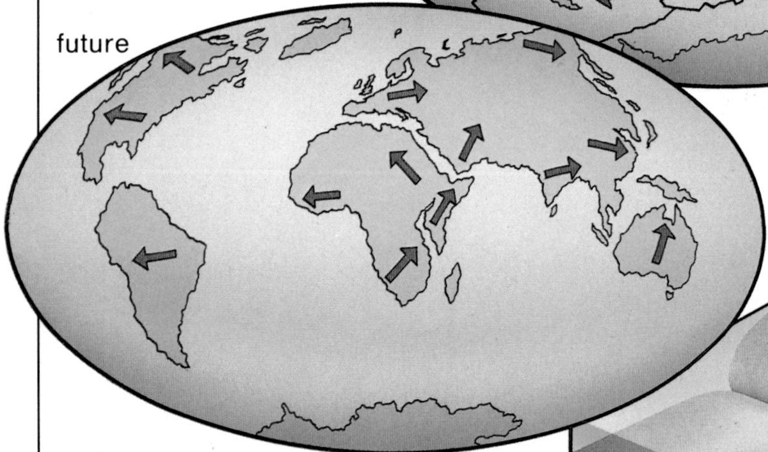

▲ Hundreds of millions of years in the future, North and South America may have spilt apart. Australia may collide with Asia.

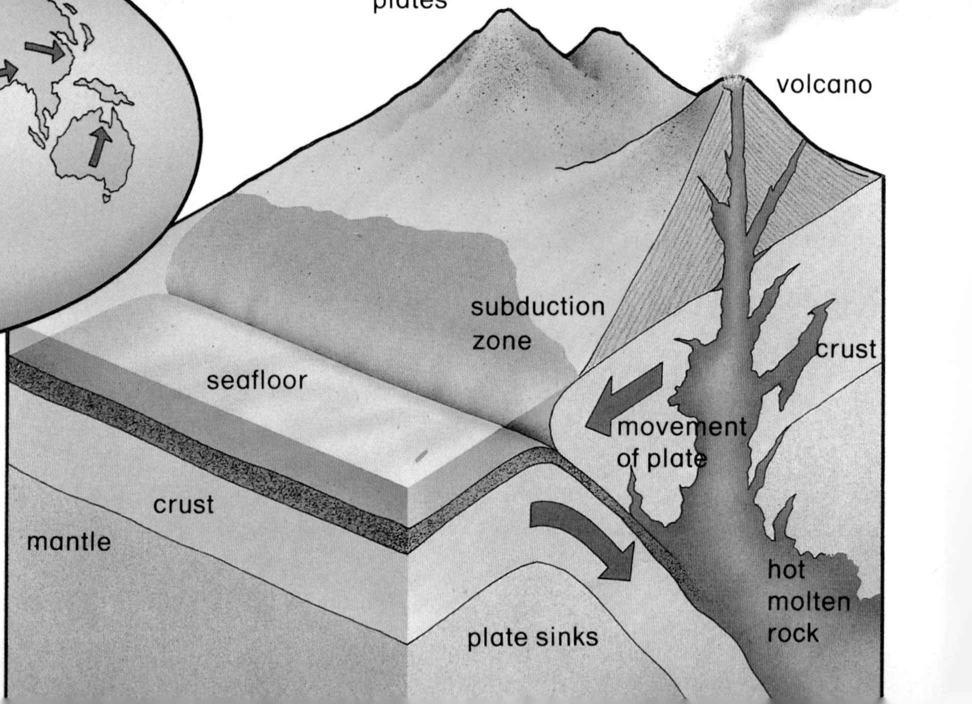

platinum
Platinum is a precious METAL of a silvery appearance. It never corrodes or becomes dull. It is used as a CATALYST in CATALYTIC CONVERTERS and is also sometimes used to make electrical contacts.

Pluto
Pluto is the outermost of the Sun's PLANETS. It is smaller than the MOON, and it takes 248.6 Earth years to orbit the SUN. See **Solar System**.

plutonium
Plutonium is a radioactive METAL with a long HALF-LIFE. Plutonium 239, its best-known ISOTOPE, breaks down easily and releases a lot of energy. It is a by-product of the FISSION of uranium 238 in NUCLEAR POWER plants, and is used to make more nuclear energy and also nuclear bombs.

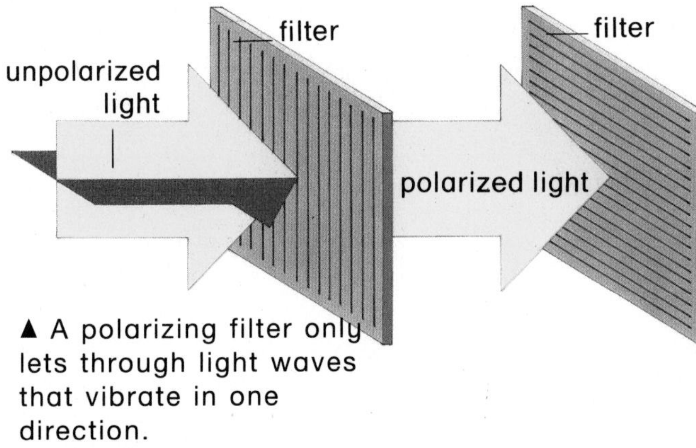

▲ A polarizing filter only lets through light waves that vibrate in one direction.

polarized light
A beam of LIGHT contains different wavelengths which vibrate at every angle. Polarized light has waves which all vibrate in only one direction. A polarizing filter polarizes light by allowing through only the light which vibrates in one direction. A second filter at right angles would stop all the light.

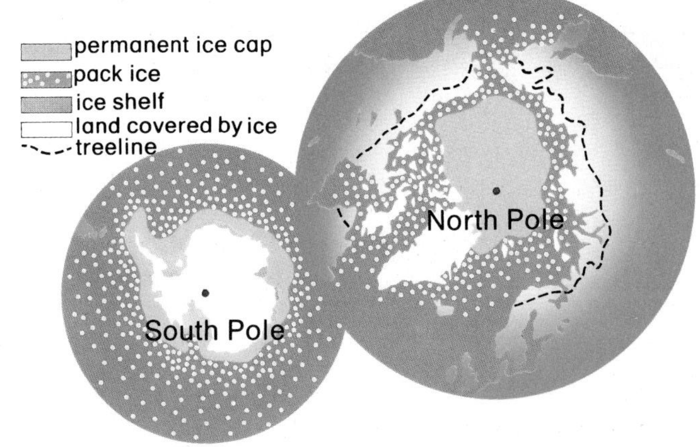

▲ The South Pole is mainly land covered by ice. The North Pole is ice floating on an ocean.

poles
If you think of the EARTH turning on a pole, you can see how the North and South geographic poles obtained their names. The Earth also has magnetic poles, just like a giant magnet. They are 11.5° away from the geographic poles. See **compass**.

pollution see **pages 108 and 109**

polygon
A polygon is a flat shape with three or more straight sides. *Hexa* means "six" in Greek, so a hexagon is a polygon with six sides.

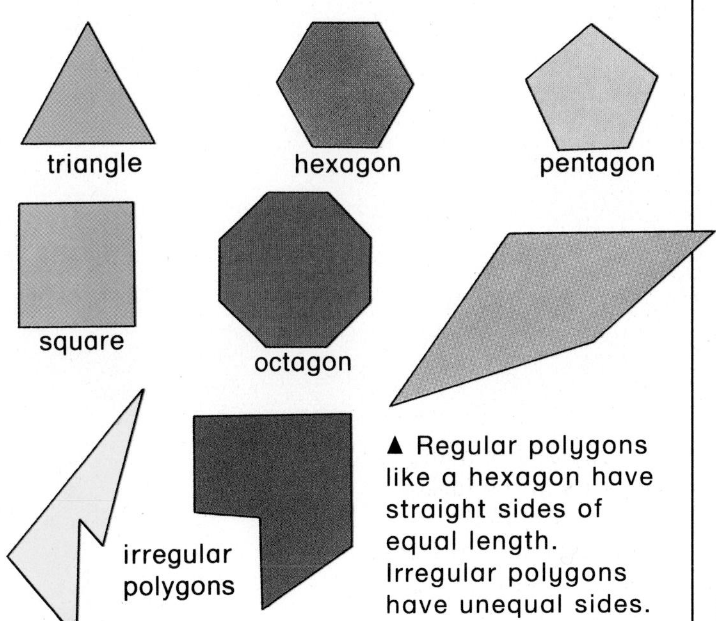

▲ Regular polygons like a hexagon have straight sides of equal length. Irregular polygons have unequal sides.

P

POLLUTION

Pollution is caused by people. It occurs when we overload the Earth with waste. Pollution has many sources. Factories, power plants, cars, and agriculture all produce harmful waste chemicals. The waste is released into the air and into the rivers and oceans. Some is buried on land. Pollution contaminates the air we breathe, kills wildlife, and destroys the environment.

Many people want the latest product. It may be new shoes or the latest car. Factories work day and night to make these goods. They use energy and pollute the air with waste gases that can be dangerous.

Every gallon of fuel burned by a car or a plane gives out more than 60 gallons of greenhouse gases. The spread of cars adds to global warming.

Noise pollution is a big problem in many cities. Airports, industries, and traffic can cause a deafening noise. Quarries, rubbish dumps, and power plants spoil the landscape. This is called visual pollution.

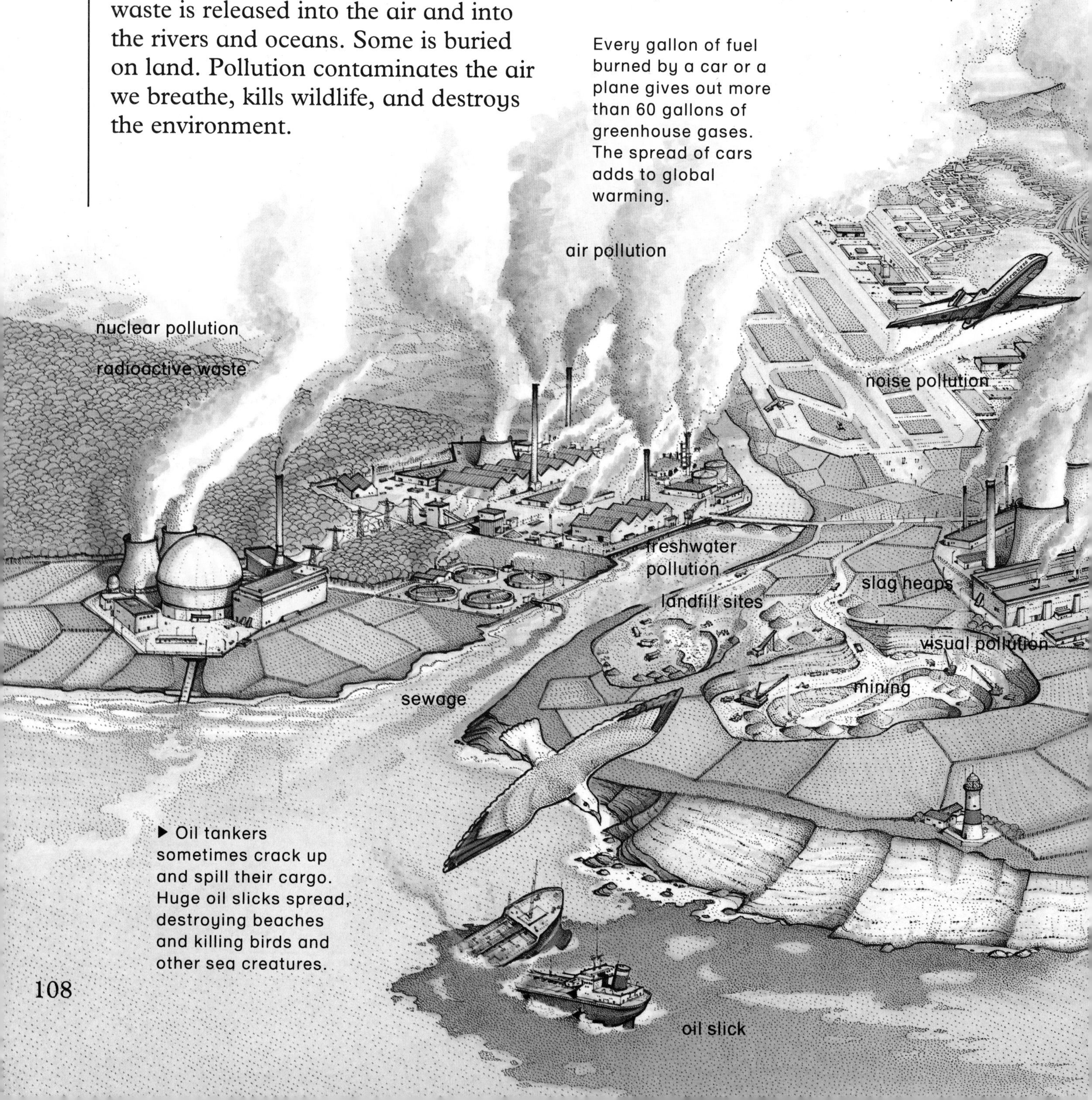

▶ Oil tankers sometimes crack up and spill their cargo. Huge oil slicks spread, destroying beaches and killing birds and other sea creatures.

Rivers are polluted by sewage, pesticides, and fertilizers from farms, and toxic waste from factories. Sometimes pollutants are dumped against the law. They harm the river's wildlife.

The huge amount of waste we produce is often buried in landfills. Many old landfill sites are leaking, and water supplies may be contaminated with poisonous chemicals. Landfills also produce methane gas.

Air pollution comes from many sources. Burning coal and oil releases toxic compounds as well as carbon dioxide. CFCs from aerosols and packaging foam harm the OZONE layer which protects life from ultraviolet radiation.

Pollution from industrial centers is found across the open countryside as well as in the seas. The poisonous elements that get into the environment include zinc, lead, arsenic, mercury, and cadmium. Waste contains materials that could be recycled instead of being thrown away.

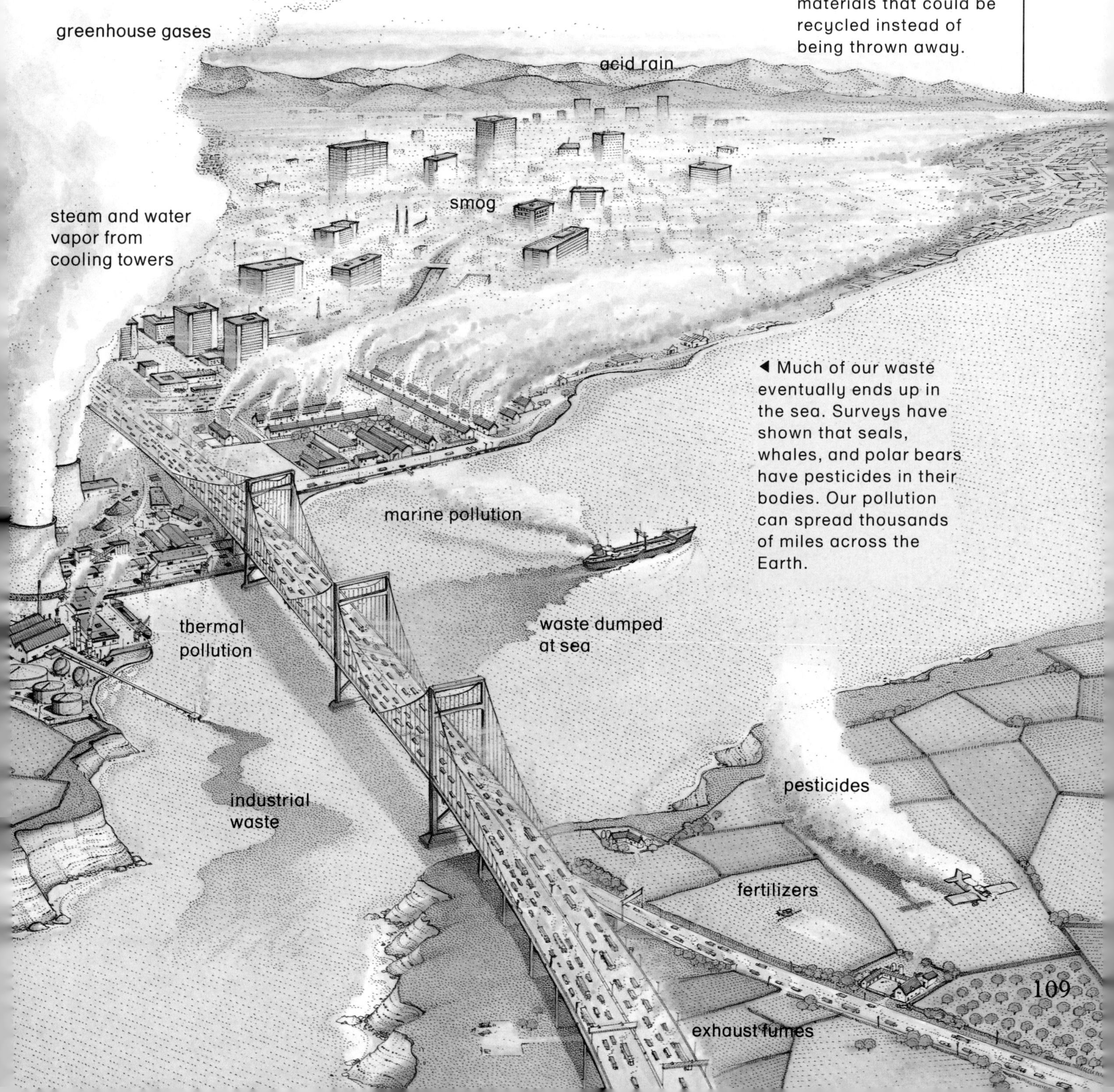

greenhouse gases

acid rain

smog

steam and water vapor from cooling towers

◀ Much of our waste eventually ends up in the sea. Surveys have shown that seals, whales, and polar bears have pesticides in their bodies. Our pollution can spread thousands of miles across the Earth.

marine pollution

thermal pollution

waste dumped at sea

industrial waste

pesticides

fertilizers

exhaust fumes

P

polymer

Polymers are formed by joining together lots of identical MOLECULES. Ethylene is a sweet-smelling gas. Join millions of ethylene molecules together and you have polyethylene, a PLASTIC.

positron

A positron is a tiny PARTICLE like an ELECTRON but with a positive charge. Positrons are antimatter because their charge is the opposite of normal MATTER.

▲ Potassium reacts violently with water. If a piece of potassium is dropped into water, it skates around the surface spitting flames.

potassium

Potassium is a light, soft METAL. Its symbol is K because the Latin for potassium is *kalium*. Potassium is such an active ELEMENT that it burns if you let air get at it. It is kept under OIL in a jar for safety. COMPOUNDS of potassium are important in the CHEMISTRY of life. They are also used in fertilizers, explosives, soap, and glass.

power

Power is the rate at which ENERGY is made to do work, or the rate at which one form of energy is converted to another form. The SI UNIT of energy is the JOULE (J). One joule used in a second equals one WATT of power. Much of the power we use comes from the COMBUSTION of PETROCHEMICALS. Electrical power can also be made from the energy of wind or waves. Dams across tidal rivers have been used to make tidal power.

▶ Light bulbs change electrical energy into light and heat. A light bulb that does this at the rate of 60 joules per second is given a power rating of 60 watts.

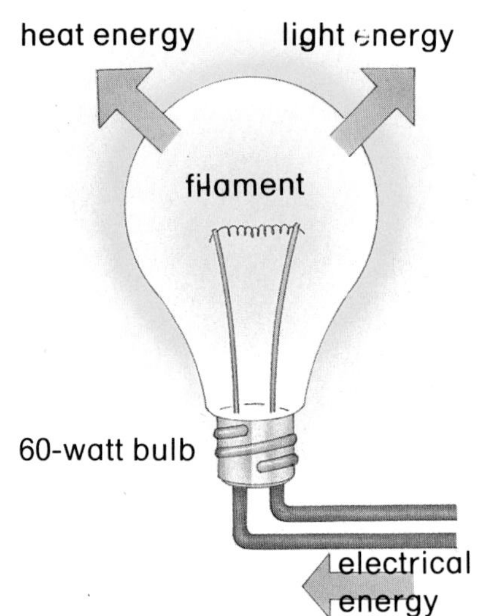

▼ Some of the immense power carried by waves in the sea can be changed into useful electrical energy by floats called ducks.

P

precipitation
Precipitation occurs when a fluid (a liquid or gas) forms as visible PARTICLES. When the water vapor in AIR turns back to drops of water to form RAIN, we have precipitation. Adding soda to hard WATER removes CALCIUM salts, causing them to form a cloudy precipitate of particles.

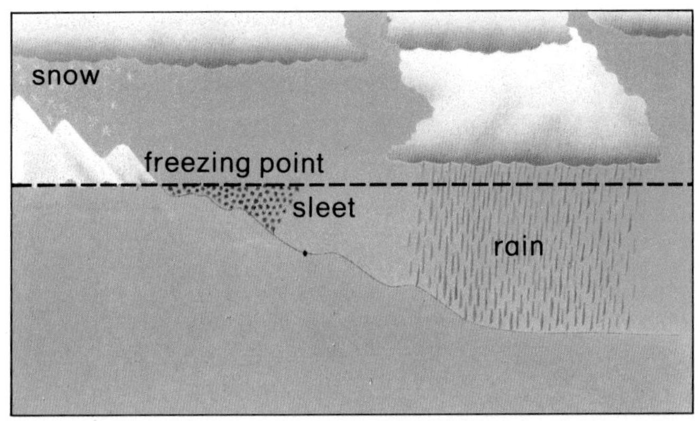

▲ Water condensing in clouds may fall as rain, snow, sleet or hail depending on the temperature of the air. These are all forms of precipitation.

pressure
Pressure is a measure of how hard a FORCE is pressing on a surface.

printing
The printing process makes many copies of text and pictures from a single original. Early methods of printing used letters (or drawings) that were higher than their background. Modern methods use a smooth printing plate. The unprinted (white) areas of the plate are kept moist, which keeps ink from sticking. The areas that are to be printed are kept dry, so the ink holds. The ink is transferred to paper as the plates roll over it.

prism
LIGHT passing through a prism is broken into its seven COLORS. Some prisms are three-sided columns of GLASS.

propane
Propane is a gas which can be DISTILLED when PETROCHEMICALS are refined. Under PRESSURE it becomes a liquid, which can be stored in metal bottles that dispense it as gas.

proton
The proton is a PARTICLE found in the nucleus of an ATOM. It is like a NEUTRON but a proton has a positive ELECTRIC charge and a neutron has no charge.

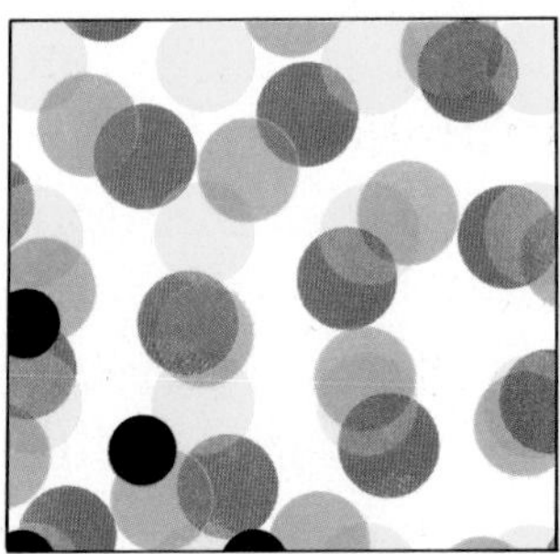

▶ A printed image is made from minute dots in only four colors. Together they give an impression that many more colors and shades are present.

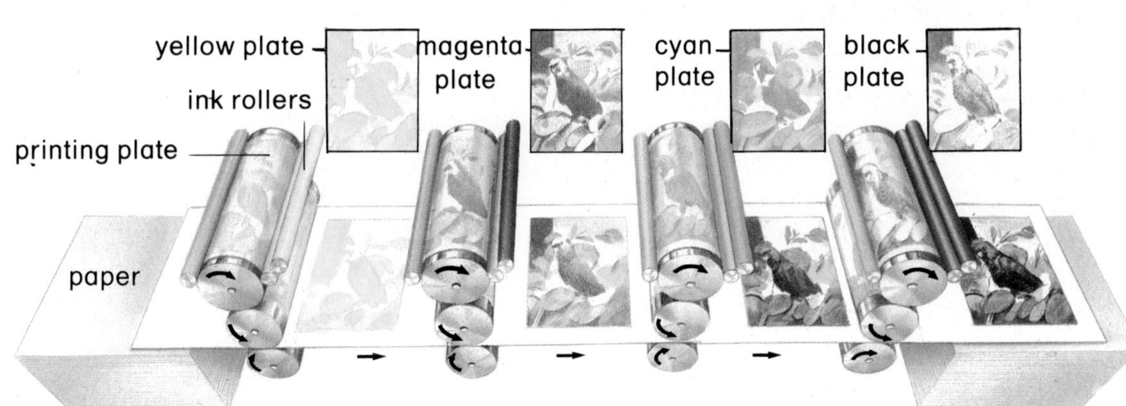

▶ Color printing uses four different colors of ink. A full-color image is built up from four different images printed one after another in yellow, magenta, cyan, and black.

pulsar

Pulsars are pulsating STARS. They give out RADIATION in pulses, usually about one pulse a second. Pulsars are believed to be spinning NEUTRON stars. Each pulsar weighs about as much as our SUN but is only 6 mi (10 km) across. This means that the DENSITY of a pulsar is very high.

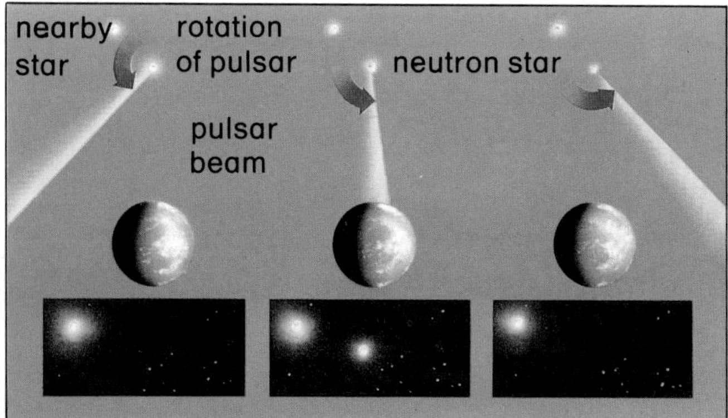

▲ As a pulsar spins, it sends a beam of radiation sweeping through space. When the beam hits Earth the pulsar appears to flash on. As the pulsar spins around, the beam goes off.

Pyrex

If normal GLASS is heated the hottest part becomes slightly larger than cooler parts. Because of this uneven EXPANSION the glass may break. Pyrex is a special glass that has about one-tenth of the silica (silicon dioxide) replaced with boron oxide. It expands much less when it is heated. This helps to protect it from cracking, so it is used as cookware and as heat-resistant glassware in laboratories.

DID YOU KNOW?

Boron is used to produce Pyrex, a heat-resistant glass. Other elements produce colored glass. Cobalt turns glass blue, manganese turns it violet, silver turns it yellow, iron turns it brown, gold turns it red, and iridium turns it black.

quark

Quarks are the smaller particles inside each PROTON and NEUTRON of an ATOM. They are held, or "glued," together by the force of massless gluons.

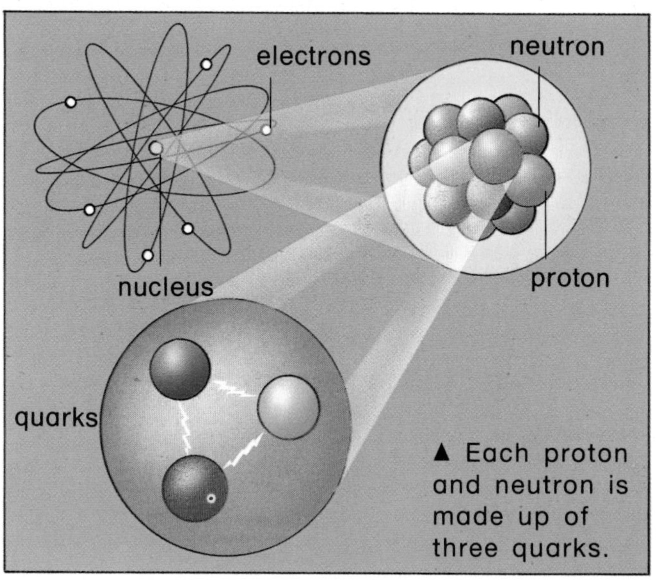

▲ Each proton and neutron is made up of three quarks.

quartz

Many of the crystals that you find in rocks at the seashore or on mountains are made of quartz. Quartz is silicon dioxide (formula SiO_2). Crystals of quartz are PIEZOELECTRIC.

quasar

Quasars occur at the centers of distant galaxies. They are millions of times brighter than normal galaxies.

radar

Radar is a system for measuring the position of distant objects such as ships or AIRCRAFT. MICROWAVES are sent out from an antenna. The REFLECTIONS from objects are picked up and used to show their position.

radiation see **pages 114 and 115**

radio

Radio waves are a form of ELECTROMAGNETIC RADIATION. The shortest radio waves measure about 0.04 in (1 mm) and the longest measure 60 mi (100 km).

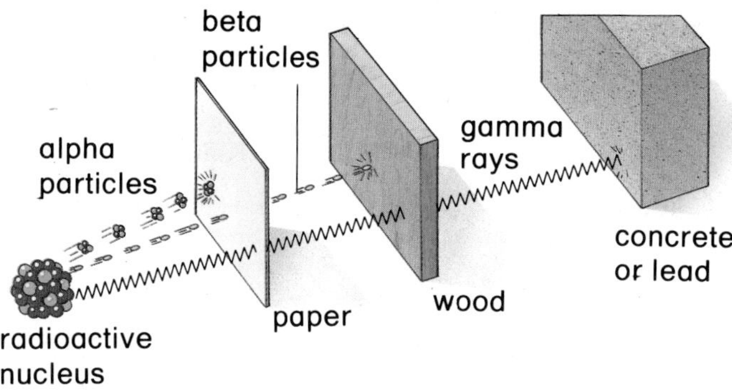

▲ Alpha particles are stopped by a thin sheet of paper. Beta particles are stopped by wood. Gamma rays are the most penetrating.

radioactivity

Radioactivity describes the RADIATION given off by nuclear materials. In 1899–1903 British physicist Ernest Rutherford found that there were three types of radiation. He called them alpha, beta, and gamma rays. Alpha rays are HELIUM nuclei. Beta rays are beams of ELECTRONS or POSITRONS. Gamma rays are similar to X-RAYS but have a shorter wavelength and can penetrate farther.

▼ To transmit live music on radio, the electrical signal from the studio microphones is combined with a radio wave, called a carrier wave. This is broadcast from a radio transmitter. The combined signal is picked up by a radio antenna and decoded to recreate the original sound.

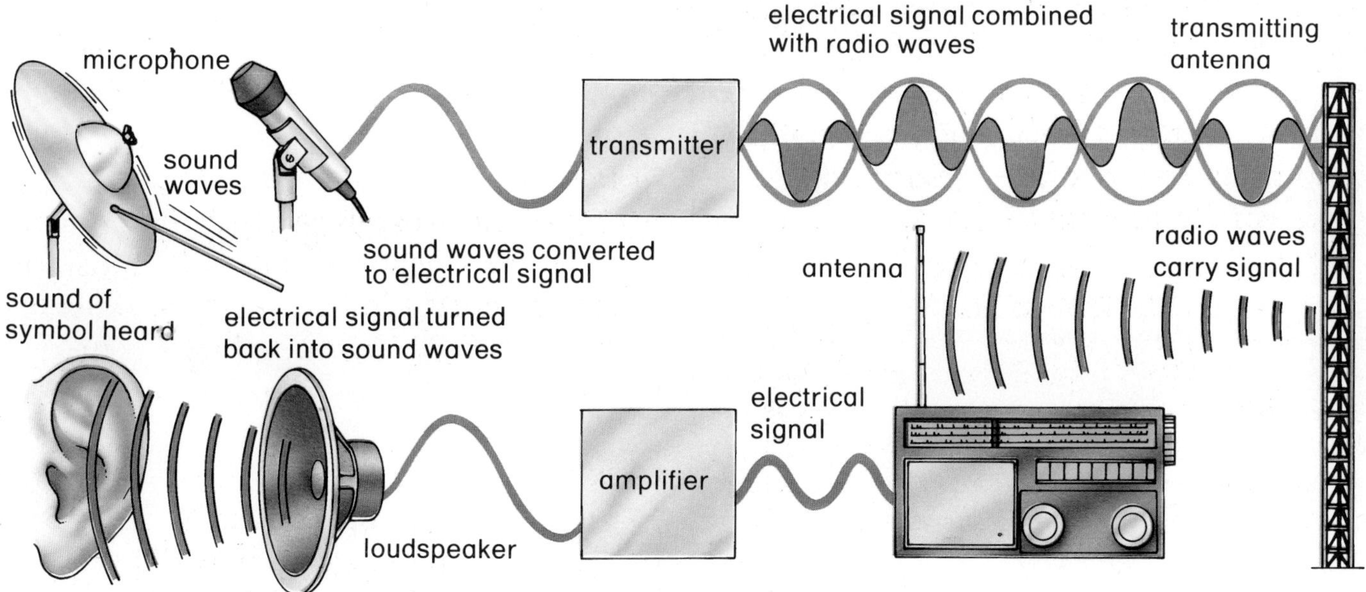

RADIATION

There are two types of radiation, radioactive and electromagnetic. There are many types of electromagnetic radiation, with enormous differences in wavelength. The longest is many miles. Radiation from a LIGHTNING flash makes your radio crackle. ULTRAVIOLET rays darken your skin. X-RAYS can shine right through your soft tissues. We can only see a tiny part of the whole range of radiation, the part we call LIGHT.

RADIO WAVES

The shortest radio waves lie next to microwaves. The shorter the wavelength, the clearer the sound that a radio transmission can carry. But longer wavelengths are less likely to be reflected by hills and buildings. VHF (FM) are very short waves. They are used for radio and TV broadcasting. Radio waves are also used in cellular telephones.

MICROWAVES

Microwaves are a type of electromagnetic radiation that can pass through many solid objects but are reflected by metal. Microwaves lie between heat rays (infrared) and radio waves. They can be produced by a device called a magnetron. A microwave oven uses microwaves to heat food. Microwaves are also used in radar.

ULTRAVIOLET

Ultraviolet radiation lies beyond violet light. The shortest ultraviolet rays are close to x-rays. The longer ultraviolet rays help make vitamin D in the skin and are used to treat people with vitamin D deficiency. The shorter rays are dangerous. The ozone layer protects the Earth from much of the ultraviolet radiation from the Sun.

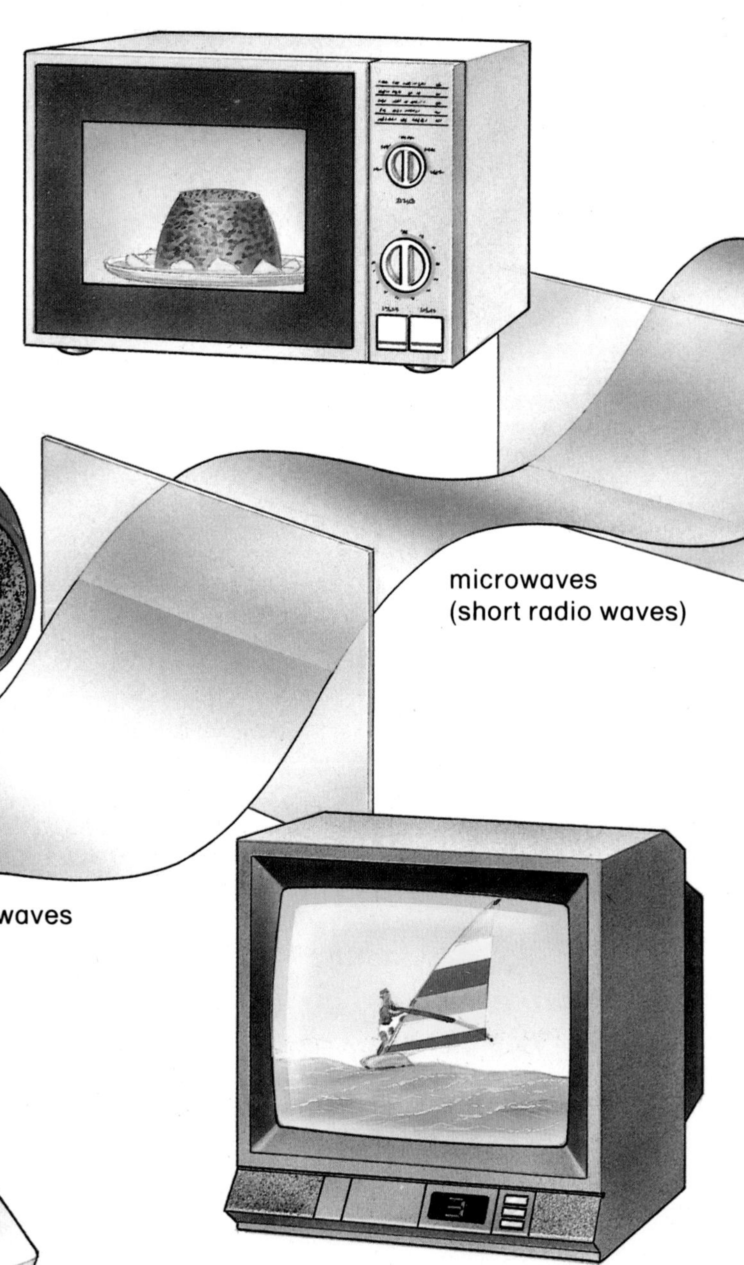

◀ Sunbathing exposes your skin to ultraviolet (UV) radiation. Longer UV wavelengths help make vitamin D in the body, by short UV rays damage the skin.

short wavelength (high frequency)

wavelength

gamma rays

ultraviolet

x-rays

visible light

infrared

▼ Radioactive materials are all around us. Even some of our food gives us radiation. This symbol is displayed wherever radioactive substances are used or stored.

X-RAYS

X-rays lie beyond ultraviolet. They can pass right through soft body tissues, so they can be used to see the bones inside your body. X-rays can harm living tissues, so doses are always kept to a minimum. Staff who operate x-ray machines use lead screens to protect them from too much radiation.

GAMMA RAYS

Gamma rays have the shortest wavelengths of all — they are measured in millionths of a millimeter. These rays can penetrate deeply into solid materials, and so they are used to obtain pictures of the inside of metal structures to check for faults. Gamma rays are highly dangerous to living cells. They are used to kill cancer cells in the human body and to sterilize certain foods.

INFRARED

Infrared radiation lies between red light and microwaves. Infrared radiation is heat. Though we cannot see infrared, we can feel the rays on our skin as heat.

LIGHT

Light rays form a very narrow band of radiation with a wavelength between 0.00016 and 0.0003 in (0.004 and 0.008 mm). These rays reflect from solid surfaces and are bent by lenses. This allows our eyes to focus light rays and see the objects around us.

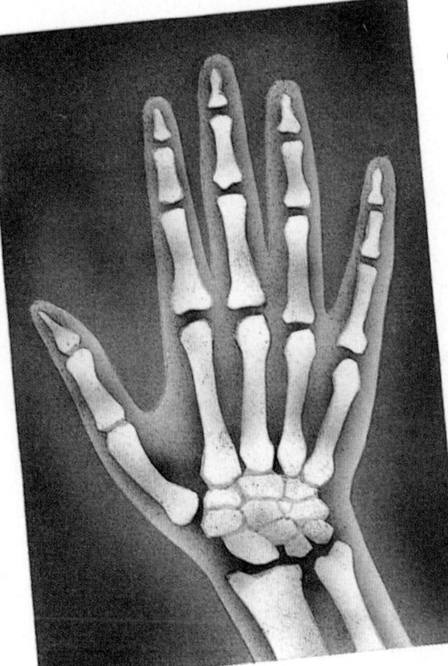

R

radio astronomy

Radio astronomy is the study of RADIO waves from space. STARS can give out RADIO WAVES more powerfully than LIGHT. Other objects may be dark but may give out strong radio signals. Radio TELESCOPES can detect the source of these waves even if the object is too far away or too dim to be seen with a normal telescope. NEBULAE, PULSARS, and QUASARS are strong radio transmitters. Telescopes that detect other forms of RADIATION, such as X-RAYS or gamma rays, are also used.

▼ The dish of a radio telescope collects radio signals from space and concentrates them onto an antenna positioned above the dish.

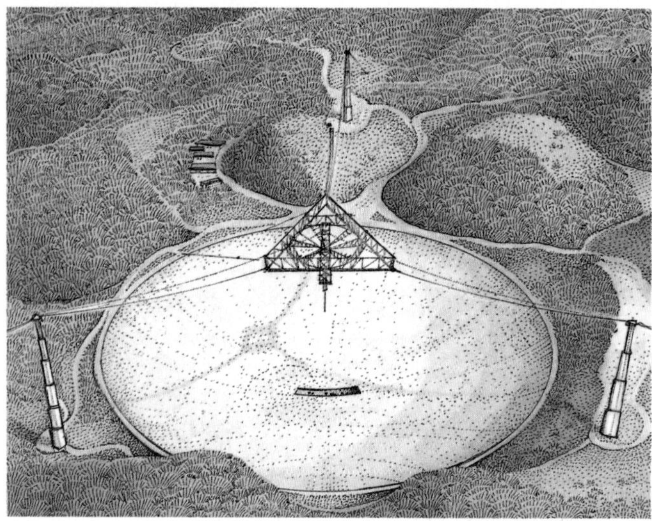

radium

Radium is a radioactive ELEMENT. COMPOUNDS of radium are always one or two degrees warmer than their surroundings because of this nuclear action. Radium was the first known radioactive material. It was discovered in 1898 by Marie and Pierre Curie. When Pierre was killed in a road accident Marie carried on the research alone. In later life she became ill because of all the harmful radiation she had absorbed.

radon

Like radium, radon is a radioactive ELEMENT. But radon is a gas. It seeps out of rocks underground. In areas where there is granite in the ground, it can collect in people's homes.

rain

Rain is a type of PRECIPITATION, formed when the TEMPERATURE is above freezing. The water vapor in the air condenses into tiny droplets around dust particles, forming clouds. When the droplets are large enough, they fall as rain.

rainbow

You see a rainbow when you look into rain with the SUN behind you. Each raindrop acts like a PRISM. As sunlight bounces off the inside of the raindrop it is split into the colors of the spectrum.

▼ A rainbow is caused by sunlight that is reflected and refracted by raindrops. The Sun must be behind you to let you see the rainbow.

recording see **pages 118 and 119**

recycling see **page 121**

red giant
A red giant is a huge, old STAR, cooler and far larger than our SUN.

reflection
A reflection is an image of an object formed in a MIRROR as LIGHT rays bounce off the shiny surface. If the mirror is distorted, so is the reflection. SOUND waves and other forms of RADIATION can be reflected off solid surfaces.

refraction
LIGHT travels at a different VELOCITY in different substances. This causes the light rays to bend. This is refraction. LENSES refract light, as light rays travel more slowly through GLASS.

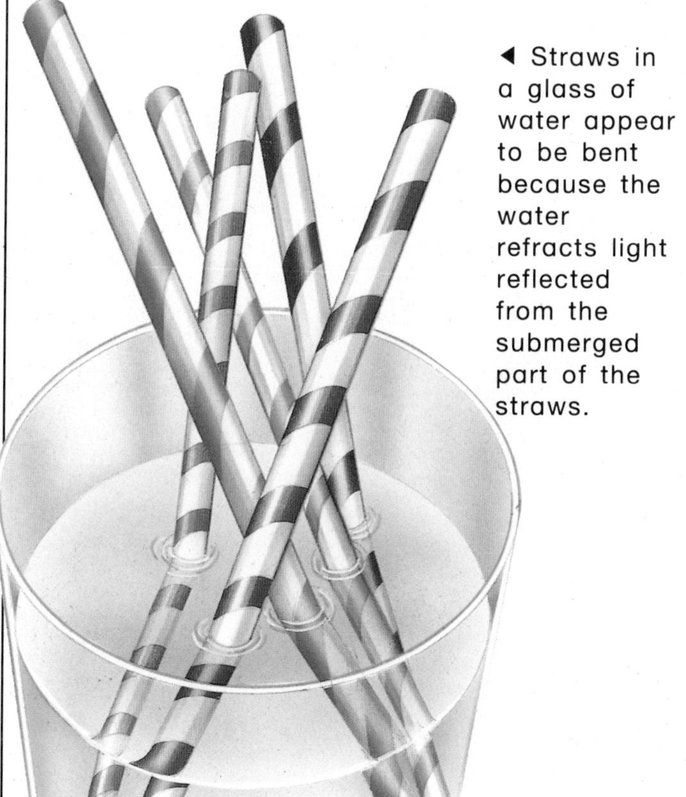

◀ Straws in a glass of water appear to be bent because the water refracts light reflected from the submerged part of the straws.

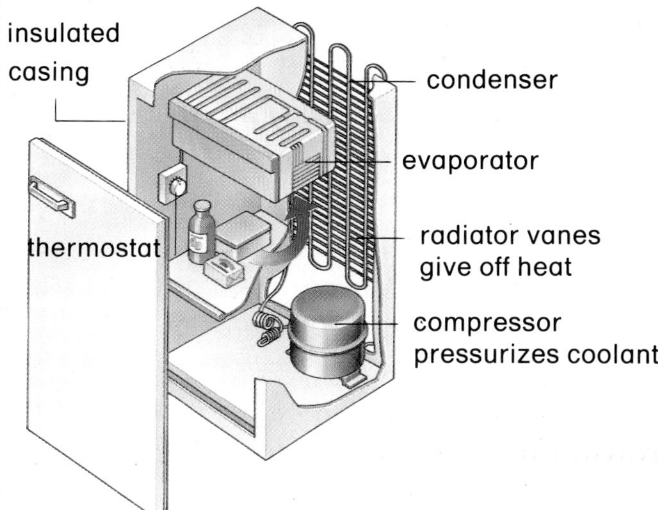

▲ Heat inside refrigerator rises to evaporator. Liquid coolant moves through evaporator and turns to gas. Compressor pumps gas to condenser, which releases the heat and changes the coolant back to a liquid.

refrigerator
When a liquid changes to a gas it takes in ENERGY. When the gas cools to a liquid, energy is given out again. These two effects are used to keep a refrigerator cool. A liquid coolant is pumped through pipes in the refrigerator. It absorbs heat from the inside and turns into a gas. The gas is compressed to a liquid in the condenser and the heat is released at the back of the refrigerator. The liquid is then pumped back inside to be used again.

relativity
The theory of relativity was developed by Albert Einstein. He proved that time on an object passes more slowly the faster the object is traveling. This can only be detected on objects moving at almost the speed of LIGHT. The theory also shows that MATTER can be converted into ENERGY. The famous equation $E = mc^2$ shows that MASS (m), multiplied by the speed of LIGHT (c) squared, produces energy (E). A tiny bit of matter can become a lot of energy.

RECORDING

Recording means making a long-lasting version of something fleeting or short-lived. The word is usually taken to mean a SOUND recording. Our ears detect sound vibrations. They are heard – and gone — in a fraction of a second. Making a recording is a way of permanently storing the sound. There are three main forms of storage. One is on a vinyl record. The second is on magnetic tape. The third method of recording is on a compact disc, which can be scanned by a LASER.

COMPACT DISCS

Tiny pits embossed in a layer of aluminum on a compact disc record a digital sound signal. A laser scans the disc.

HI-FI SYSTEMS

A stack system has a radio, turntable for vinyl discs, a CD unit, and a cassette unit below. Some hi-fis have a second cassette.

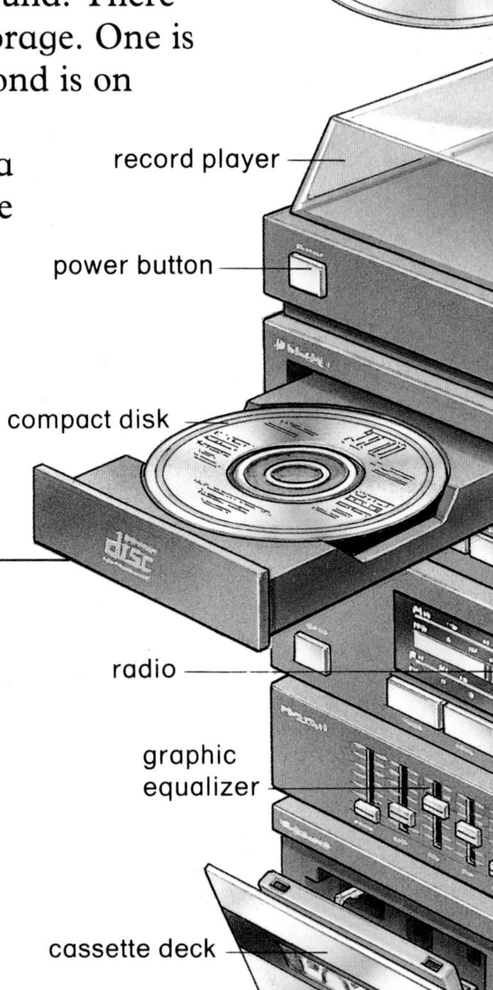

TAPE CASSETTES

Tape cassettes are used for analog recordings and also for high-quality DAT (digital audio tape). Signals are stored as magnetic impulses on the tape. The tape is drawn past the head by a pinch-wheel at a carefully controlled speed.

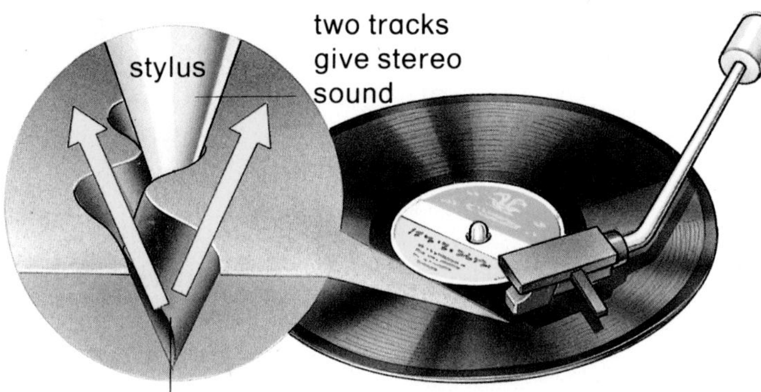

DID YOU KNOW?

The first recording of human speech was made by Thomas Edison in 1877. He said the words: "Mary had a little lamb." The first tape recorder was patented in Denmark in 1898. The long-playing (LP) vinyl disc was first sold in 1948. Vinyl records have now started to go out of production. They are being replaced by CDs.

R

VINYL RECORDS

The groove on an LP is a copy of the sound wave made at the time of the recording. The stylus moves in two directions to give separate signals for the two speakers.

LOUDSPEAKERS

The loudspeaker changes the electrical signals (from the CD, disc, or cassette) back into sound. The speaker producing low notes is the woofer; high notes are recreated by the smaller tweeter.

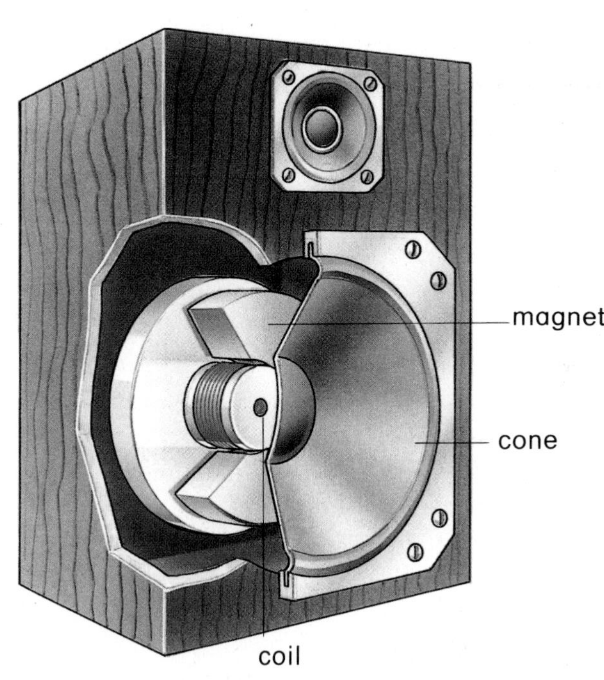

RECORDING SOUND

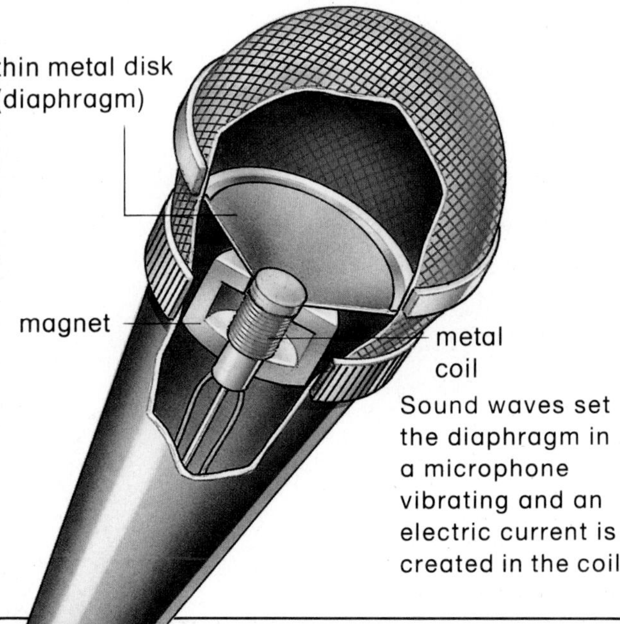

Sound waves set the diaphragm in a microphone vibrating and an electric current is created in the coil.

DIGITAL RECORDING

A digital recording system breaks the smooth sound wave down into separate bits of information. The sound wave is "sampled" against a grid. Each point on the wave is given a digital value. The digital code is stored and may be used to make a recording.

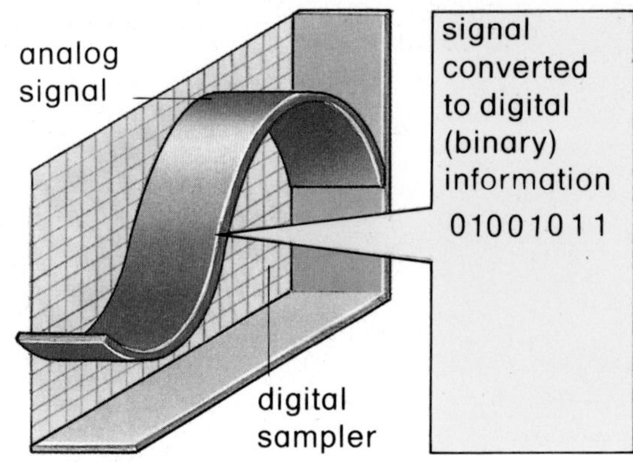

R

resonance

An object vibrates if it moves back and forth. A series of "pushes" at exactly the right time makes the vibration stronger. This is resonance. You can see it work in a playground. If you push a swing once as it starts each swing forward, it will go higher and higher.

Richter scale

The Richter scale measures the strength of an EARTHQUAKE. Each number up the scale represents an earthquake ten times more powerful than the previous one. The scale was invented in 1935 by geologist Charles Richter. See **seismograph**.

rivers

When RAIN falls, some of it soaks into the ground until it meets a layer of ROCK. This is groundwater. When hilly ground is waterlogged the rainwater runs down the slopes and forms small streams. Each stream collects more water off the slopes as it flows down and joins with other streams. Eventually a river is formed. The river slowly cuts a valley out of the hills by EROSION as it flows down the slope. As the river flows over the flatter ground towards the coast it becomes wider and slower. Eventually it flows into the ocean.

▼ The course of a river changes as the water carves new channels through the ground. Bends in the river sometimes form oxbow lakes.

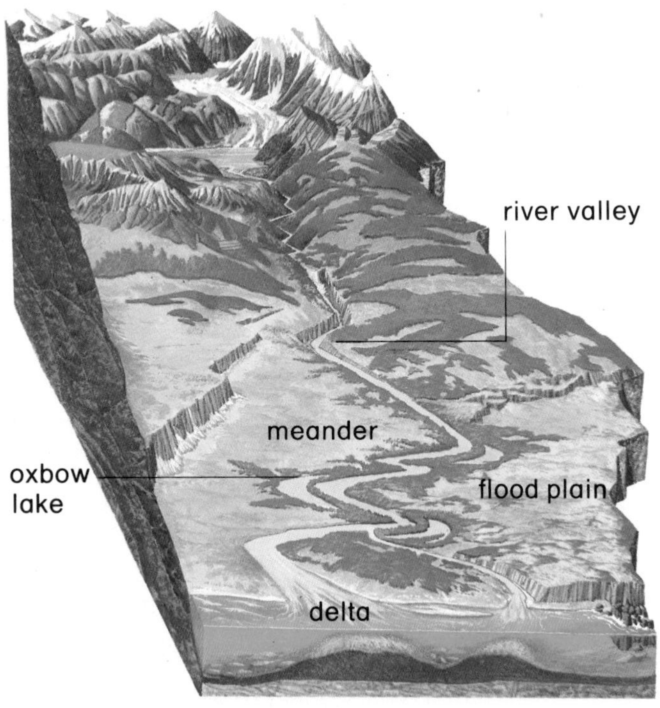

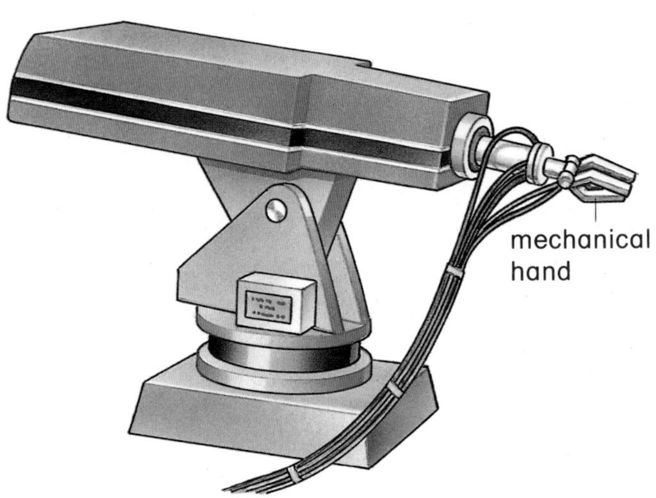

▲ Robots are often used in factories to carry out a precise series of operations. Their actions are controlled by a computer program.

robot

A robot is a machine that can carry out MOVEMENTS which look like those of a human arm or hand. The movements are produced by little pumps or levers. These actions are controlled by a COMPUTER. Robots are widely used in factories. Some assemble cars, for example.

rock

Rock is a hard substance found in the EARTH's crust. Stones and sand are broken pieces of rock. Many rocks are made up of tiny MINERAL grains.

RECYCLING

In nature, waste materials are regularly recycled, keeping the system balanced. Modern society throws unwanted items away. This is a waste of useful land and resources. Recycled goods take less energy to produce than items made from raw materials, so recycling saves ENERGY and resources.

▼ A large proportion of our garbage consists of paper and cardboard, which can easily be recycled. Vegetable matter comes next — this can become compost to fertilize soil.

▼ Glass, metals, and plastics are valuable materials which end up as garbage. They could be reclaimed and reused. There is very little in our waste that could not be put to use.

DID YOU KNOW?

Layers of garbage in a dump are covered with clay or soil. Perforated pipes collect the methane gas produced as the waste decays. The methane can be used to provide power.

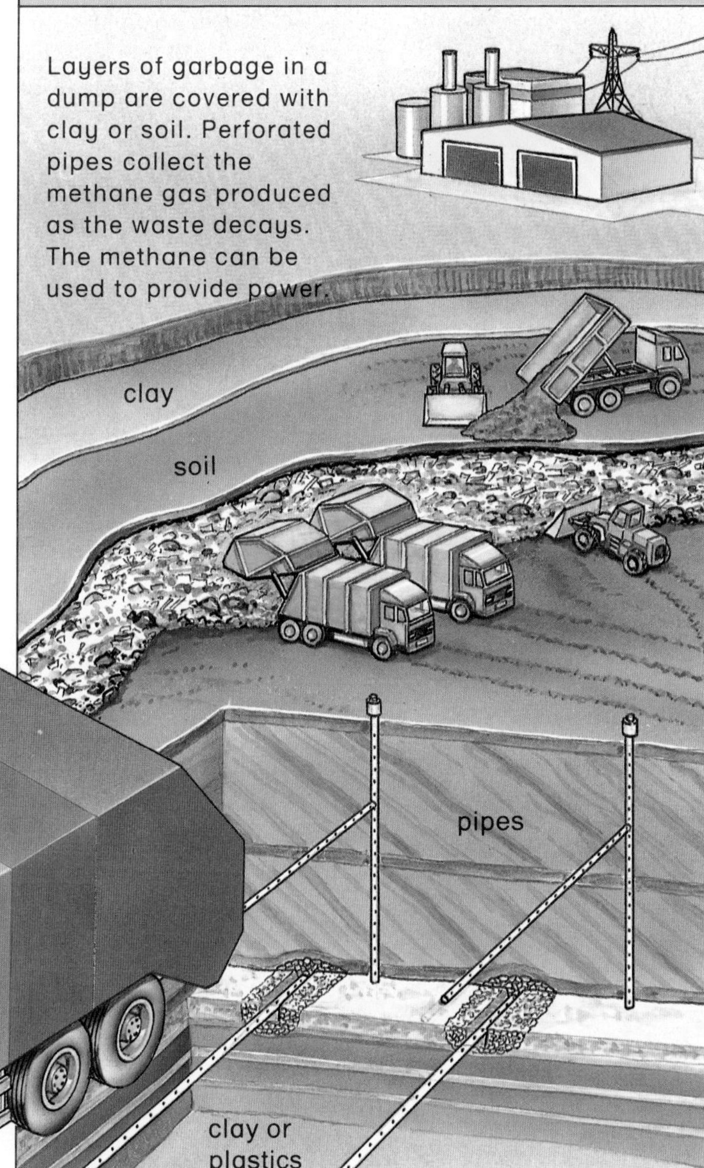

▶ Some towns have a policy for recycling waste. People separate out aluminum cans, glass bottles, and newspapers for recycling. But only one percent of our garbage is recycled. We each throw away more than a pound of trash every day!

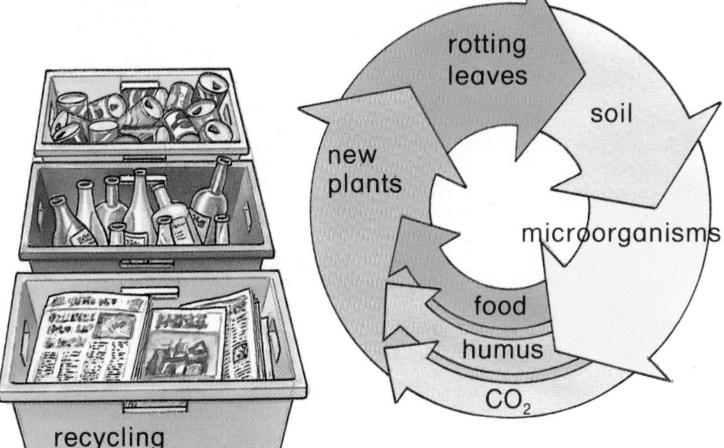

◀ In nature, a waste material from one form of life becomes food for the next in line. When a plant dies it is broken down into its basic components by tiny organisms in the soil. These raw materials are taken up by other forms of life. In this way the organic wastes are recycled through the system.

R

rocket

The simplest rockets are FIREWORKS. They were invented in ancient China and spread to Europe almost 1,000 years ago. Inside a rocket is a FUEL and an OXYGEN source. As the fuel burns it expands and produces PRESSURE on the inside of the rocket. The pressure on the front of the rocket is not balanced by pressure at the tail, because the bottom is open and the hot gases can escape. As a result, a jet of gas is created at the tail and the rocket is forced upward. A fireworks rocket uses a solid fuel, like GUNPOWDER. For better control, a rocket needs liquid fuel so that the supply can be turned on or off. The first liquid-fuel rocket was launched in 1926 by Robert Goddard, in Massachusetts. Modern space rockets are built in sections, or stages, each with its own engine and fuel supply. The first stage is huge and is used to push the rocket off the ground. The next stage carries the rocket out of the Earth's atmosphere. The third stage gives the rocket enough speed to go into ORBIT. The rocket drops the first two stages when their fuel has been used up.

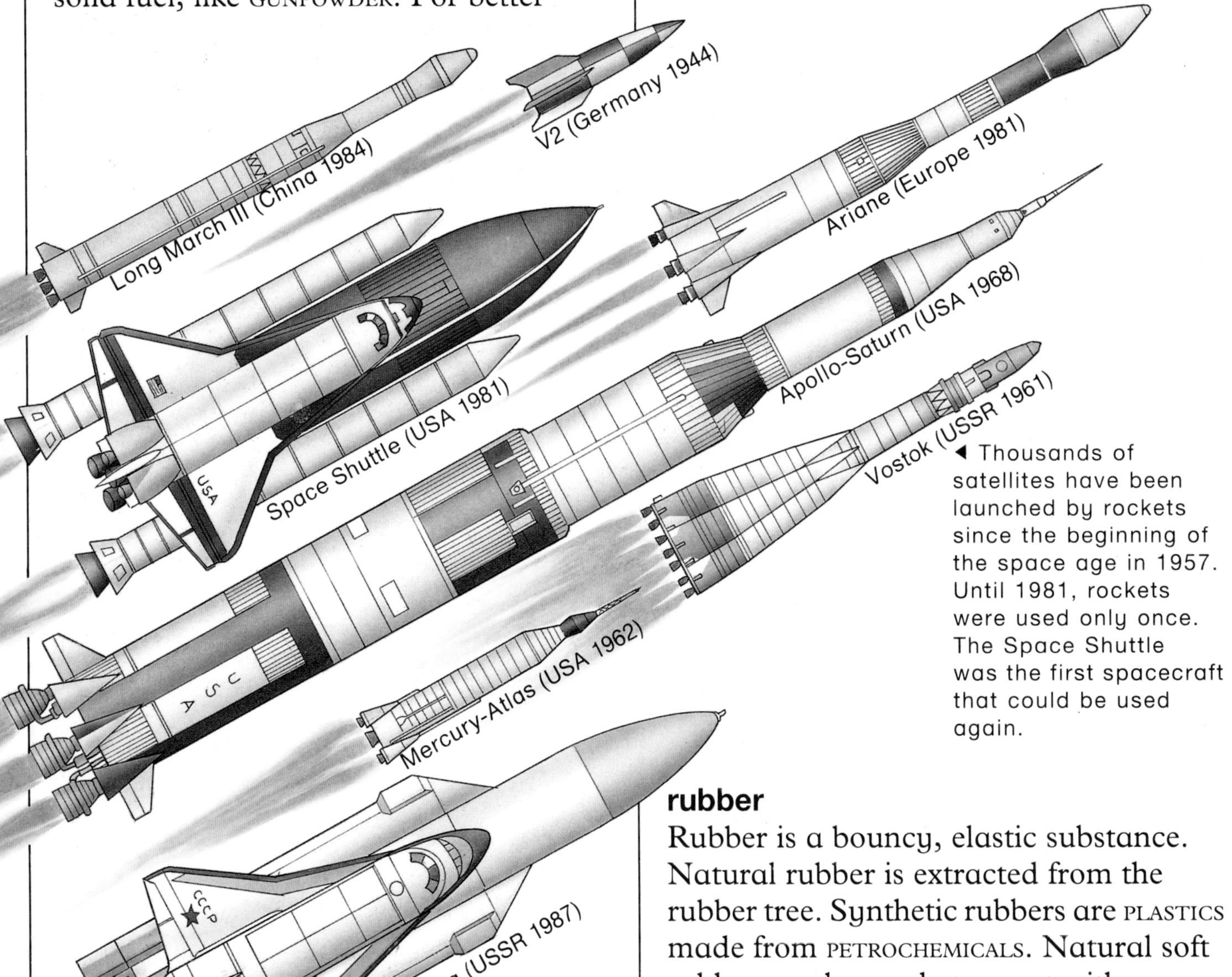

◀ Thousands of satellites have been launched by rockets since the beginning of the space age in 1957. Until 1981, rockets were used only once. The Space Shuttle was the first spacecraft that could be used again.

rubber

Rubber is a bouncy, elastic substance. Natural rubber is extracted from the rubber tree. Synthetic rubbers are PLASTICS made from PETROCHEMICALS. Natural soft rubber can be made to react with SULFUR to strengthen it.

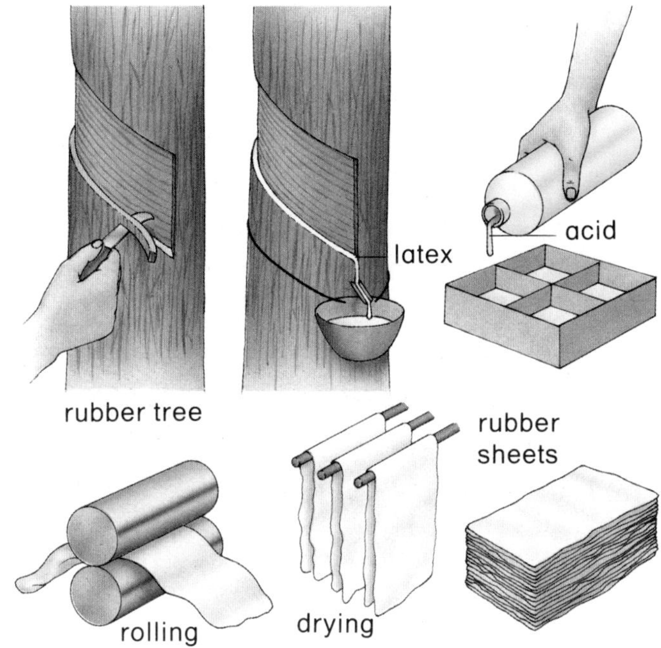

▲ Natural rubber begins its life as latex collected from rubber trees. It is then thickened by adding acid or sulfur, rolled into sheets and dried.

rust

Rust forms when IRON reacts with OXYGEN and WATER. The iron forms a flaky brownish crust of iron oxide. This is a form of corrosion. Iron ORE in the Earth's crust is iron combined with oxygen. In an ironworks, the oxygen is removed to leave us with pure iron. So when rust forms the iron is returning to its original state. Stainless steel is an iron ALLOY containing CHROMIUM, which does not rust.

▼ The steel in a car's body reacts with moist air to form rust. Cars are therefore covered with a protective coat of paint. If this is damaged, the car begins to rust.

salt

Common table salt that we use on food is sodium chloride, a COMPOUND of atoms of SODIUM and CHLORINE. Salt is important for keeping the body healthy. There are many other chemical salts. All ACIDS contain HYDROGEN, and if the hydrogen atom is replaced with a METAL atom a salt is formed. Sodium chloride is produced when an acid (hydrogen chloride) reacts with an alkali (metallic sodium hydroxide). See **acids and alkalis**.

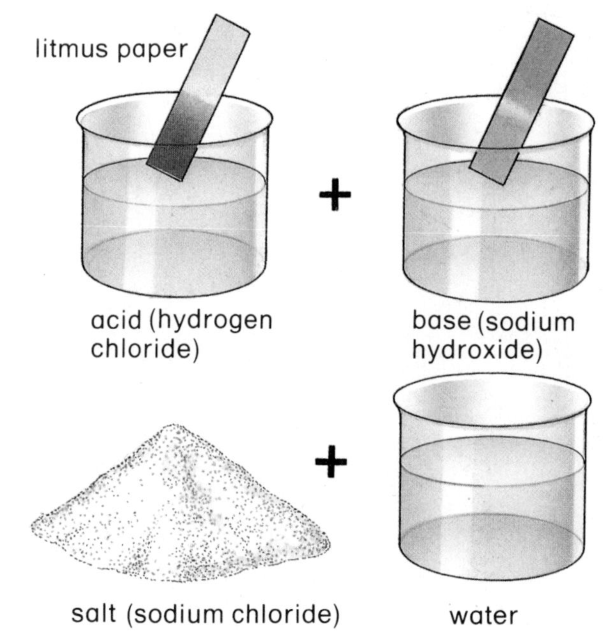

▲ The reaction to produce common salt is shown above. Water is the by-product of the reaction and is evaporated to obtain the salt crystals.

▲ Artificial satellites relay telephone calls and television programs around the world. They also record the world's changing weather and collect information for scientists.

satellite

Satellites are small bodies that are in ORBIT around larger ones. The MOON orbits the Earth. It is the Earth's natural satellite. In 1957, the USSR launched the first artificial satellite, *Sputnik 1*, which orbited the Earth. Since then many other satellites have been launched. The most important uses of satellites are surveying the Earth, helping ships and planes to navigate, and transmitting RADIO and TELEVISION signals from one country to another.

Saturn

Saturn is the sixth planet, famous for its rings. It is the farthest planet known to ancient astronomers. It is big enough to contain 752 planets the size of our EARTH. See **Solar System**.

seismograph

A seismograph is used to measure MOVEMENTS of the EARTH. It has a large weight on a bar suspended by a spring. As the Earth trembles in an EARTHQUAKE, the weight has enough INERTIA to keep still while the rest of the equipment moves. A pen traces the movements onto paper.

▼ Seismographs measure the shock waves produced by an earthquake. Both horizontal and vertical movements of the Earth's crust are measured. A pen traces out the pattern of movement on a roll of paper.

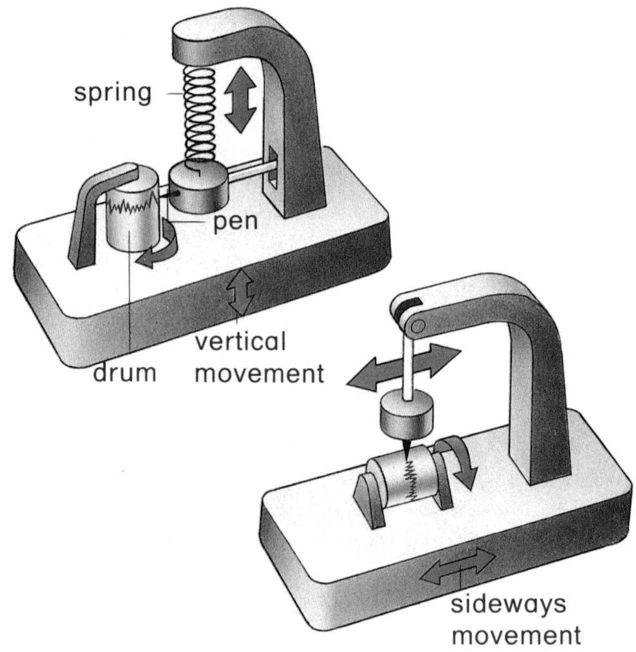

semiconductor

Semiconductors are special minerals that allow the ELECTRONS that produce an ELECTRIC CURRENT to flow in one direction, but not in the opposite direction. In some semiconductors the direction of the current can be switched by an electric charge. Computers are made up of a large number of semiconductors. The way they control and switch the flow of electricity enables computers to store data and make calculations at high speed. See **transistor**.

SHADOWS

Shadows form when solid objects block the LIGHT. Your own body casts a shadow on a sunny day. A RAIN shadow is the area of land downwind from a line of hills. The rain falls on the hills, and the rain-shadow area has little rainfall. TELEVISION "shadows" are areas where a TV signal is blocked by mountains or tall buildings and reception is poor.

▶ The length of a shadow depends on the angle between the Sun and the ground. At the equator near midday the Sun is overhead, and people stand in their own shadows. North of the equator the Sun is in the east at dawn and in the west at dusk. At midday it is to the south. If you remember this you can tell which direction you are facing when the Sun is shining.

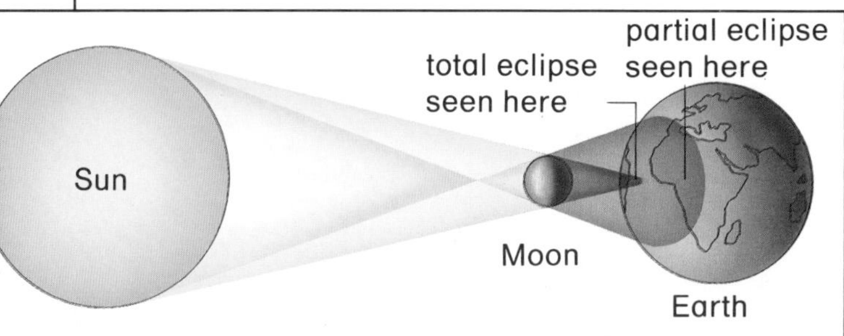

▲ The Moon sometimes blocks out the Sun, and its shadow falls on the Earth. We see a solar eclipse. The whole scene goes as dark as night until the Sun peeks past the Moon again. If the Moon is on the far side of the Earth, the Earth's shadow can fall on the Moon and the Moon disappears. This is a lunar eclipse.

▼ Shadows can be used in theater. There is a strong tradition of shadow puppets in Thailand, for example. You can cut paper shapes to produce shadow puppets, and even your hands can make many animals. Rabbits, dogs, and even a flying bird are easy to make and use to illustrate a story.

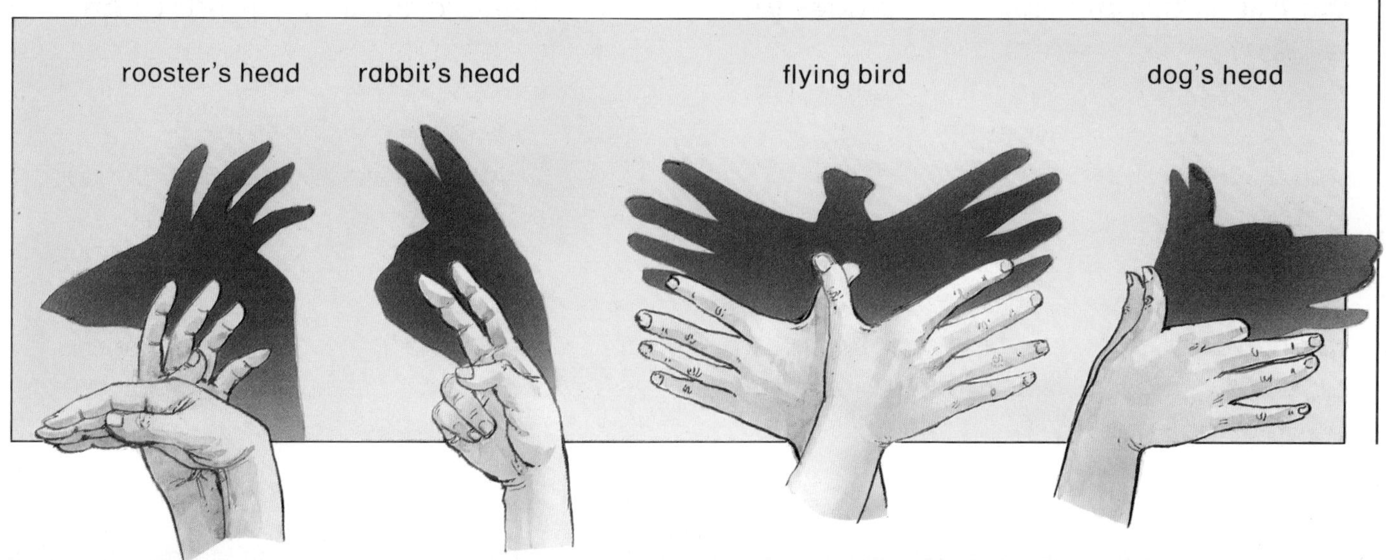

S

SI units

SI stands for Système International. It describes the international system of units of MEASUREMENT which is used by scientists around the world. There are seven basic units, each of which has a standard definition. For example, the standard kilogram is a cylinder of a platinum ALLOY. SI units have been used since 1960.

unit name and symbol	physical quantity
meter (m)	length
kilogram (kg)	mass
second (s)	time
ampere (a)	electric current
Kelvin (K)	thermodynamic temperature
candela (cd)	luminous intensity
mole (mol)	amount of substance

▲ These are the seven basic SI units. All other units used in science and technology, such as watts and joules, stem from these basic units.

silver

Silver is a white shiny precious metal. It is quite soft, but does not react with OXYGEN, so it lasts a long time. Silver eventually turns black because it reacts with sulfur gases in the air to form silver sulfide, which is dark.

siphon

Water sometimes flows uphill, for example in a pipe if the far end of the pipe hangs below the water's surface. You can siphon a liquid by sucking it into a tube and then placing the end of the tube in another container lower down. The water will flow into the second container until both containers have the same level of liquid.

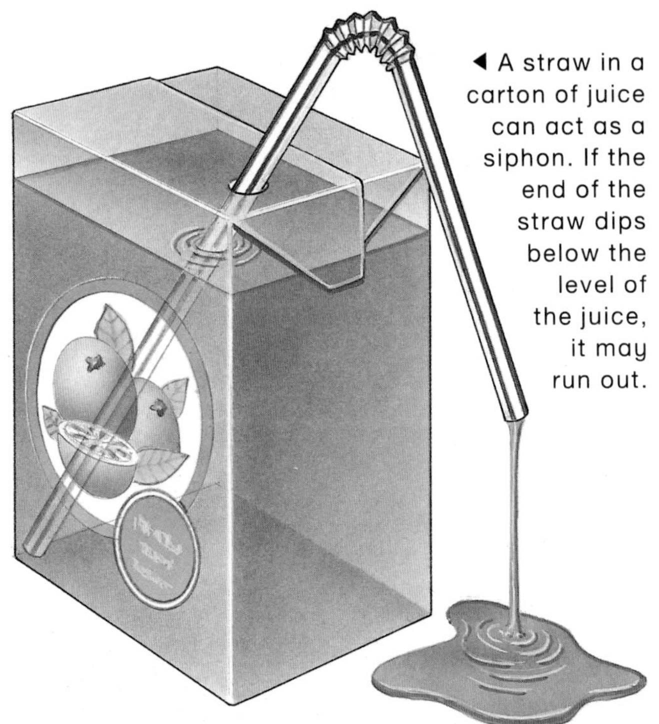

◀ A straw in a carton of juice can act as a siphon. If the end of the straw dips below the level of the juice, it may run out.

soap

Soaps are alkali SALTS of fatty ACIDS (MOLECULES found in animal fat and plant OIL). Soaps made with POTASSIUM are soft. Soaps of SODIUM are hard, and soaps of other metals do not dissolve in WATER. Soaps lift grease from skin and clothes.

sodium

Sodium is a soft white METAL. It is very reactive, and it burns if it comes into contact with WATER. Sodium is used in NUCLEAR REACTORS to carry heat. Your body needs a little bit of sodium to stay healthy.

software

Software is the name given to the programs that you run in a COMPUTER. The computer system itself is the HARDWARE.

▲ The solar panels on this car trap the energy of sunlight and use it to make electric power. Solar energy does not cause pollution.

solar energy
Most ENERGY comes from the Sun. Humans are powered by this stored energy when they eat food. A COAL fire is releasing ancient solar energy, too. Modern solar cells collect sunlight and turn it directly into ELECTRICITY. They provide solar power for SPACECRAFT. Solar cells have also been used for small cars.

Solar System see **pages 128 and 129**

sonar
Sonar is like RADAR. But instead of using RADIO waves, sonar uses ULTRASOUND. A "ping" is sent out by a ship and its ECHO is recorded. COMPUTERS measure the time between the sound and the echo to work out how far an object is from the ship.

▼ Sonar is used by ships to measure water depth. The seafloor is shown on a TV screen.

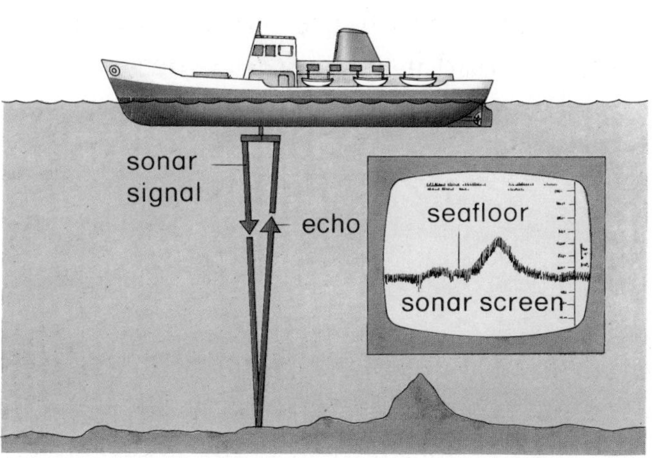

sound see **page 131**

sound barrier
SOUND waves move away from an AIRCRAFT in all directions. If the plane is flying at the speed of sound it catches up with the sound waves. They build up in front of the plane as a shock wave — the sound barrier. Planes flying faster than sound leave a loud bang, called a sonic boom, behind them. It is caused as the plane breaks through the sound barrier and the shock waves reach the ground.

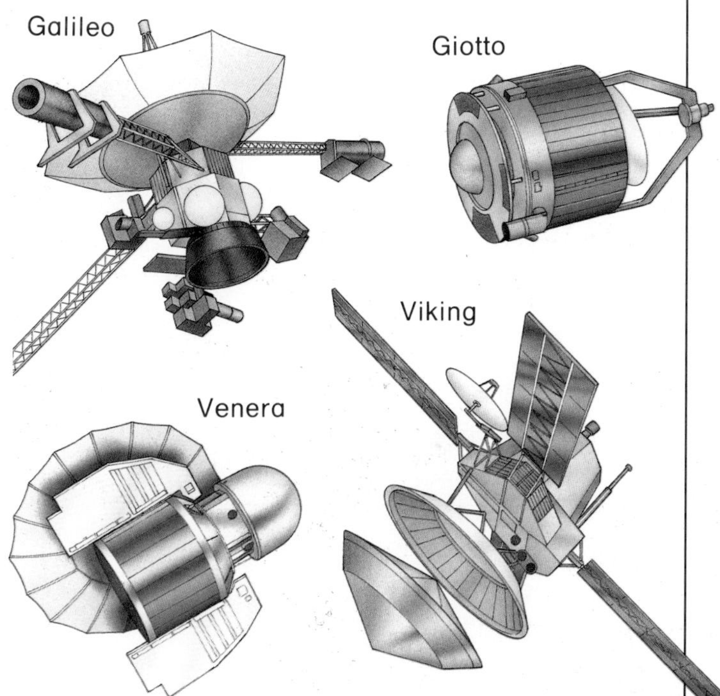

▲ *Giotto* was the first spacecraft to fly alongside a comet, Halley's Comet, in 1986. *Venera* landed on Venus, *Viking* searched for life on Mars, and *Galileo* is the latest spacecraft to visit Jupiter.

spacecraft
A spacecraft is an object designed to fly through space. Spacecraft include SATELLITES, which are launched by a ROCKET into ORBIT around the EARTH, and vehicles that travel far into the SOLAR SYSTEM to send back information about the PLANETS.

SOLAR SYSTEM

The Solar System measures 7.5 billion mi (12 billion km) from one side to the other. It consists of nine planets which orbit the SUN, plus millions of asteroids, METEORS, and COMETS. Most of the PLANETS have moons of their own. The surface of the Sun is covered with waves of hot gas. Some project out from the surface. These huge FLAMES are often larger than the Earth.

DID YOU KNOW?

Most of the planets are named after the gods of ancient times. Mars was the god of war, and Venus the goddess of love and peace. Mercury was the winged messenger of the gods, and Saturn was the ancient god of farming. Saturn was the outermost planet known to the ancient world. Jupiter was lord of them all. Pluto, the outermost planet known, was discovered in 1930. Its orbit sometimes brings it closer to the Earth than Neptune. There may be another planet beyond Pluto!

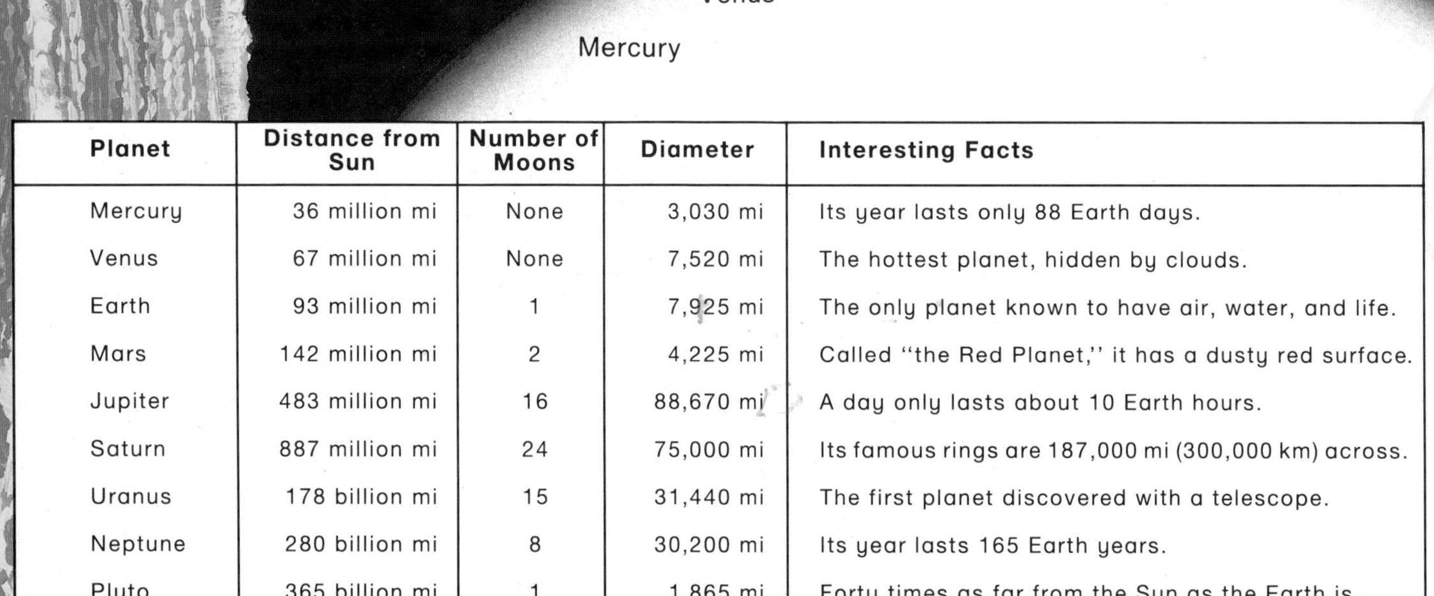

Planet	Distance from Sun	Number of Moons	Diameter	Interesting Facts
Mercury	36 million mi	None	3,030 mi	Its year lasts only 88 Earth days.
Venus	67 million mi	None	7,520 mi	The hottest planet, hidden by clouds.
Earth	93 million mi	1	7,925 mi	The only planet known to have air, water, and life.
Mars	142 million mi	2	4,225 mi	Called "the Red Planet," it has a dusty red surface.
Jupiter	483 million mi	16	88,670 mi	A day only lasts about 10 Earth hours.
Saturn	887 million mi	24	75,000 mi	Its famous rings are 187,000 mi (300,000 km) across.
Uranus	178 billion mi	15	31,440 mi	The first planet discovered with a telescope.
Neptune	280 billion mi	8	30,200 mi	Its year lasts 165 Earth years.
Pluto	365 billion mi	1	1,865 mi	Forty times as far from the Sun as the Earth is.

JUPITER'S RED SPOT

A gigantic swirling mass of red gas that can be seen near the equator of Jupiter is known as the Great Red Spot. It was first seen over 300 years ago when primitive telescopes were used. Jupiter also has a smaller Yellow Spot.

ASTEROIDS AND RING SYSTEMS

Between Mars and Jupiter there is a belt of rocky bodies called asteroids. They range up to 620 mi (1,000 km) in diameter. Some, like Eros, have passed quite close to Earth. Saturn became famous for its giant ring system when Galileo discovered it with his new telescope in the early 1600s. In recent years other ring systems have been found. There is even a very fine ring around Jupiter.

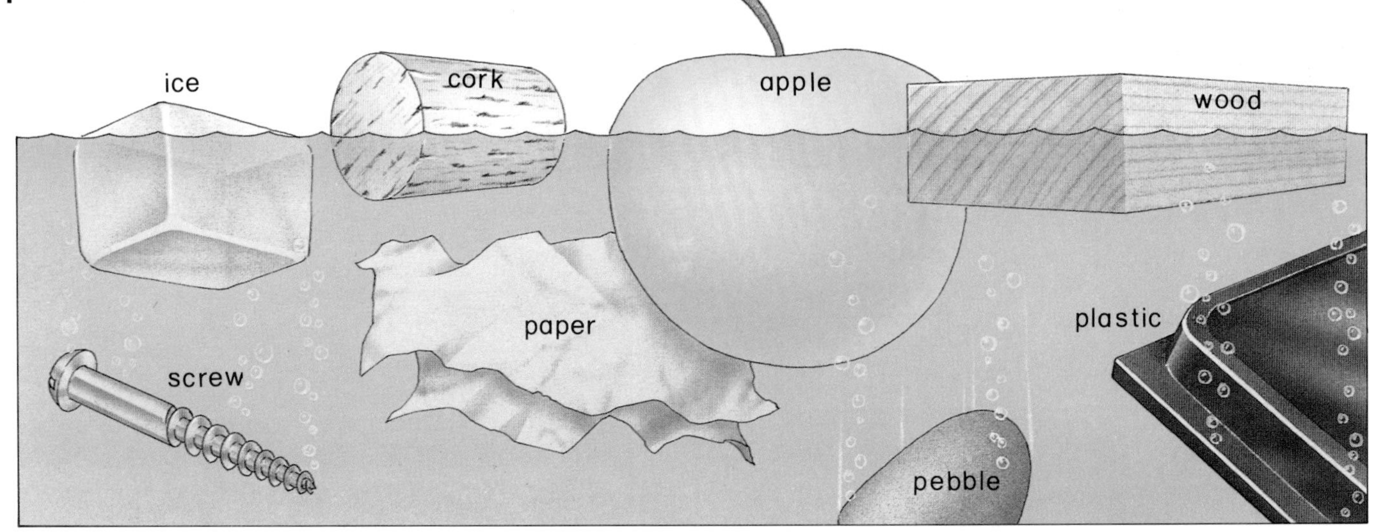

▲ Ice, apples, and most woods have a specific gravity lower than that of water, so they float. Stone and most metals have a specific gravity which is higher than water's, so they sink.

Space Shuttle

The Space Shuttle is a special SPACECRAFT which can be sent into space and then land back on Earth like a plane. The Shuttle can be used for many flights, whereas normal ROCKETS can be used only once. The Shuttle is used for launching SATELLITES or space probes. It can stay in ORBIT for a few days, then re-enter the Earth's ATMOSPHERE and glide back to land on a special runway. The first Shuttle was *Columbia*, which was launched by the U.S. in 1981.

specific gravity

Specific gravity is the MASS of a volume of any substance compared with the mass of the same volume of WATER. Something with a specific gravity of more than 1.0 has a greater DENSITY than water, and it sinks. At less than 1.0 it has a lower density, and it floats. Specific gravity is also called relative density.

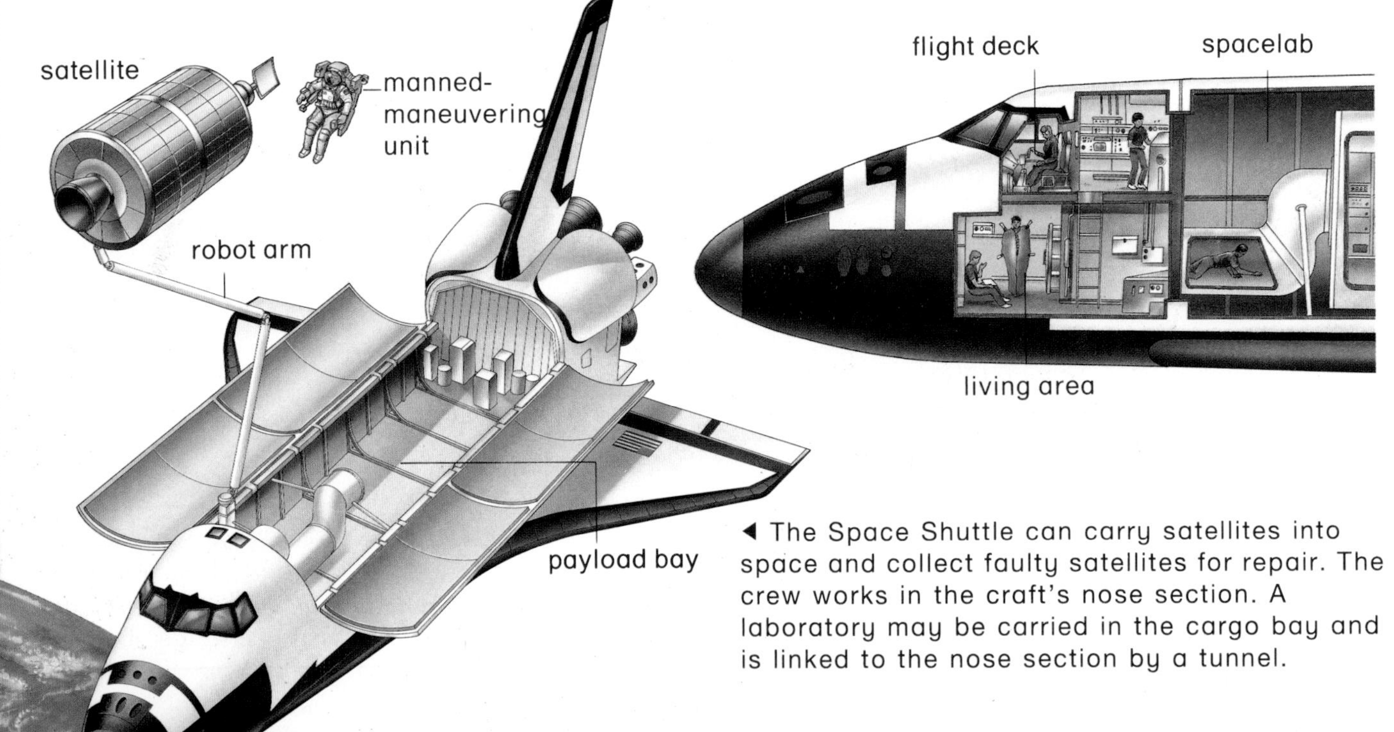

◄ The Space Shuttle can carry satellites into space and collect faulty satellites for repair. The crew works in the craft's nose section. A laboratory may be carried in the cargo bay and is linked to the nose section by a tunnel.

SOUND

Sound waves are vibrations that travel through a medium (which can be solid, liquid, or gas). They cannot travel in a vacuum or across empty space. Space is silent! Sound waves travel out in a spreading circle, getting weaker (so the sound becomes quieter) the farther they go. Sound waves are a bit like ripples in a pond.

Sound travels millions of times slower than light, so it can take a while before the sound of a distant explosion reaches you. Watch someone burst a balloon or bang a piece of wood at the far end of the street, and you will see the action a split second before you hear it.

DID YOU KNOW?

The speed of sound at sea level is about 750 mph (1,200 km/h). At high altitudes it is 660 mph (1,060 km/h). Sound travels three times as fast though helium, and four times as fast in hydrogen.

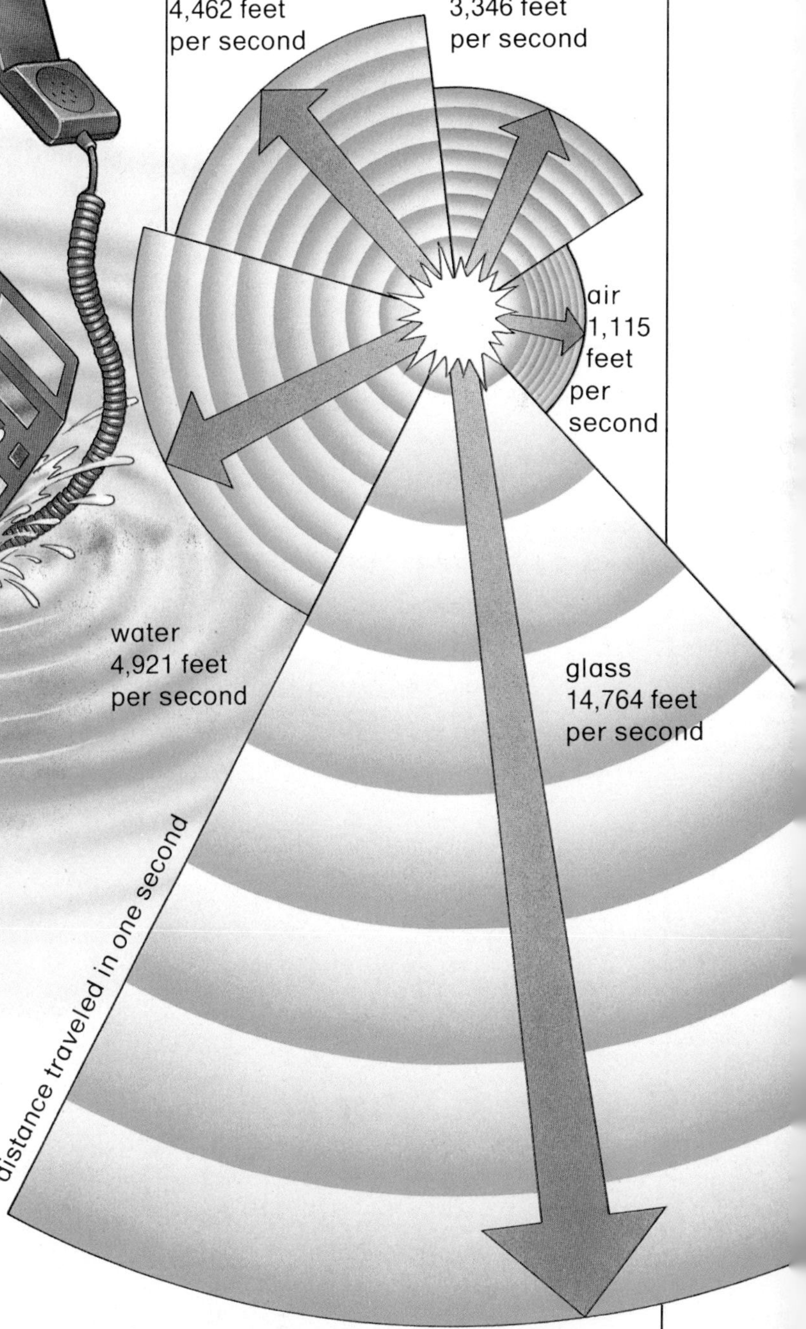

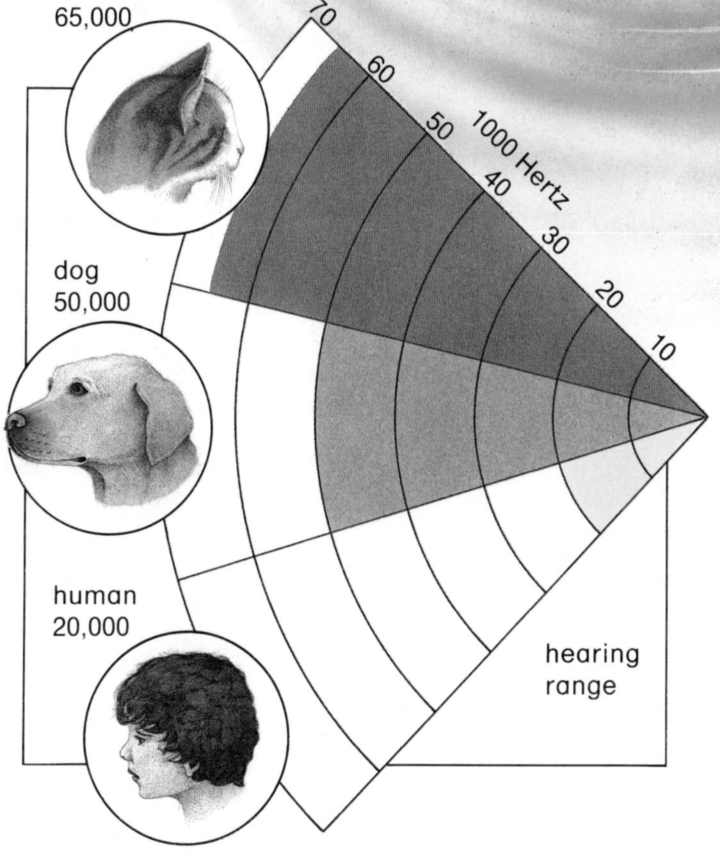

◄ Animals can hear sounds that are higher than we can detect. Cats can hear sounds with a frequency of up to 65 kHz. Dogs have an upper range of 50 kHz. Young people can hear up to 20 kHz.

S

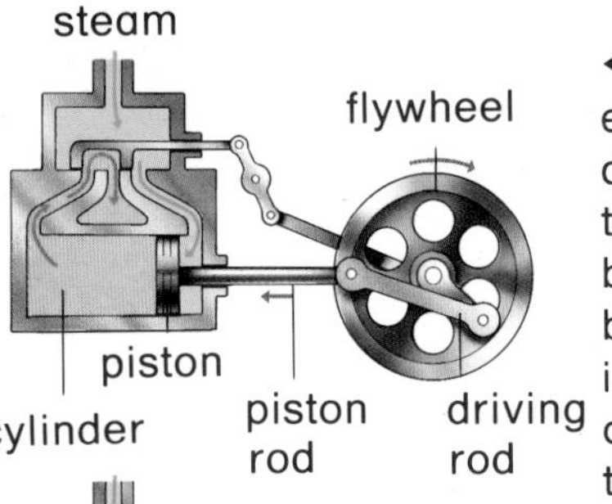

◀ Inside a steam engine, steam is directed in front of the piston and then behind it to push it back and forth. This is then changed into a rotating motion to turn the wheels of a vehicle such as a steam locomotive.

stars see **page 133**

static

Static is a form of ELECTRICITY. LIGHTNING is caused by a buildup of static electricity in the atmosphere.

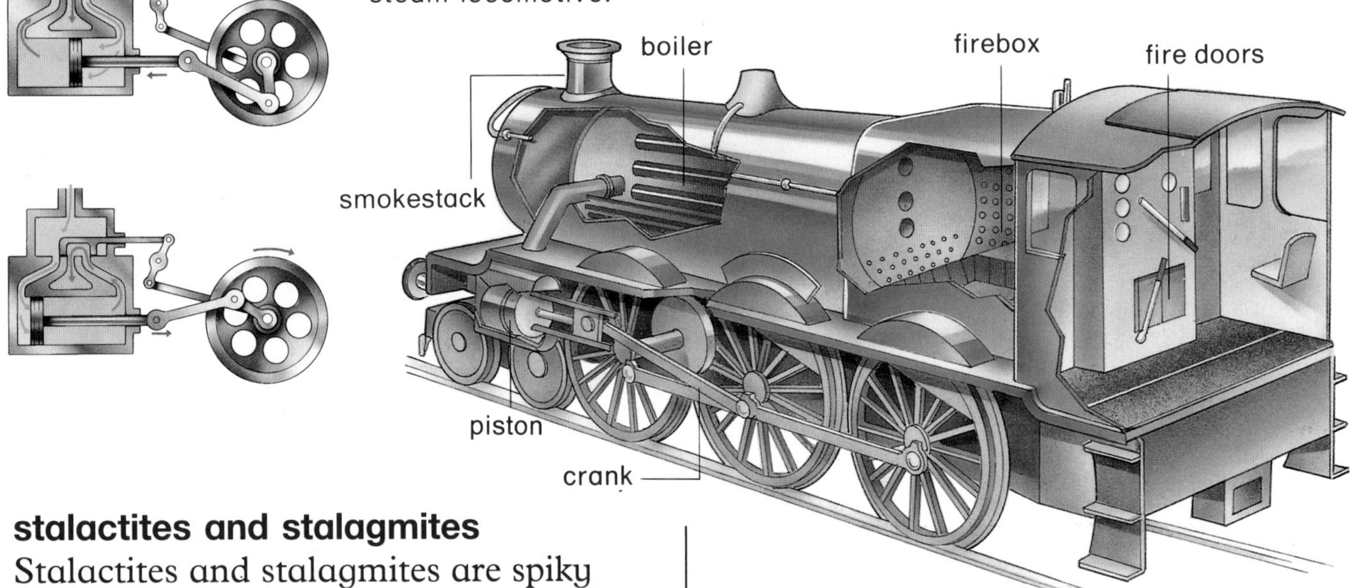

stalactites and stalagmites

Stalactites and stalagmites are spiky deposits of CALCIUM that form in limestone caves. As rainwater drips through the caves, the dissolved calcium is deposited and builds up into tall stone spikes.

▼ Stalactites hang down from the cave's ceiling. Stalagmites grow from the ground upward. And sometimes they meet in the middle.

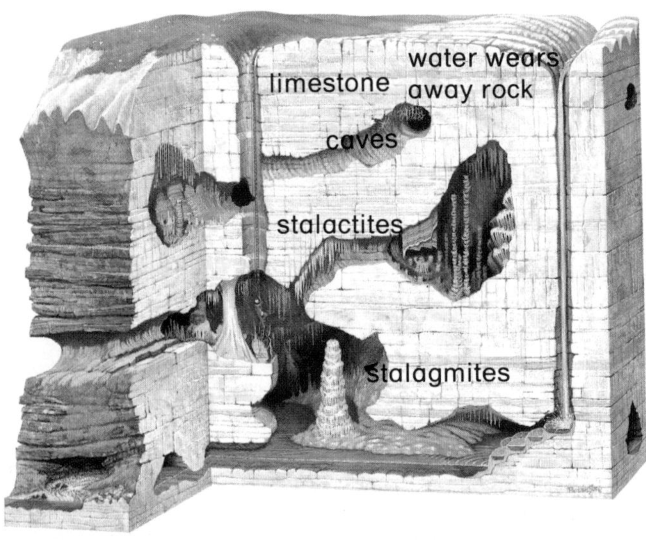

steam

Steam is the vapor produced when WATER boils. It contains much stored ENERGY and can easily scald people. A steam engine uses steam to push a piston. It produces high POWER even when turning very slowly because it generates the most TORQUE at low speeds. Modern engines have to turn over at high speed to produce most energy.

steel

Steel is made by adding a small amount of CARBON to IRON. It is harder than iron but still rusts. Stainless steel contains CHROMIUM to protect it from CORROSION.

stereo

Stereophonic, or "stereo" RECORDINGS are made with separate tracks for the sound heard by each ear.

STARS

Stars are massive luminous bodies in space. You can see 5,780 stars with an unaided eye. But some stars are invisible and emit RADIATION in wavelengths we cannot see. Many of the bright objects in the night sky are not stars but whole GALAXIES. The nearest star to us is called the SUN. It is halfway through its life cycle and will last another five billion years.

▼ Our own star, the Sun, is halfway through its life. Inside, it is a giant nuclear reactor powered by fusion. The Sun is about 80 percent hydrogen and 20 percent helium.

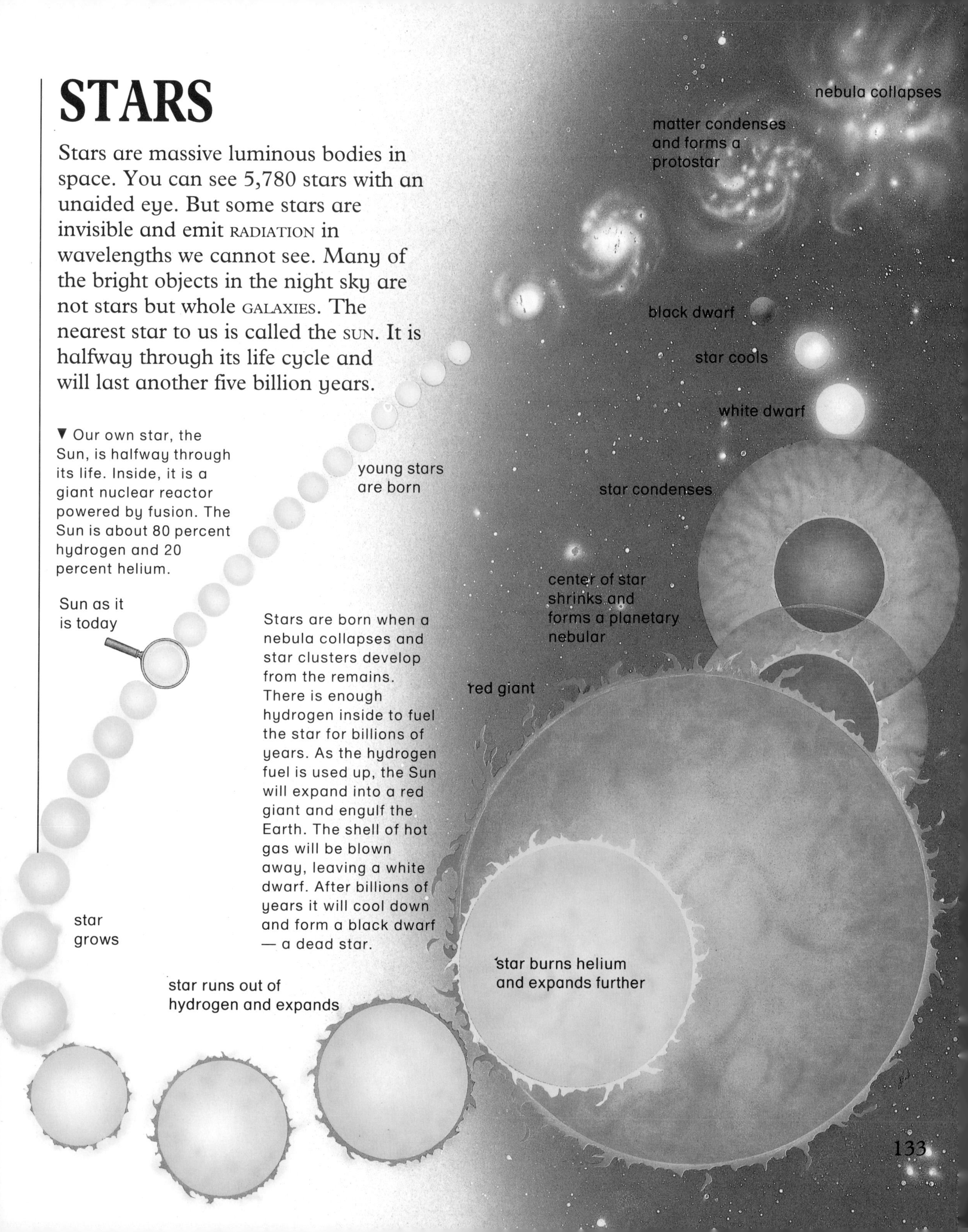

Stars are born when a nebula collapses and star clusters develop from the remains. There is enough hydrogen inside to fuel the star for billions of years. As the hydrogen fuel is used up, the Sun will expand into a red giant and engulf the Earth. The shell of hot gas will be blown away, leaving a white dwarf. After billions of years it will cool down and form a black dwarf — a dead star.

nebula collapses

matter condenses and forms a protostar

young stars are born

Sun as it is today

star grows

star runs out of hydrogen and expands

star burns helium and expands further

red giant

center of star shrinks and forms a planetary nebular

star condenses

white dwarf

star cools

black dwarf

S

stratosphere

The stratosphere is the second layer of the ATMOSPHERE. It starts about 6 mi (10 km) above the ground. The SUPERSONIC Concorde and other long-distance AIRCRAFT fly this high.

strobe

A strobe is a flash of LIGHT that makes a moving object appear still. This effect is seen when a moving object is glimpsed for a split second. A flashing light in a disco seems to freeze a moving dancer. In some MOTION PICTURE Westerns, the wagon wheels seem to turn backward. This strobe effect is seen as the spokes nearly catch up to each other in the time between each separate frame.

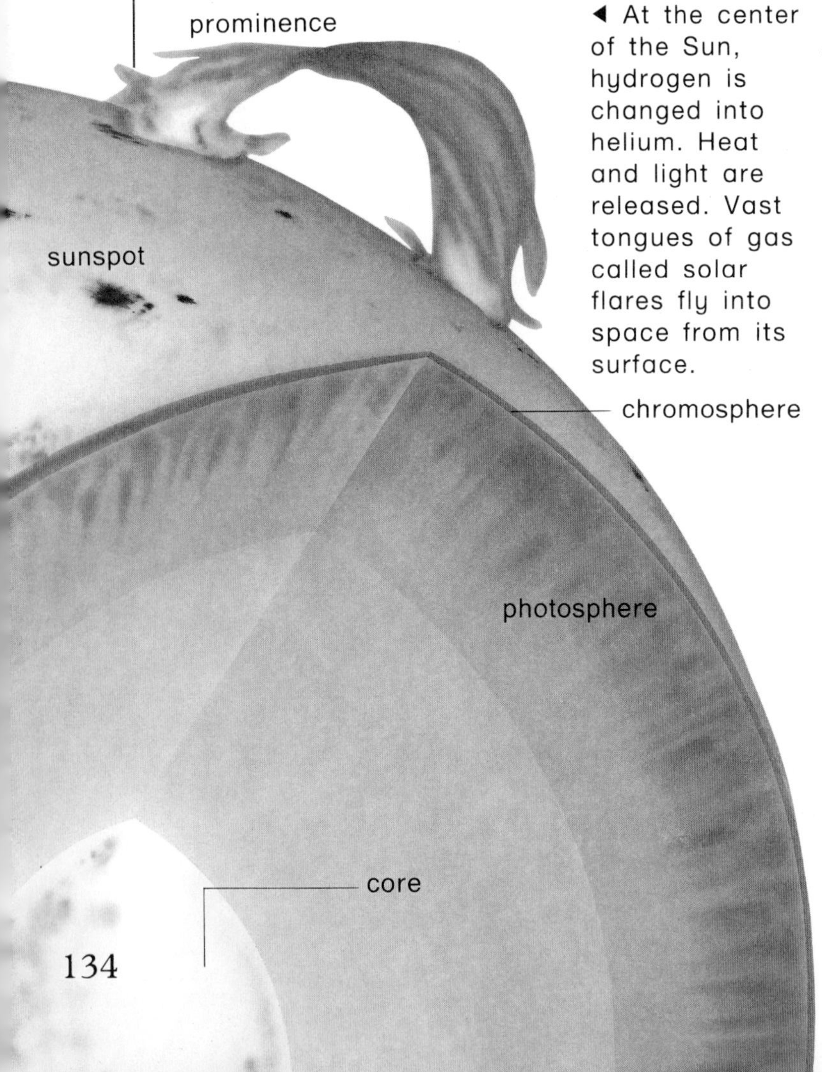

◀ At the center of the Sun, hydrogen is changed into helium. Heat and light are released. Vast tongues of gas called solar flares fly into space from its surface.

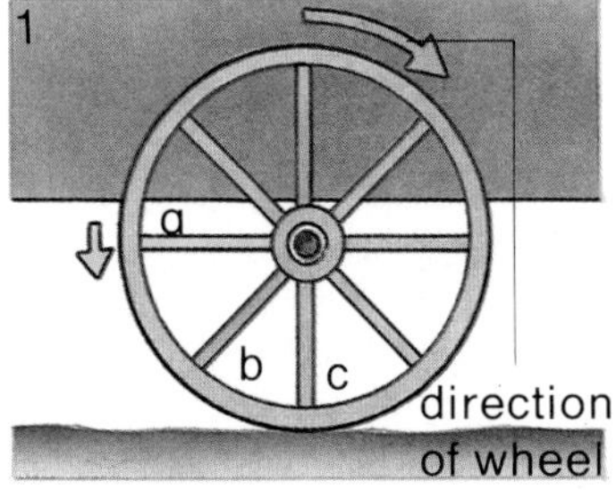

◀ Wagon wheels seem to turn backward on film because of the strobe effect. A film is made up of a series of still frames. Note the position of spoke *a* in frame 1.

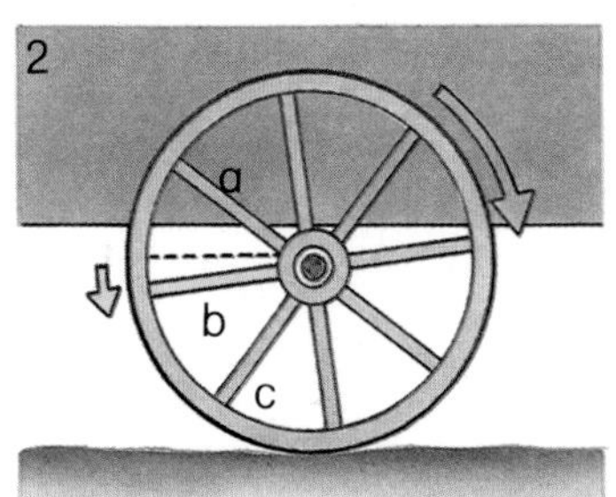

◀ In the time between each frame, the wheels continue to turn. In the second frame spoke *b* has moved almost to where spoke *a* was originally.

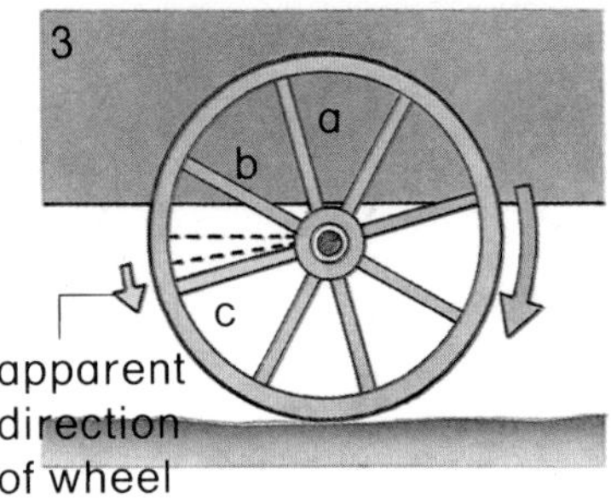

◀ To your eye it looks as though the spokes have moved back a little in each frame, and it appears that the wheels are turning backward.

Sun

The Sun is an ordinary, and not very important, STAR. At least, that's how it would seem to any alien scientist! It is important to us because it is our source of ENERGY. The Sun is 93.2 million miles (150 million km) from the Earth. It is a huge nuclear reactor. In its center, the temperature is about 25 million°F. The surface is at 10,832°F. Cooler areas show through as sunspots. They can sometimes be seen when the Sun is setting. (*Never* use BINOCULARS or a TELESCOPE to look at the Sun. You can be blinded.)

supernova

A supernova is a massive nova produced by the collapse of a giant STAR. A small NEUTRON STAR is usually formed when the supernova has ended.

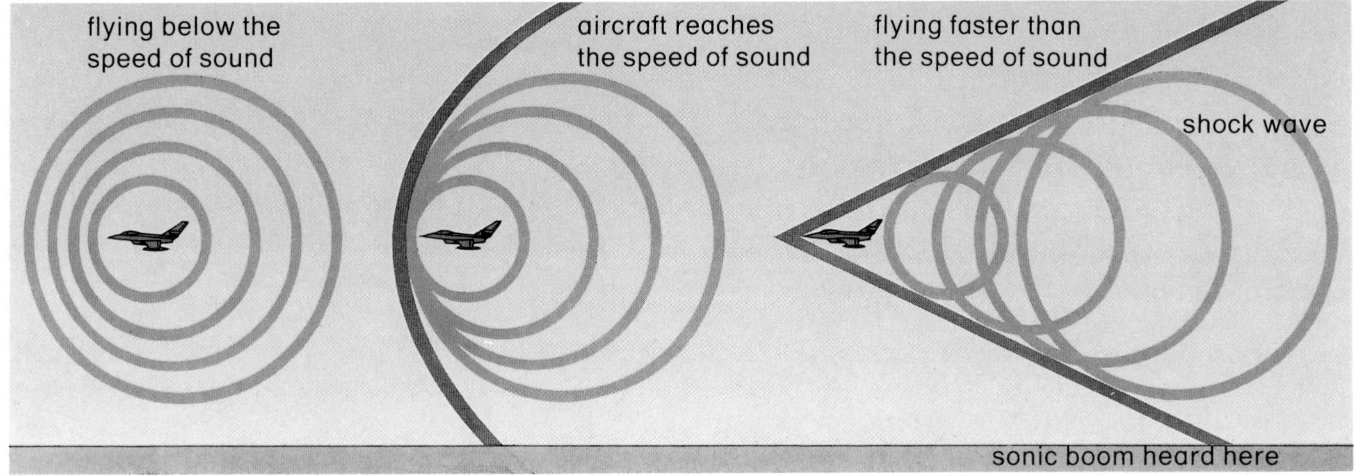

▲ Sound waves spread out from a plane flying below the speed of sound. As it nears the speed of sound, it catches up with its own sound waves. As it passes the speed of sound, they form a shock wave, heard as a sonic boom.

supersonic

Supersonic planes travel faster than the speed of SOUND. They must be specially designed to withstand the heat caused by air friction and shock waves. See **Mach, sound barrier**.

surface tension

The MOLECULES of water pull each other in all directions. At the surface they are only pulled back toward the other water molecules, and this makes a kind of skin. The effect is known as surface tension.

▶ Surface tension pulls a droplet of water into a spherical (ball) shape. Gravity squashes it a little. Surface tension is firm enough to allow an insect called the water strider to glide on top of the water without falling in.

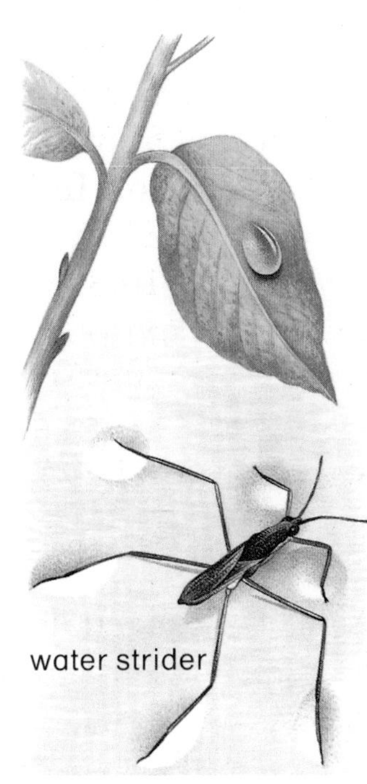

suspension

PARTICLES that are very tiny can stay suspended in a liquid for a long time. Milk is a suspension of fat in water. A suspension is the liquid version of an AEROSOL.

synthesizer see **page 136**

synthetic

A synthetic product is one that people make. A natural product is one that occurs in nature. Synthetic products are often based on natural ones; for instance, many DRUGS were first found in plants.

DID YOU KNOW?

Many synthetic materials were discovered by accident. Polyethylene was first made when the apparatus sprang a leak. Modern dyes were discovered by accident, during research on quinine. The hardening of rubber to make tires was a chance discovery by Charles Goodyear.

SYNTHESIZER

A synthesizer creates SOUND vibrations that imitate musical instruments (and other sounds). Technologists analyze the patterns of a sound and then program HARDWARE to set up the same patterns artificially. A synthesizer can sound like an organ or a guitar, and some can manage a roaring lion or a space alien as well.

The keyboard is based on a piano keyboard. The white notes, played in sequence, give the scale of C. The note of C is always to the left of the pair of black notes. Groups of notes are chords. The lower notes of your synthesizer probably play chords automatically.

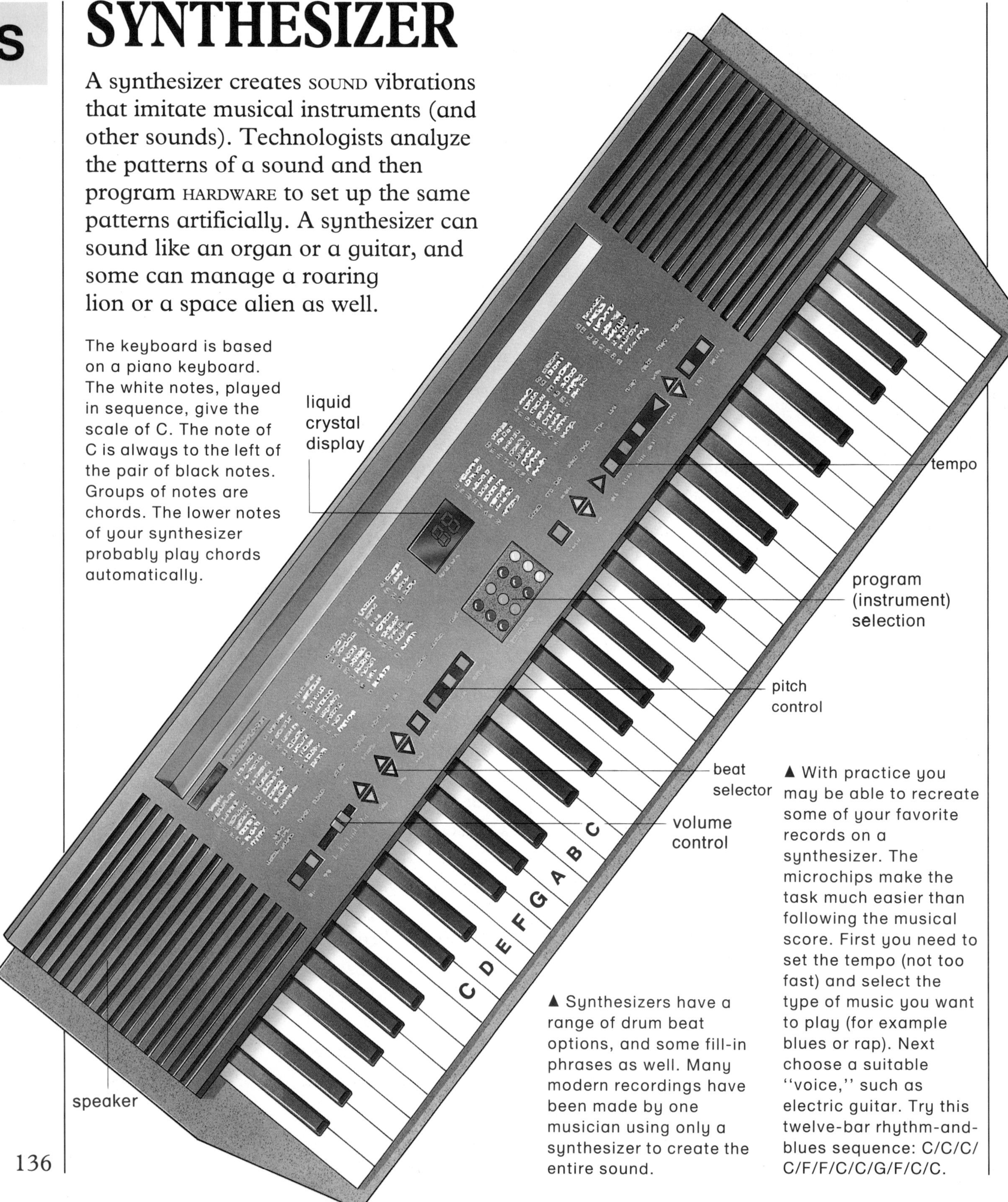

▲ Synthesizers have a range of drum beat options, and some fill-in phrases as well. Many modern recordings have been made by one musician using only a synthesizer to create the entire sound.

▲ With practice you may be able to recreate some of your favorite records on a synthesizer. The microchips make the task much easier than following the musical score. First you need to set the tempo (not too fast) and select the type of music you want to play (for example blues or rap). Next choose a suitable "voice," such as electric guitar. Try this twelve-bar rhythm-and-blues sequence: C/C/C/C/F/F/C/C/G/F/C/C.

tape see **recording**

telephone

The first commercial telephone was made by Alexander Graham Bell in 1876. Modern telephones are similar to Bell's early designs. There is a MICROPHONE which picks up SOUND signals. The ELECTRICAL signal it creates is sent to a distant phone. There the signal is changed back to sound in an earpiece, and the original words can be heard.

▼ A telephone mouthpiece has a microphone which changes the speaker's voice into an electrical signal. A loudspeaker in the earpiece turns the signals back into sound.

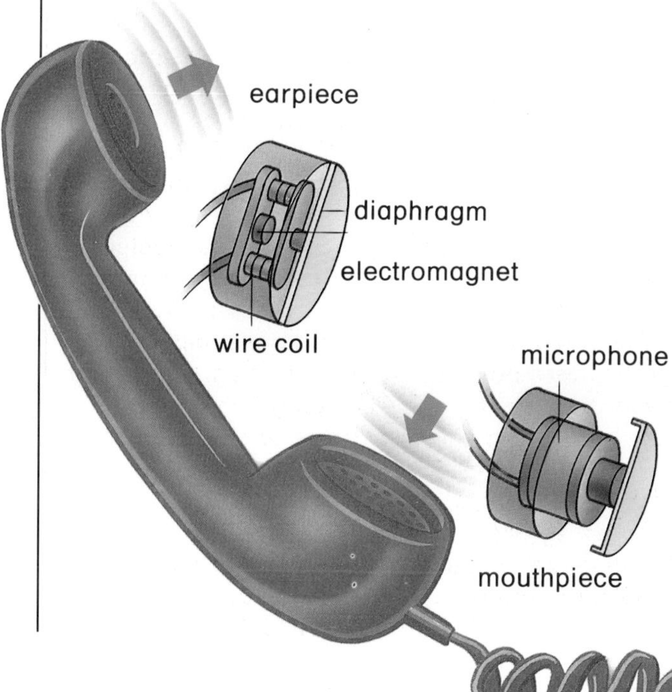

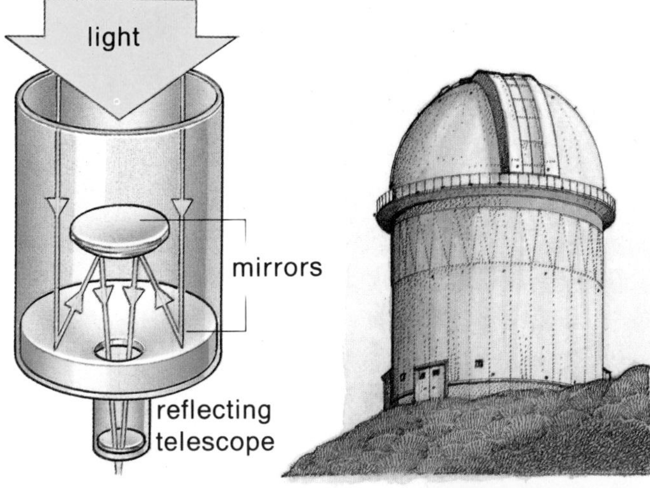

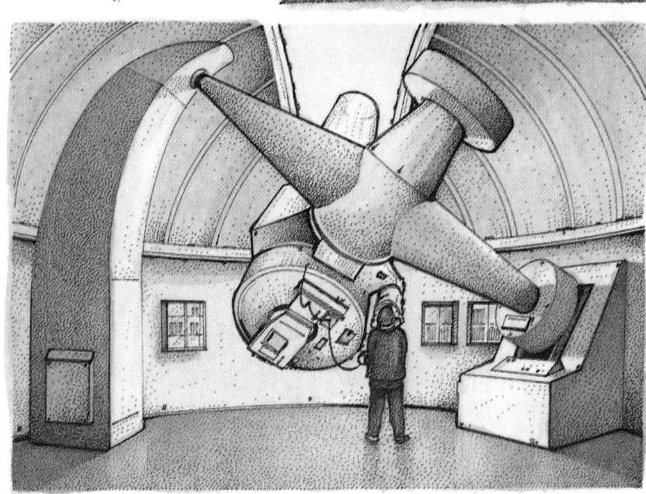

▲ Large telescopes for studying the planets and stars magnify these distant objects by means of curved mirrors. They are called reflectors. Telescopes that use lenses instead are called refractors.

telescope

Telescopes make distant objects appear nearer. One that magnifies ten times (written 10 ×) would make an object ten miles away look as though it was only one mile away. Large telescopes have a magnifying MIRROR to enlarge the image. Smaller telescopes use LENSES to produce the magnification. The largest telescope in the world is the Kech telescope in Hawaii, which has a 400 in (1,000 cm) mirror.

television see **page 138**

T

TELEVISION

The first successful demonstration of moving images on TV was given in 1926 by John Baird, a Scottish engineer. The pictures, however, were blurred. Modern TV pictures are built up on screen line by line. The start of public television was in Berlin in 1935, with 180 lines across the screen. Clearer TV pictures (with 405 lines) were transmitted from London in 1936.

▼ The electronic signals from the studio are sent to a transmission station. Here they are amplified, and sent out from the transmission mast. The signal travels hundreds of miles. Some television transmitters are on satellites orbiting the Earth. With no houses or mountains in the way, these signals can be broadcast over an entire continent.

▼ Light from an object is scanned by the TV camera. Modern cameras split the picture into 525 lines. Each line is converted into three sets of signals, one each for red, blue, and green, the primary colors of light. The strength of the signal depends on the amount of each color reflected by the object. In this case it is a vase, but it can be a news anchor or a rock star.

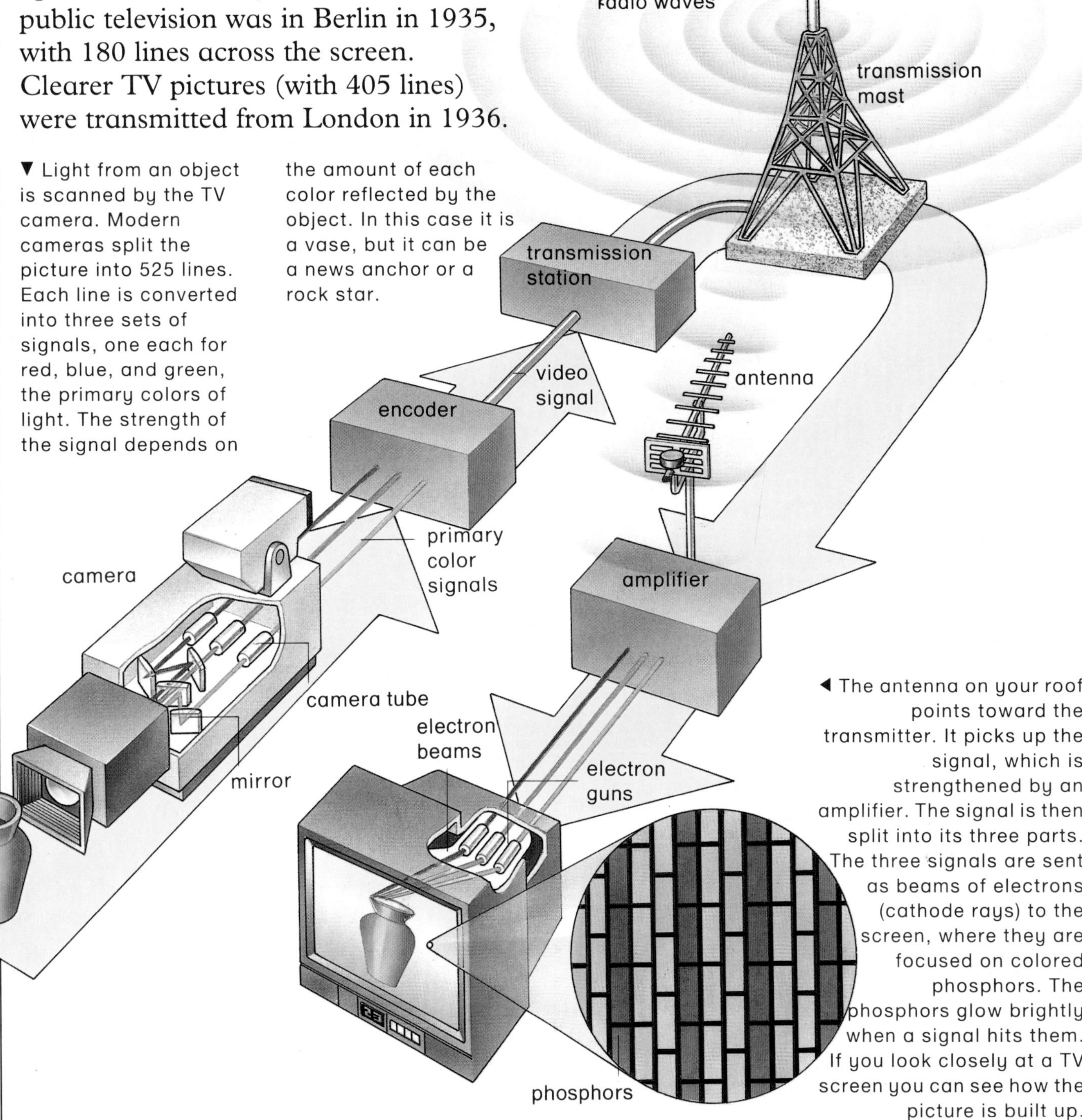

◀ The antenna on your roof points toward the transmitter. It picks up the signal, which is strengthened by an amplifier. The signal is then split into its three parts. The three signals are sent as beams of electrons (cathode rays) to the screen, where they are focused on colored phosphors. The phosphors glow brightly when a signal hits them. If you look closely at a TV screen you can see how the picture is built up.

T

temperature

Temperature measures how hot something is. Traditionally temperature was measured in degrees Fahrenheit, with the freezing point of water at 32°F and its boiling point at 212°F. The CELSIUS scale was then adopted, with freezing at 0°C and boiling at 100°C. The Kelvin is the SI UNIT for temperature. Degrees Kelvin are the same size as degrees CELSIUS, but the scale begins at ABSOLUTE ZERO (0 K or −273°C), which is the point at which molecules can be cooled no further. Freezing is at 273 K.

	Celsius	Fahrenheit
freezing point (0°C)	**0**	**32**
	10	50
	20	68
	30	86
	40	104
	50	122
	60	140
	70	158
	80	176
	90	194
boiling point	**100**	**212**
	110	230
	120	248
	130	266
	140	284
	150	302
	200	392
	250	482
	300	572

◀ A temperature on one scale can be converted to another scale by doing a simple calculation. Multiply degrees Celsius by nine, divide it by five, and add 32 to give the temperature in degrees Fahrenheit.

DID YOU KNOW?

The highest surface shade temperature ever recorded was 135.9°F (57.7°C) at Al'Aziziyah, Libya, on September 13, 1922. The coldest was −128.6°F (−89.2°C) at Vostok, Antarctica, on July 21, 1983.

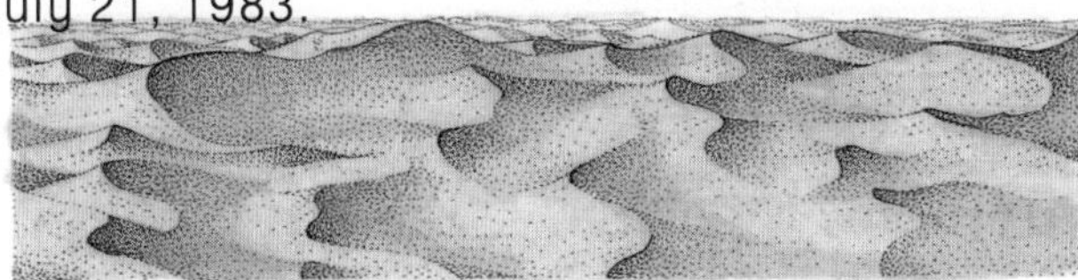

theodolite

A theodolite is an automatic surveying instrument with a prism TELESCOPE. It finds the height or distance of a point by measuring its angle with known points. Newer devices beam a LASER to a mirror and measure the time it takes to return.

thermocouple

If two wires of different metals are joined together in a loop, they may produce ELECTRICITY if one end of the loop is heated. The more it is heated, the more electricity is produced. This idea can be used to measure TEMPERATURE with ELECTRICAL instruments. IRON and COPPER act as a thermocouple.

thermometer

A thermometer is a device for measuring TEMPERATURE. Liquid inside GLASS thermometers expands as temperatures rise. LIQUID CRYSTAL thermometers show temperature by a change of color. Other thermometers contain a THERMOCOUPLE.

▼ When a thermometer is taken out of a patient's mouth, it begins to cool down. A small kink at the bottom of the mercury channel breaks the thread of contracting mercury and stops it from falling, so an accurate reading can be taken.

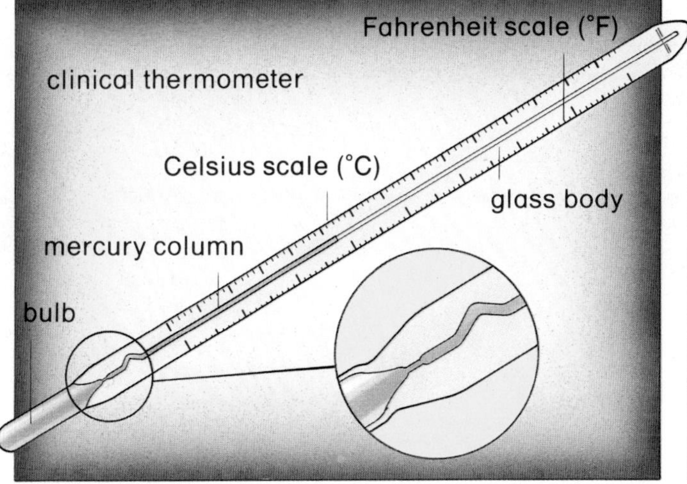

▶ Tomato ketchup is thixotropic: It is normally thick, but it becomes thinner when the bottle is shaken.

thixotropism

Some substances are quite stiff if you leave them standing. But they become runny if you move them. This effect is known as thixotropism. Gel paints are thixotropic. They are solid until you begin painting, when they turn into a liquid and are easier to spread.

tide

Tides are the regular rise and fall of ocean levels. High tide is caused by the Moon's GRAVITY, which pulls up the waters directly below the MOON. It also pulls the solid Earth up a bit, leaving a bulge of water — a second high tide — on its opposite side. As the Moon travels around the Earth, the high tides follow it. The highs and lows arrive at each place about $6\frac{1}{4}$ hours apart. Every two weeks, at the new moon and full moon, the Sun's pull combines with the Moon's, causing very high tides called spring tides. At the half moons the high tides are weakest; these are neap tides.

▼ High spring tides occur when the Sun and Moon are in line with the Earth and pull in the same direction. Neap tides, the lowest high tides, occur when the Sun and Moon are at right angles.

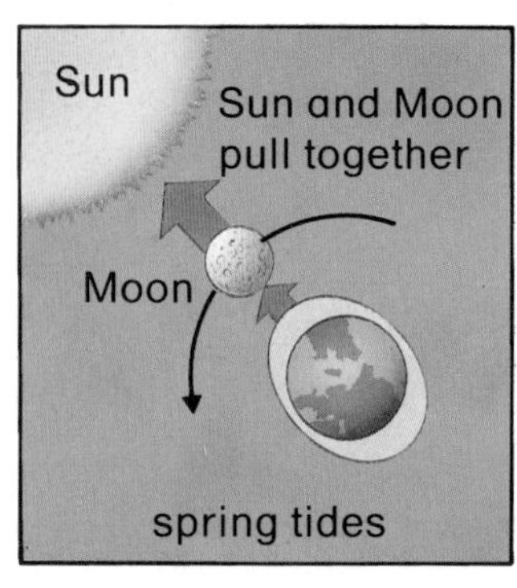

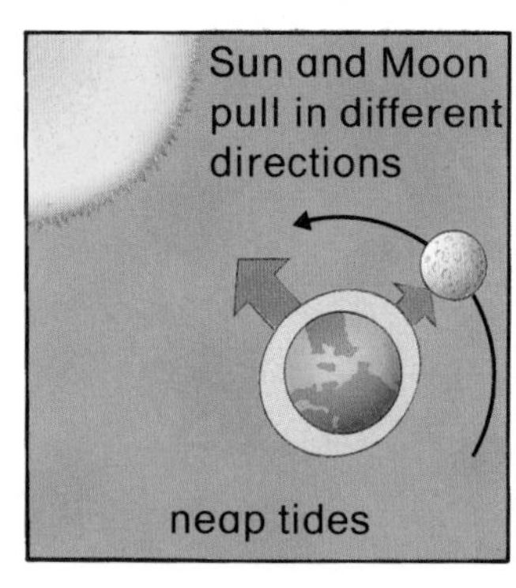

time

Time is the passing of the present into history. It is measured by comparison with natural events. A day is the time it takes the EARTH to spin round once,

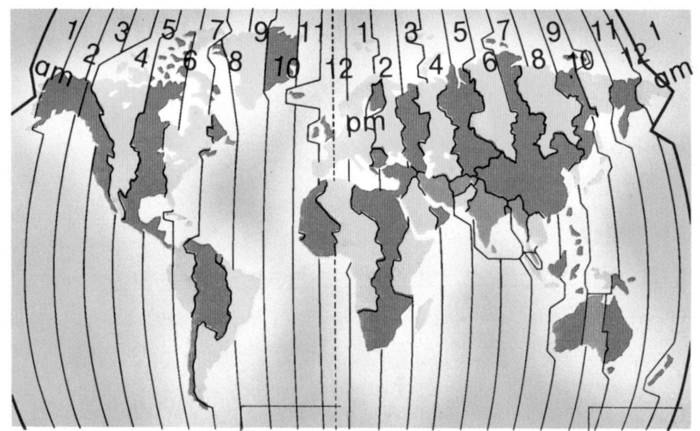

▲ The world is divided into 24 time zones. The time is one hour later in each zone to the east.

▼ In this clock, the rod burns slowly, dropping balls on the cymbal at regular intervals.

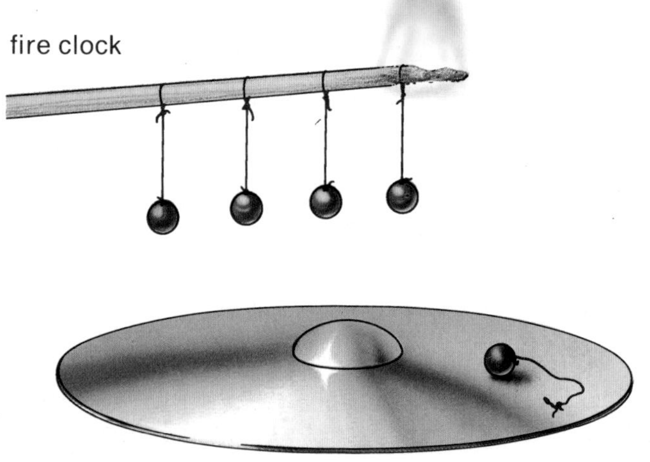

marked by the SUN rising in the sky. A year is the time the Earth takes to make an ORBIT of the Sun. Before there were clocks and watches, people used SHADOWS or candles to tell how time was passing.

tin

Tin is a soft silvery metal. A rod of tin squeaks as you bend it, because it is made of CRYSTALS which rub together. Tin is used to coat STEEL to keep RUST from forming. It is also used to make many useful ALLOYS.

titanium

Titanium is a very hard light METAL. It is present in almost all ROCKS. Titanium is a useful metal for making ALLOYS in the aerospace industry.

tornado

A tornado is a twisting narrow wind that moves at up to 40 mph (65 km/h). At the center of the tornado, the PRESSURE of the air is very low and winds may swirl at 400 mph (640 km/h). Buildings sometimes EXPLODE when a tornado passes over, because the low air pressure outside the building pulls it apart. Tornadoes are most common in the U.S. and Australia.

torque

Torque is the FORCE of twisting. A screwdriver develops torque as it turns. A car engine twists, or applies torque, to the crankshaft. High-performance cars have high-torque engines.

transformer

A transformer is a device for changing ELECTRICITY from a high to a low VOLTAGE, or the other way round. Transformers are

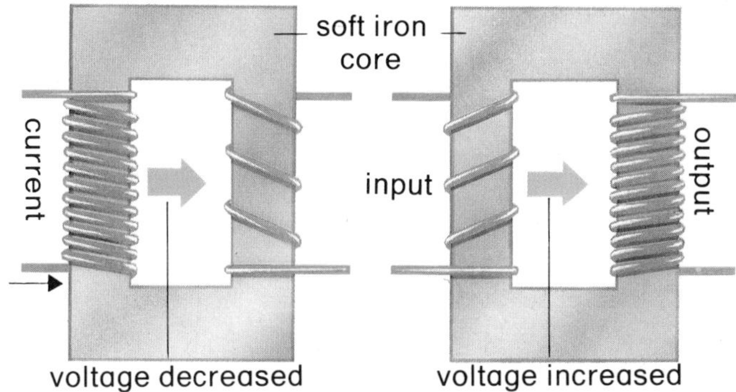

▲ The way a transformer changes voltage depends on the numbers of coils of wire on each side. The transformer on the left reduces the voltage. The one on the right increases it.

made by wrapping two coils of COPPER wire around an IRON core. The voltage produced depends on the number of coils in each set. If the second set has twice as many coils as the first set, the voltage will be doubled. Or, if it has half as many coils as the first set, the voltage will be halved.

transistor

A transistor is a sandwich of SEMI-CONDUCTORS. Transistors were invented at Bell Laboratories in 1947. Many new ways were found to make semiconductors control ELECTRIC currents. They are used as switches or to amplify an electric current. They are very small and are now used in RADIO and TELEVISION equipment.

▼ A weak electric current flowing into the middle, or base, connection of a transistor produces a larger change in the emitter-collector current.

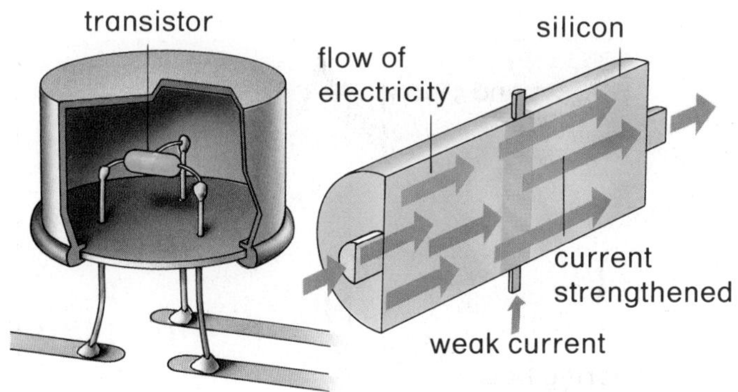

T

trinitrotoluene

Trinitrotoluene is a powerful EXPLOSIVE made up of CARBON, HYDROGEN, NITROGEN, and OXYGEN. It is known as TNT for short.

tungsten

Tungsten is a very hard, brittle METAL with a very high melting point, 6,116°F (3,380°C). It is used to make ALLOYS and is also used in ELECTRIC light bulbs.

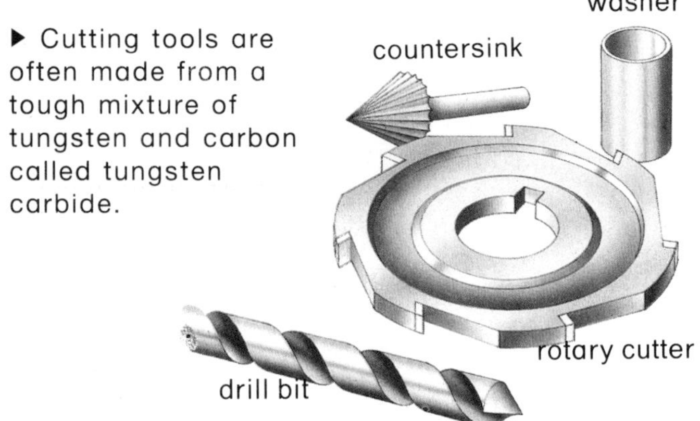

▶ Cutting tools are often made from a tough mixture of tungsten and carbon called tungsten carbide.

turbine

A turbine is a fan turned by the PRESSURE of gas or water. A JET engine is a turbine. A power station GENERATOR is often POWERED by a turbine.

▼ In this steam turbine, stationary blades direct the steam onto the turbine wheels. The fans spin round and drive the shaft.

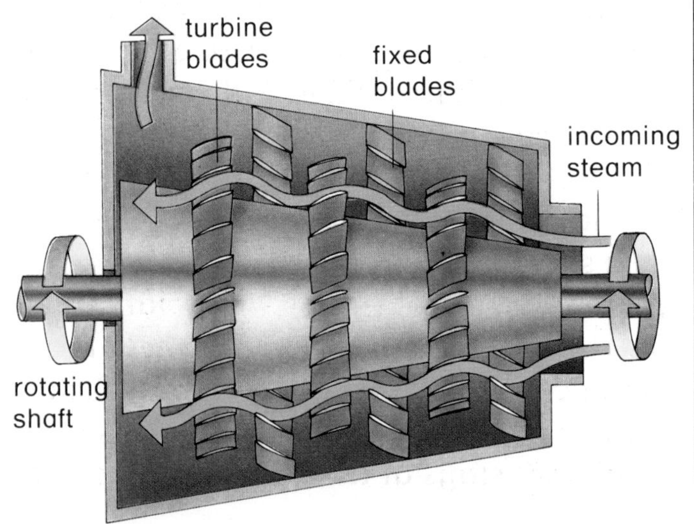

ultrahigh frequency

Ultrahigh frequency waves are RADIO waves between 300 and 3,000 megahertz. They are known as UHF for short. UHF waves are used to broadcast TELEVISION signals. See **hertz**, **very high frequency**.

ultrasound

Ultrasound is sound too high for people to hear. Humans can hear SOUNDS up to about 20,000 HERTZ. Anything above this is ultrasonic. Early remote control units for TELEVISION sets produced ultrasonic beams. But they frightened cats and dogs, which can hear these high noises. So remote controls now use INFRARED or RADIO signals.

ultraviolet radiation

Ultraviolet is the RADIATION that lies beyond the blue end of the COLORS of a rainbow. Though it is invisible to us, many insects can see in ultraviolet as LIGHT. Shortwave ultraviolet rays from the sun can damage eyes and skin.

universe

"Universe" is the word we use to describe everything we know to exist. It includes all the STARS, the PLANETS in the SOLAR SYSTEM, and the GALAXIES. Between all these bodies is interstellar space, with a small amount of gas and dust spread very, very thin.

▼ The universe is mostly empty space with galaxies, stars, planets, moons, comets, asteroids, gas, and dust scattered throughout it.

uranium

Uranium is a hard, white, naturally RADIOACTIVE METAL with many ISOTOPES. For example, uranium atoms have 92 PROTONS but 142–146 NEUTRONS; this makes between 234–238 total PARTICLES in each ATOM. Uranium 238 makes up 99 percent of the natural uranium found in the ORE in rocks. Uranium 235 makes up less than 1 percent of the ore. It is used in nuclear reactors and nuclear weapons.

Uranus

Uranus is the seventh PLANET from the SUN, discovered in 1781 by William Herschel. It was the first planet to be discovered by telescope. Uranus has 10 dark rings with bright dust between them. See **Solar System**.

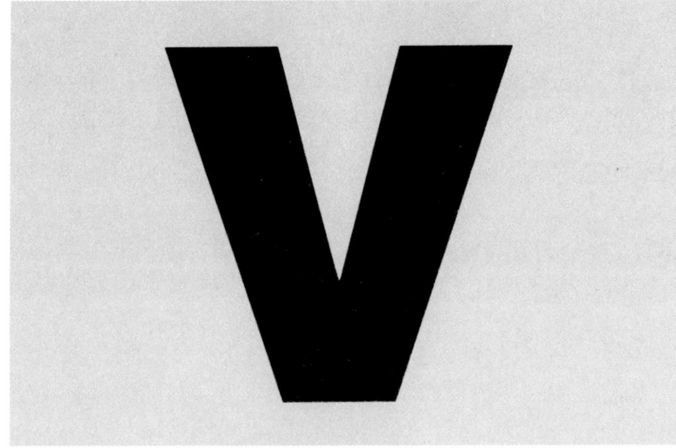

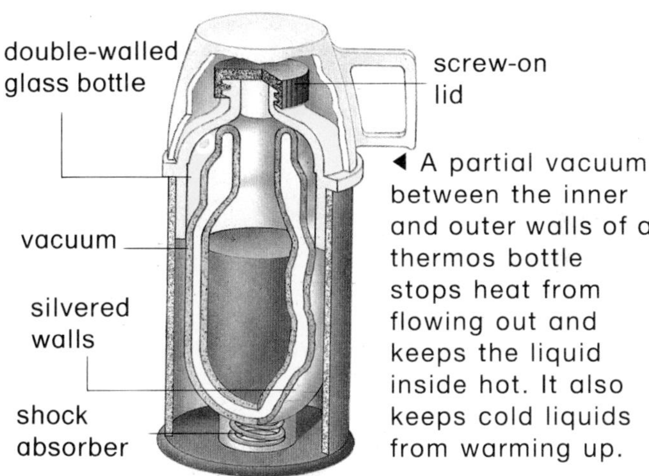

◀ A partial vacuum between the inner and outer walls of a thermos bottle stops heat from flowing out and keeps the liquid inside hot. It also keeps cold liquids from warming up.

vacuum

A vacuum is completely empty space. A perfect vacuum does not exist. Even out between the distant STARS there are always ATOMS and MOLECULES floating around. A vacuum cleaner, or vacuum brakes on a train, work with AIR at low PRESSURE, called a partial vacuum. A partial vacuum is created inside a vacuum cleaner, and air and dust rush in to fill it. A thermos has a partial vacuum between two walls of silvered GLASS. Most of the air between the two layers of glass has been pumped out. The silvering reflects back HEAT, preventing loss of ENERGY by radiation. The vacuum space prevents the heat from being conducted away. And the lid helps stop its escape upward. The result is a drink that stays at the same temperature.

velocity
Velocity is speed in a certain direction. A car has velocity as it drives along a road, but a spinning wheel does not have velocity. Only things in linear motion have velocity. See **movement**.

Venus
Venus is a hot PLANET, veiled by thick clouds. It is about the same size as EARTH but nearer to the SUN. In 1992 the Magellan space probe was sent into ORBIT around Venus to survey it in detail.

very high frequency
Very high frequency (VHF) waves are radio waves below ULTRAHIGH FREQUENCY. They have a frequency of about 100 megahertz. See **hertz**.

video see **page 145**

volcano
Volcanoes are formed when molten ROCK from under the crust of the EARTH escapes through a weak point. They are often found at the boundaries between parts of the Earth's crust. There are 500 active volcanoes around the world, some up to 20,000 ft (6,000 m) high. Molten rock, called LAVA, can flow for more than 40 mi (65 km). See **plate tectonics**.

volt
The volt is an SI UNIT for measuring the amount of ENERGY needed to move an electric charge from one point to another — it is the potential difference between the two points. A portable BATTERY labeled 1.5 V tells you it can generate 1.5 volts of energy, or electromotive FORCE, to move an electric current through a circuit. Household electricity is usually 120 or 240 volts. The volt is named for the Italian scientist Alessandro Volta (1745–1827).

▼ When a volcano erupts, hot molten rock called lava pours out of the central and side vents. Layers of ash and lava build up a cone-shaped mountain. Dikes, sills, and laccoliths are formed when lava hardens underground.

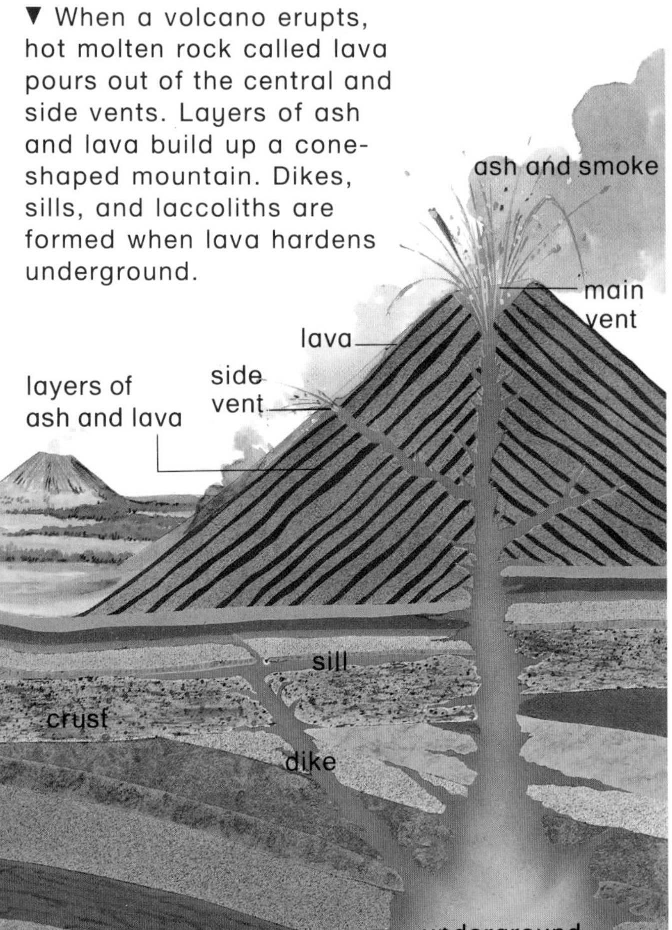

VIDEO

A video camera captures LIGHT and focuses the image onto a sensitive target plate, usually a SEMICONDUCTOR device. The target produces electrical signals which are stored on magnetic tape. Part of the signal is fed to a viewfinder, so you can see what the lens is seeing. The whole device — with camera and recorder in one body — is known as a camcorder.

▼ A microphone beside the lens picks up the sound. Camcorder microphones are very sensitive. A separate microphone is used for professional results.

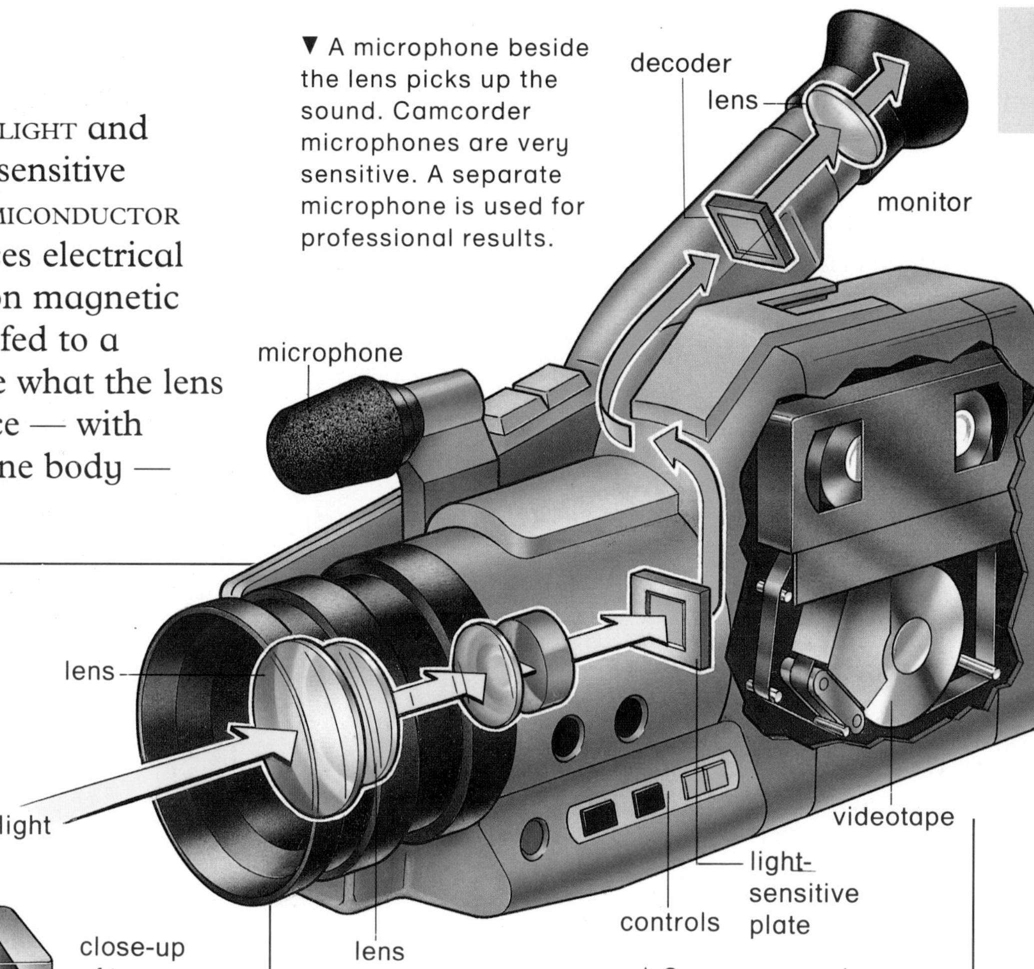

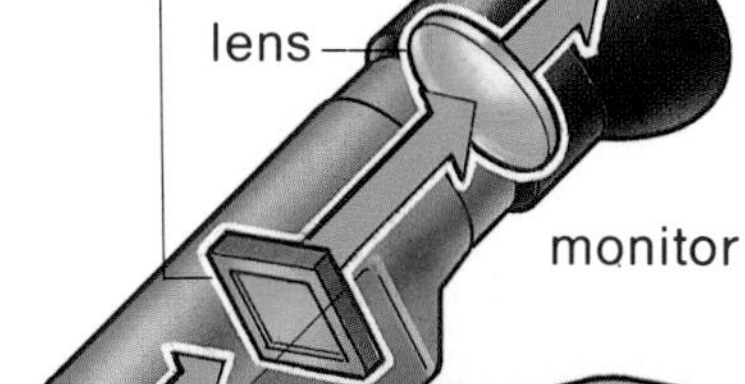

▲ Some camcorders are fitted with a color viewfinder. But a black-and-white screen often gives a sharper image. It is best to focus the camera lens manually, because the automatic setting will drain the batteries very quickly.

VIDEOTAPE

The record/playback head lays down the picture track as a series of slanting lines on the tape. The sound track and a time code are laid down alongside.

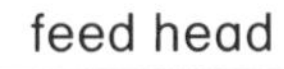

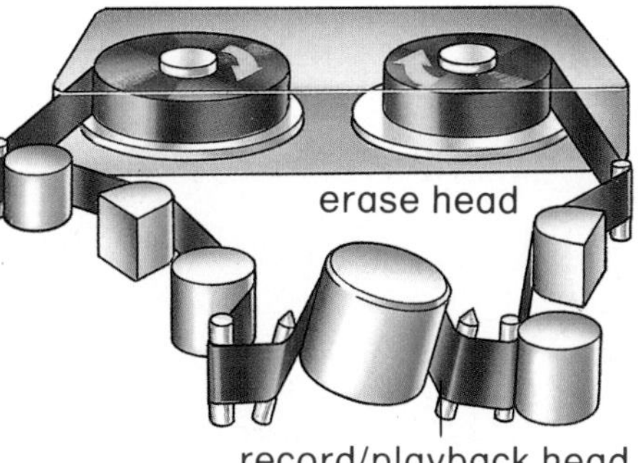

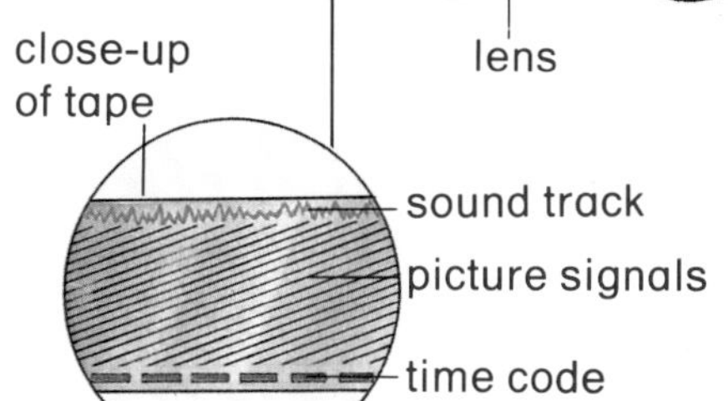

HOME VIDEO

When you make a video, do not film the same scene for long. Always change the position of the shot before you turn the camera on again if you want to avoid a sudden jump in the action. Shoot short closeups to break up long scenes.

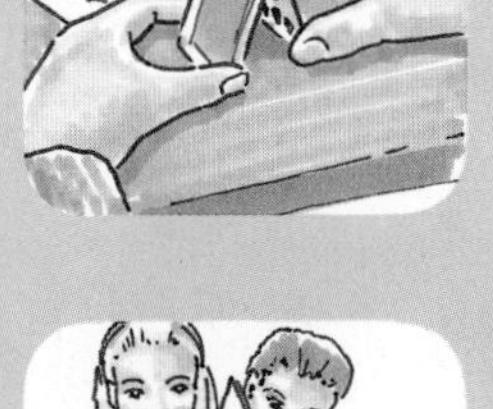

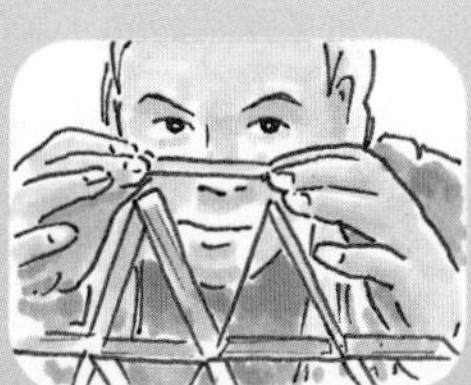
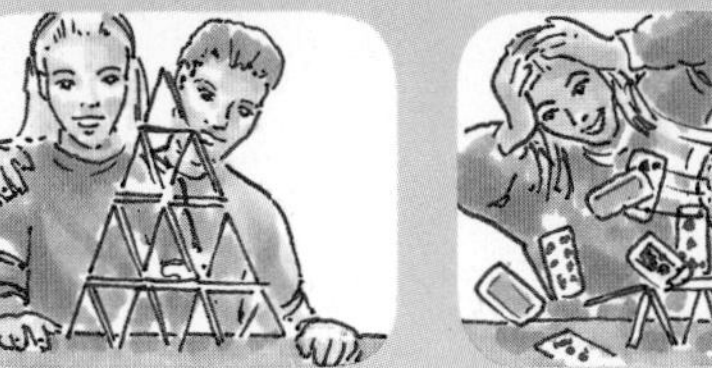

V

W

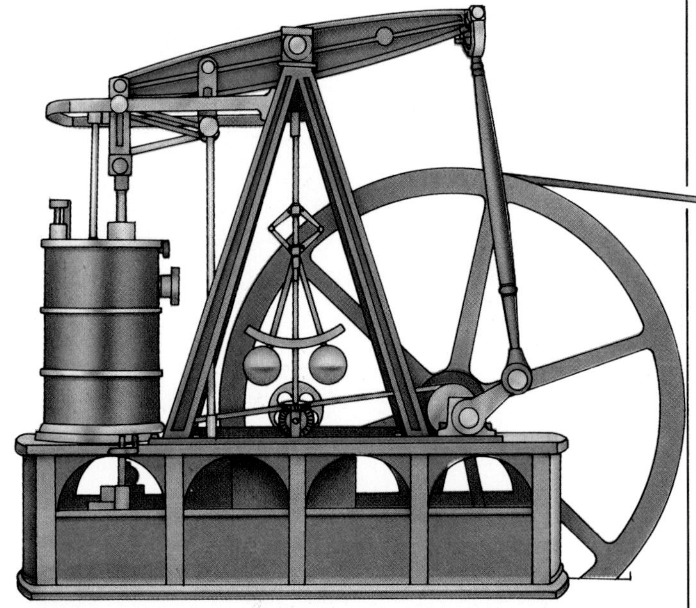

▲ The British engineer James Watt (1736–1819) improved the design of steam engines in the 1770s. The SI unit of power is named after him.

waste
Waste is material that you do not need. Most of the waste from homes and factories is buried at landfill sites or burned in an incinerator. Many waste products are dangerous, and strict laws are needed to make sure they are disposed of safely. RECYCLING is a good way to dispose of waste.

water see **page 148 and 149**

watt
A watt is the SI UNIT of POWER. It measures the rate at which ENERGY is used up or converted to another form. One watt represents the use of one JOULE of energy per second.

wave
A wave is a steady rise and fall, like water at sea. Wavelength is the distance from the peak of one wave to the peak of the next. The height is the distance between the peak and the trough. The power waves may be used to generate ELECTRICITY.

▼ As waves roll onto the seashore from far out to sea, the water particles circle up and down. The water itself does not move forward, but the wave travels toward the shore.

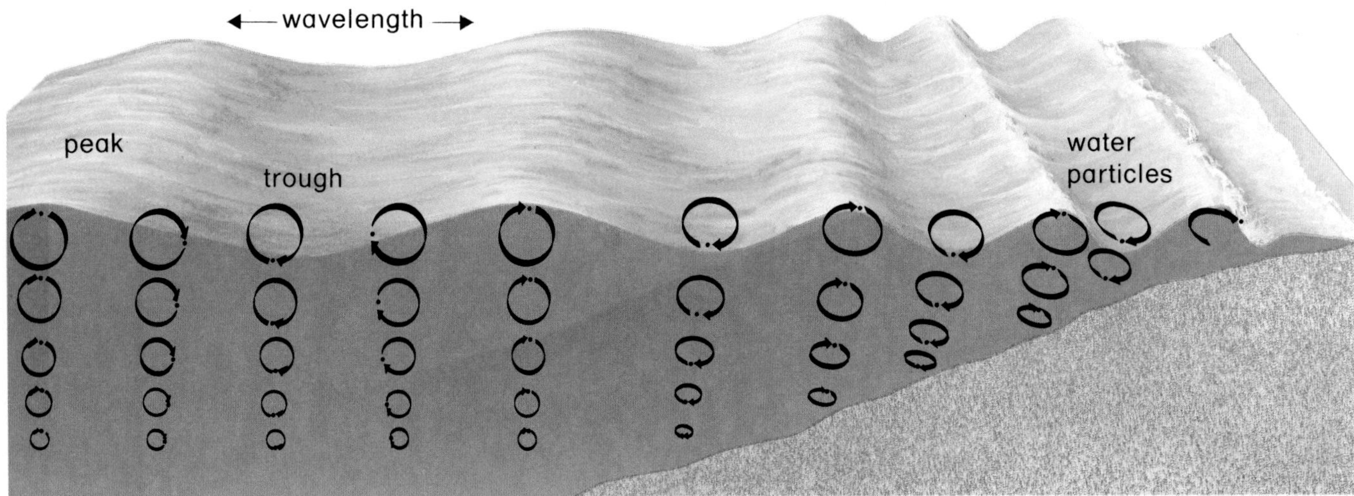

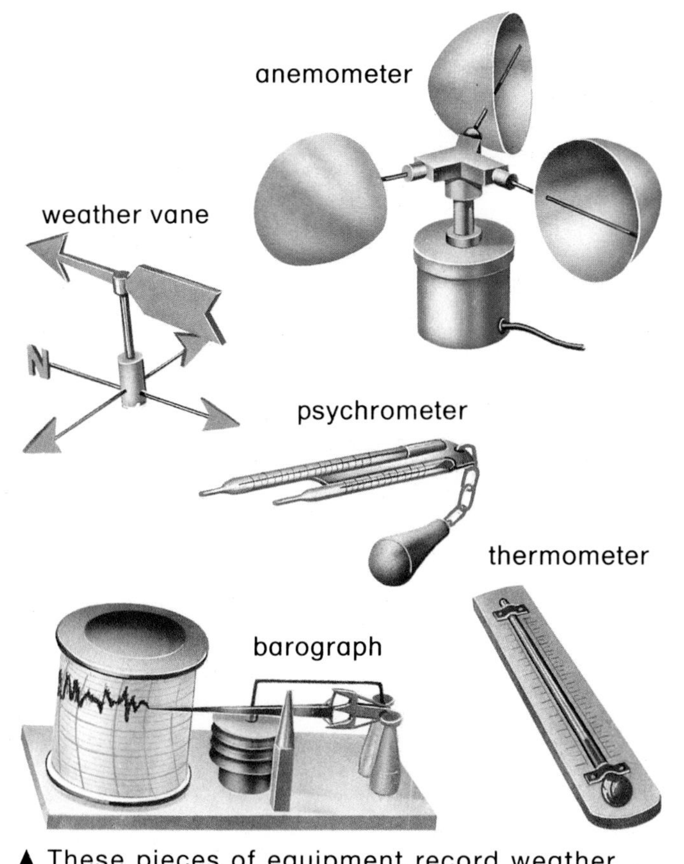

▲ These pieces of equipment record weather conditions of air temperature and pressure, humidity, and wind speed and direction.

▼ Annual rainfall around the world ranges from less than an inch in desert regions to more than 118 in (3,000 mm) in places like the Amazon rainforest.

weather

Weather is the name given to the changing conditions that result from the ENERGY of the SUN acting on the WATER and the AIR around us. They include TEMPERATURE, PRECIPITATION, air PRESSURE, HUMIDITY, sunshine, cloud cover, and WIND. Near the POLES of the EARTH the air is cold. Around the Equator it is much hotter. Where the two air masses meet, the weather is very changeable. The cold air can move across countries as a cold front. Warm air can push it back, bringing a warm front. There are usually clouds and rain where the two air masses meet. Sometimes the two air masses swirl around each other, like eddies and whirlpools in a stream. These are depressions, where the pressure of the air is low. Still and calm air has high pressure and is called an anticyclone. When the pressure is falling (you can see it on a BAROMETER) poor weather is likely. See **climate**, **meteorology**.

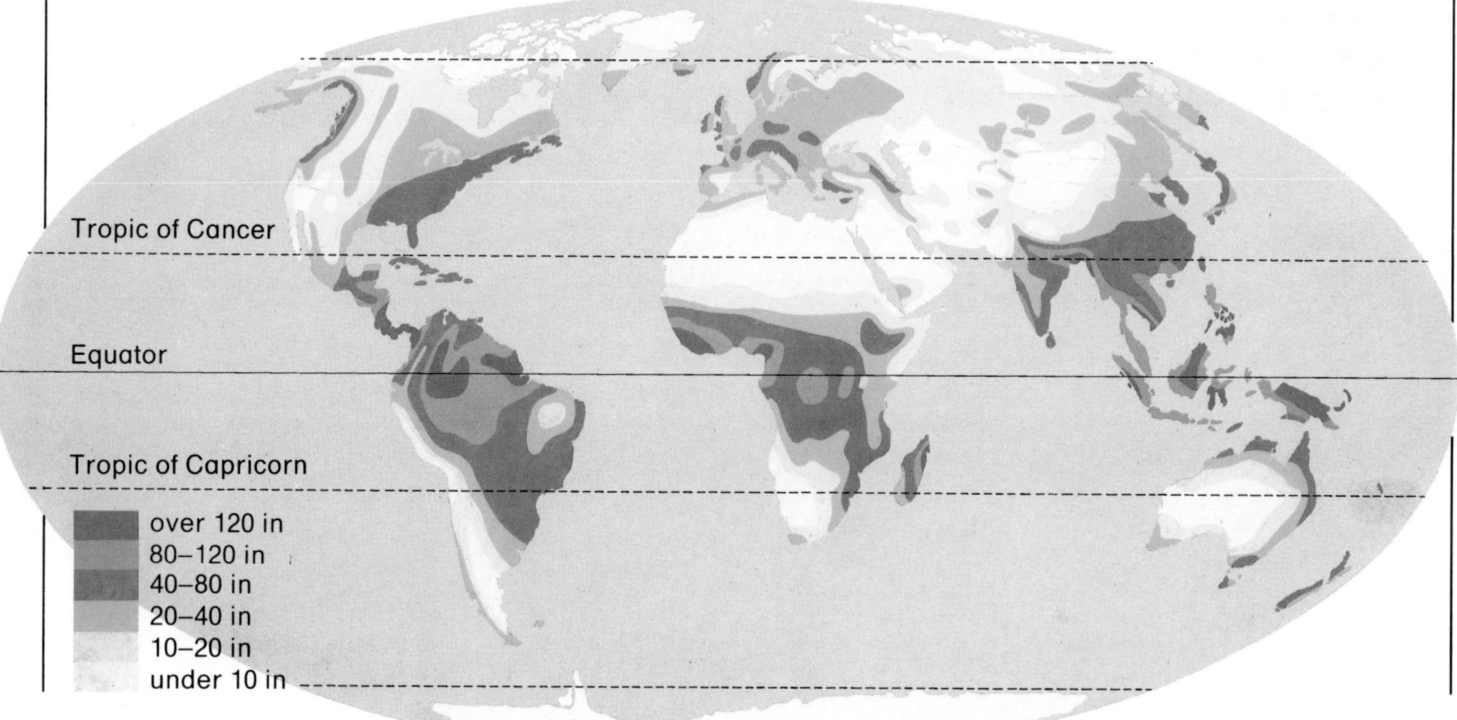

WATER

There are almost a billion cubic miles of water on our planet. At the North and South poles it is frozen into permanent ICE, and in the air it exists as colorless water vapor. Together all this water makes up 7 percent of the Earth's mass. Water is made of two atoms of HYDROGEN bonded with one atom of OXYGEN. Its formula is H_2O. Water can dissolve more different chemicals than any other liquid known.

▼ Water exists on Earth in all three states of matter. Ice and snow on the mountains melt to water under the heat of the Sun. Vapor is given off as the water is heated up for cooking. Water is vital for life. Human bodies are two-thirds water, and some plants contain more than 90 percent.

▼ You could say that if ice sank, life would never have evolved. Life began in the sea; originally there were no living things on land. If ice did not float, the sea would freeze from the bottom up. This would mean that all the living things would have been stranded on the top and would have died.

DID YOU KNOW?

Water has an amazing property: Other liquids slowly contract as they cool, but when water freezes solid it expands. A frozen water-pipe may split because of this. Nothing happens until the ice melts — that's when you find the leak!

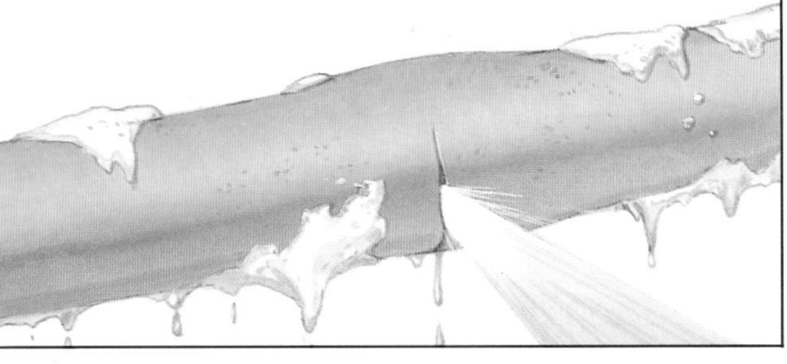

▲ Ice from the North and South Poles breaks off to form icebergs. The largest can be larger than Belgium! We see only the tip of the iceberg — nine tenths of it lie below the surface. This is why icebergs are a danger to ships.

ice water steam

▲ Ice takes in a lot of energy to melt, just as water does to become vapor. This latent heat is given out again when vapor condenses to water and when water freezes to ice.

◄▼ Water attacks many things. A stream can dissolve away limestone to form caves. The solid steel of a car can be attacked by water and changed to powdery rust. Even the washing of waves on the shore wears away tall cliffs.

DID YOU KNOW?

Think what happens when you hang a T-shirt over a radiator to dry. The radiator heats the T-shirt and evaporates the water. You can see the window misting as the vapor condenses on the cold glass.

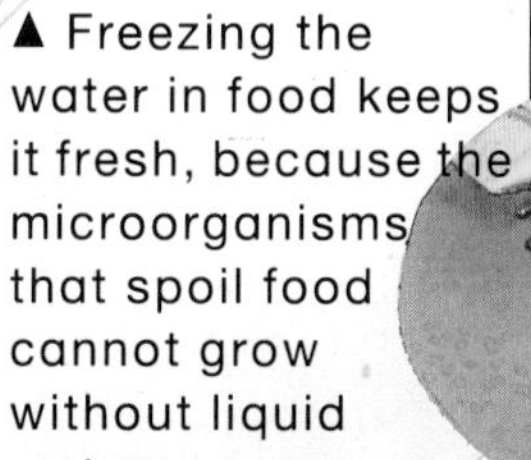

▲ Freezing the water in food keeps it fresh, because the microorganisms that spoil food cannot grow without liquid water.

▲ Inside a seed is a plant embryo. When water is added, the embryo grows and bursts out of the seed case. Try growing some seeds in a pot, and watch water at work.

▲ The invention of the wheel 5,000 years ago led to the development of vehicles and machines of many different kinds.

wheel
The earliest method of moving huge blocks of stone was on wooden rollers. Later, people used solid wooden wheels instead. The wheel is one of the most important early inventions.

weight
Weight is a measure of how heavy something is. A 10-pound weight always has the same MASS, but on the MOON it will weigh only 1.7 pounds, because the force of GRAVITY is only one-sixth as strong on the Moon as it is on EARTH. In ORBIT its weight would be zero, because the VELOCITY in orbit is enough to balance the pull of gravity.

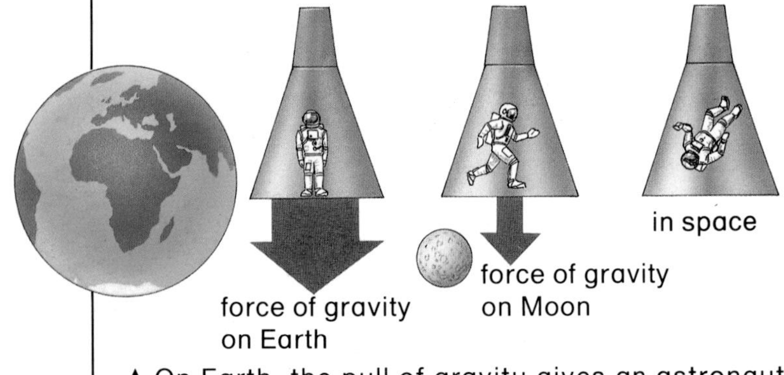

▲ On Earth, the pull of gravity gives an astronaut weight. Gravity on the Moon is weaker, so the same astronaut will weigh less. Floating free in space or in orbit, the astronaut is weightless.

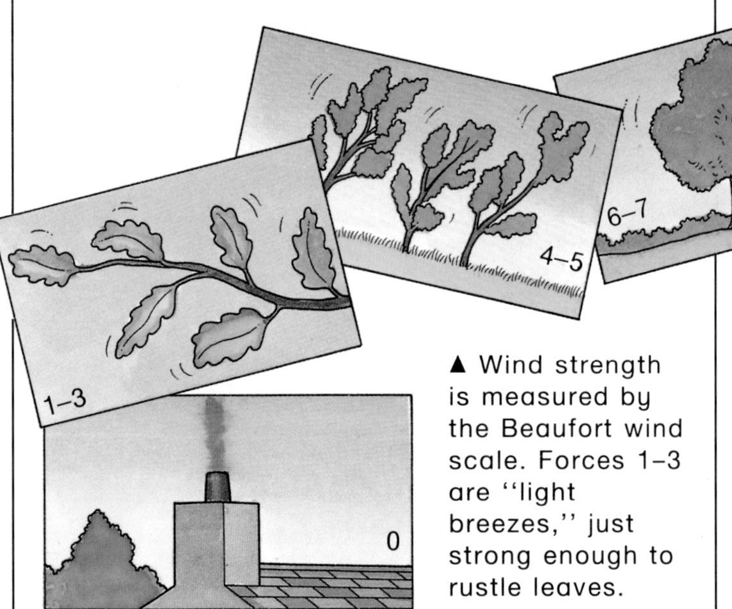

▲ Wind strength is measured by the Beaufort wind scale. Forces 1–3 are "light breezes," just strong enough to rustle leaves.

wind
Winds are air CURRENTS produced by AIR moving between areas of different PRESSURE in WEATHER systems. In the Northern Hemisphere they swirl counterclockwise around a low-pressure

W

area. But in the Southern Hemisphere of the EARTH the movement is the other way around. Wind power is a way of using windmills as GENERATORS of ELECTRICITY. A wind tunnel is a chamber with a powerful fan. It is used to test the air resistance of cars, AIRCRAFT, and ROCKETS.

▶ Force 10–11 are "storm winds" that cause damage to buildings. The strongest wind in the Beaufort scale is force 12, a hurricane. Hurricanes have wind speeds over 74 mph (120 km/h).

◀ Force 4–5 winds are "moderate winds," making trees sway and raising small waves on lakes.

◀ Winds blowing at up to 38 mph (61 km/h) are classified as "strong winds." They make large trees sway and make walking difficult. A force 8 gale can blow shingles off roofs.

word processor

A word processor is a COMPUTER that is used to create and print documents. The SOFTWARE allows you to correct what has been typed. Word processors have a keyboard similar to that of a typewriter but with extra keys to edit and move text and save text in the computer's memory. The words are shown on a screen, and in many systems there is a dictionary facility to check spelling automatically.

Wright Flyer

The Wright brothers' *Flyer* was the world's first successful powered plane. It was built by Wilbur and Orville Wright. The Wright brothers were bicycle builders who went on to design planes. They experimented with gliders and then on December 17, 1903 they made the first controlled FLIGHT in a heavier-than-air craft. It took place at Kitty Hawk in North Carolina and lasted 12 seconds.

▼ The *Flyer 1*, built by Orville and Wilbur Wright, was the first successful powered airplane. Their achievements influenced aircraft designers in Europe and the United States for many years.

x-rays

X-rays lie between ULTRAVIOLET and gamma RADIATION in the electromagnetic spectrum. They have a wavelength of less than a billionth of a meter. This is smaller than an ATOM, and x-rays can pass through soft materials. X-rays cannot pass through bone, so they are used to photograph broken bones. They can show up the lining of the stomach and intestines if the patient swallows BARIUM.

xylene

Xylene is a PETROCHEMICAL. It can dissolve some PLASTICS and is used in preparing specimens for the MICROSCOPE.

year

A year is the time it takes the EARTH to move in ORBIT once around the SUN. A year is exactly 365.25636 days long. To make up the extra quarter day, the month of February has 29 days (instead of 28) every four years. This is known as a leap year. As this makes the year slightly too long, there is no leap year in the first year of a century unless the year can be evenly divided by 400.

▼ A year is the time taken by the Earth to orbit the Sun, about 365.25 days. Because the Earth is tilted on its axis, the two hemispheres lean toward the Sun and have summer at different times of year. Summer begins on June 21 in the Northern Hemisphere, and on December 21 in the Southern Hemisphere.

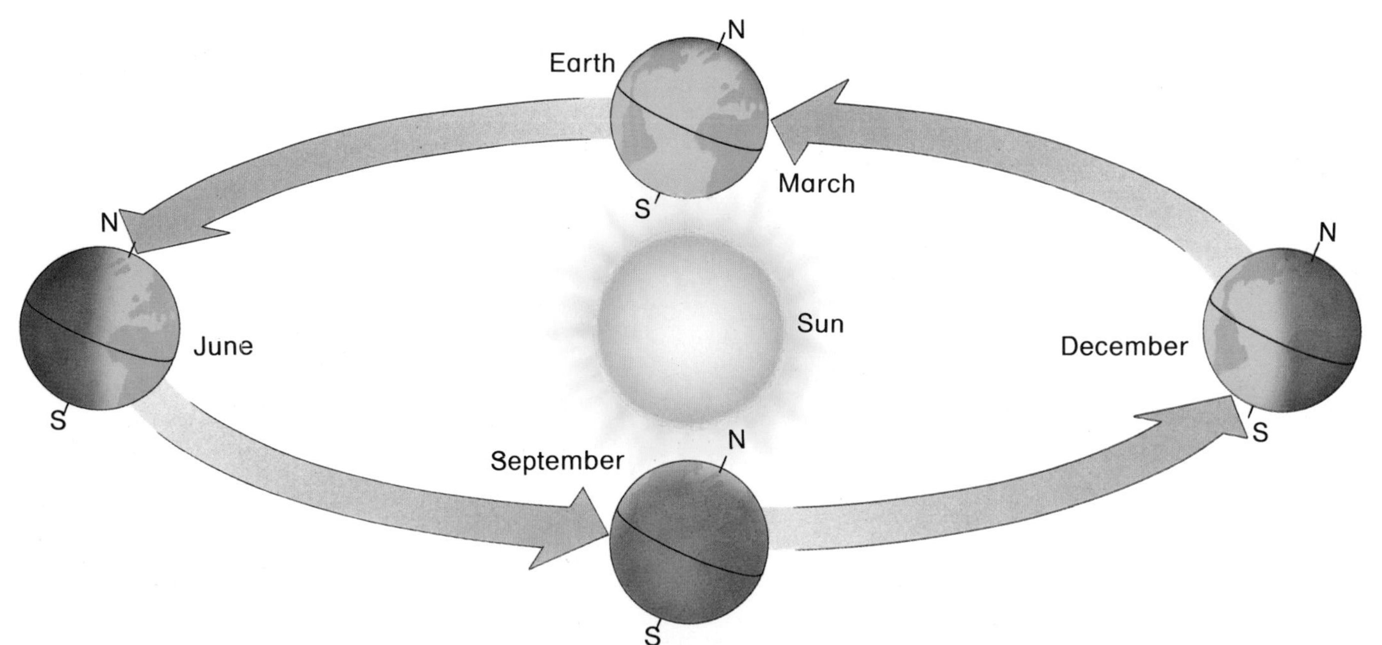

zero
Zero means "cipher" or "nil." It was invented by Hindus about 300 BC and reached Europe about AD 1200. It has profoundly advanced all NUMBERS systems.

zinc
Zinc is a soft, white METAL which does not react with the AIR. If sheets of STEEL are dipped into molten zinc, they are said to be GALVANIZED. The steel does not rust for many years. Zinc is used to make old-fashioned carbon BATTERIES.

▼ Zinc and zinc alloys are used to make dry battery cases, machine parts, and some coins.

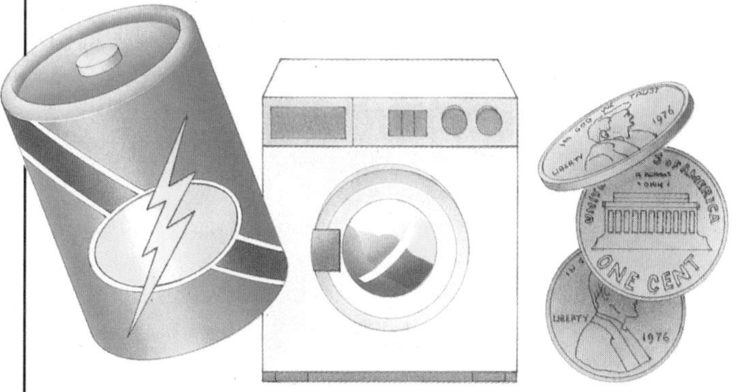

zircon
Zircon is a semiprecious stone. It is a form of ZIRCONIUM silicate and can be found in many different colors.

zirconium
Zirconium is a metallic ELEMENT with the very high melting point of 3,866°F (2,130°C). It is used in NUCLEAR reactors and in the lining of JET ENGINES.

zone
A zone is a region with a recognizable character. The term is used in GEOGRAPHY to divide up the land.

zoom lens
A zoom lens is one that allows you to close in and magnify one part of a picture without changing your position. The distance between a lens and the image it forms of an object is the focal length. In technical terms, a zoom is a LENS in which the focal length can be changed without altering the focus. See **photography**.

▼ A zoom lens can produce different pictures of the same scene. A 210 mm setting magnifies part of the picture taken on a 75 mm setting.

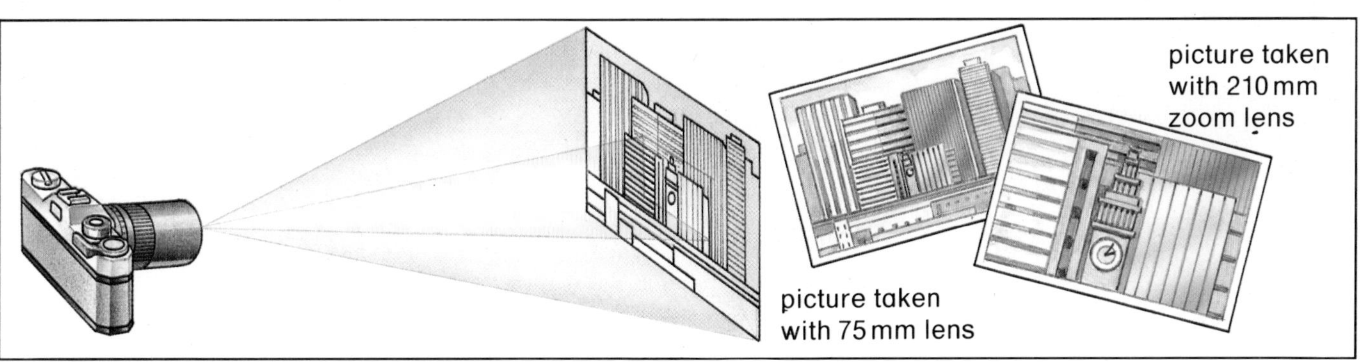

Index

Page numbers in italics refer to illustrations.